JAVA ENTERPRISE EDITION: A PRACTICAL APPROACH

JAVA ENTERPRISE EDITION: A PRACTICAL APPROACH

J2EE – JDBC with Oracle – HTML – Java Servlets – JSP – JSTL – SOA and Web Services – JMS with Apache ActiveMQ – Project Management with Apache Maven

By

B. Mohamed Ibrahim MCA., M.Phil., MBA.,
Software Technical Consultant

UNIVERSITY SCIENCE PRESS

(An Imprint of Laxmi Publications Pvt. Ltd.)

BANGALORE • CHENNAI • COCHIN • GUWAHATI • HYDERABAD
JALANDHAR • KOLKATA • LUCKNOW • MUMBAI • RANCHI
NEW DELHI • BOSTON, USA

Published by :

UNIVERSITY SCIENCE PRESS

(An Imprint of Laxmi Publications Pvt. Ltd.)

113, Golden House, Daryaganj,
New Delhi-110002

Phone : 011-43 53 25 00
Fax : 011-43 53 25 28

www.laxmipublications.com
info@laxmipublications.com

Price : ₹ **250.00** *Only.* *First Edition* : 2013

OFFICES

Bangalore	080-26 61 15 61	**Chennai**	044-24 34 47 26
Cochin	0484-237 70 04, 405 13 03	**Guwahati**	0361-254 36 69, 251 38 81
Hyderabad	040-24 65 23 33	**Jalandhar**	0181-222 12 72
Kolkata	033-22 27 43 84	**Lucknow**	0522-220 95 78
Mumbai	022-24 91 54 15, 24 92 78 69	**Ranchi**	0651-2214764

UJE-9671-250-JAVA ENTER PRAC APP-IBR **C—5400/012/06**

Typesetted at : Shubham Composer, New Delhi. *Printed at :* Ajit Printing Press,

PREFACE

The web has grown very fast, and the rate of its growth continues to be exponential. Many enterprises were already sunset to standalone desktop applications, and started working on web-based applications. And they can access their applications throughout the world, mainly without installing any special client applications.

Currently, a new trend in technology for Enterprise Application Interaction (EAI), which uses web protocols for data transmission. And every module can be accessed via web as services. This Service Oriented Architecture (SOA) with Web Services breaks platform and implementation software dependency.

Java platform is one of the best choices of the web developers, which supports many attractive features including rapid development and platform independent. Due to the rapid growth, the Sun Microsystems released the second generation of Java with three major divisions: J2SE (Java 2 Platform Standard Edition), J2EE (Java 2 Platform Enterprise Edition) and J2ME (Java 2 Platform Micro Edition). The J2SE consists of Application Programming Interfaces (APIs) needed to build the Java applications and applets. The J2ME supports the development of Java applications for mobile/wireless devices. And, the J2EE is a replacement for the traditional CGI (Common Gateway Interface) technologies and is used to build dynamic and enterprise web applications. The J2EE components are modified and enhanced time to time, and released to the users. Due to maturity, stability, scalability, security and enhanced features, the generation indicator (the number "2" in J2EE) is removed and now J2EE is referred as JEE (Java Enterprise Edition). The latest version of this Java Enterprise Edition is Java EE 6.

This book is composed of ten chapters. All the chapters and the concepts in each chapter are properly ordered, and the readers are advised to read them sequentially as some chapters / sections use the concepts explained in the previous chapters / sections. The following are the brief introduction to the chapters in this book.

Chapter 1 (J2EE – An Introduction): This chapter briefly introduces Java Enterprise Edition. The Component Technologies, Service Technologies, Integration Technologies, and Communication Technologies of the Java Enterprise Edition platform are briefed. Further, it also lists the supported technologies of JEE 6 platform with their individual version numbers. The Client-Server architecture with its logical layering is explained. Then, the JEE Architecture is introduced.

Chapter 2 (Working with Oracle Database): This chapter illustrates SQL and PL/SQL commands/logic to work with Oracle database. This chapter is given for the readers to gain experience in the database operations which is required while reading database based examples, especially JDBC examples. Oracle installation procedure for Windows operating system is given with screenshots. This chapter explains Data Definition Language, Data Manipulation Language, and Transaction Control Language SQL commands with syntaxes and examples.

Chapter 3 (JDBC): This Chapter explores the JDBC API. The Java Database Connectivity (JDBC) APIs are used to interact with RDBMS. The JDBC Architecture, supported types of drivers and their features are described. The common data types in database and their corresponding data types in Java are given for reference. The JDBC APIs are listed with brief explanation. The advanced concepts such as Scrollable Result Set, Batch Updates, Transaction Management, and Calling Stored Procedures are explained with sample code and screen output.

Chapter 4 (Understanding HTML FORM Elements): This chapter aims to list and explain the form input / output elements in HTML. To create dynamic web applications, the HTML form elements are used to get and to set the data. And these data are accessed and processed by server-side web applications. The output of any web application is in HTML format. The web client such as browsers can understand these HTML content and display the information by interpreting the HTML elements. This chapter also explains some basic elements that are used frequently such as formatting elements, listing elements and frameset elements. Some samples with code and their corresponding output are given at the end of the chapter to get hands-on experience.

Chapter 5 (Java Servlets): This chapter explains Java Servlet API. It briefly explains the importance of Java Servlets in the dynamic webpage development. The life-cycle of a Servlet is given, and the programmer can do appropriate actions at each stage of the life-cycle. The Important Servlet APIs are listed with brief explanation. Both Generic Servlets and HTTP Servlets are explained with their features. The advanced concepts including Session Tracking and Manipulating Cookies are given with code samples. Apache Tomcat is used as Servlet Container in executing the examples given this chapter. The installation procedure of Tomcat, configuration, deployment descriptor format for web applications, and the procedure for deploying web applications on Tomcat are given for reference. A list of sample programs with their correspond screen output are given at the end of the chapter, and these samples uses almost all the explained Servlet APIs in this chapter.

Chapter 6 (Java Server Pages): This chapter explains the very important and most used component of Java Enterprise Edition: Java Server Pages, simply called JSP. All JSP code support Java Servlet API, and it simplifies the development process by providing support to the developers to embed Java code in HTML documents. And all JSP code will be converted into Java Servlet code before execution. This chapter analyses the aspects of JSP and compares with other competitive technologies such as Active Server Pages (ASP). The components of JSP are grouped and explained as JSP Tags, Implicit Objects, and Standard Actions. Java code can be embedded with JSP Tags, and JSP provides frequently used important objects implicitly that those objects should be created in case of Java Servlets. These directives are used to provide page-specific global information about JSP pages to the JSP engine before compilation. A list of sample programs that use the JSP concepts is given for illustration at the end of this chapter.

Chapter 7 (JSTL): This chapter focuses on standard tag libraries for JSP. JSTL adds customized tags features to JSP. This chapter explains with code samples the core tags, formatting tags, XML tags, and SQL tags. The developers can easily accomplish by using these JSTL tags, rather than using complex JSP Scripting code. JSTL also provides many implicit objects that these objects can also be used with the implicit objects provided by JSP. JSTL is not an alternate to JSP, but provides additional support and features to JSP; otherwise they should be achieved through complex JSP code. Data formatting tags in JSTL are very much handy, and also these data are formatted based on locale (Internationalization). JSTL supports sufficient tags for database manipulation, and these tags are given with syntaxes and code samples. XML provides a flexible means for representing structured data. Since the XML format is just simple text, it is well suited for exchanging data particularly between loosely coupled systems. The XPath is used to navigate through elements and attributes in an XML document. This chapter explains briefly the JSTL support for parsing and manipulating XML data.

Chapter 8 (Service Oriented Architecture and Web Services): This chapter is given for Web Services. A service is a self-contained software component (subroutine) that performs a specific task. A Service Oriented Architecture is essentially a collection of services; these services communicate with each other and each service does not depend on the context of any other services. A Web Service is an application functionality service that can be accessed by any application via standard Internet Protocols such as HTTP. This chapter explains the SOA with Web Services with the supporting technologies such as WSDL and SOAP. A complete working example is given, which uses Apache Axis2 (Web Services Engine) and Web Tool Platform (Eclipse extension for code generation).

Chapter 9 (Message Oriented Middleware and Java Messaging Service): This chapter focuses on the Java Messaging Service IJMS). The JMS is one of the Message Oriented Middleware implementation, supporting asynchronous communication between client and server in a Client-Server application. This chapter uses Apache ActiveMQ as JMS provider and given examples based on this provider. This chapter explains more elaborately with working examples the two JMS domains: Point-To-Point Messaging and Publish/Subscribe Messaging. The important JMS APIs are listed with explanation.

Chapter 10 (Project Management with Apache Maven): This chapter deals with Project Management activities including creation, build, deployment of Java standard applications and Web applications. Apache Maven is a project management tool, more than a build tool such as Apache Ant. This chapter takes Apache Maven as the project management tool and explains how to do the operations with this tool. Three complete examples are given in this chapter to create a Java standalone application project, a Java web application project, and a multi-module application project.

The core component of Java Enterprise Edition, Enterprise Java Beans (EJB) is not covered in this book, as it requires many pages and I want to restrict the number of pages of this book. I am planning to write a separate book for EJB 3. And, it is not a complete book for JEE. This book is for beginners and intermediates to quickly understand the important JEE components.

I thank the Almighty Allah, who gave me the soul, strength, knowledge and everything. All praise is due to him. Salutations on the Prophet (may Allah's blessings and peace be upon him) and his descendents. I thank all the well wishers of mine, who prayed the Almighty for me.

—Author

CONTENTS

1

J2EE: An Introduction

1.0 INTRODUCTION

This chapter introduces the generation of Java. The components of Java Enterprise Edition and their features are briefly explained. It further explains the client-server technology and how it fits in application software. This chapter ends by giving you introduction to J2EE Architecture.

1.1 JAVA GENERATION

Java was developed at Sun Microsystems, Inc. headed by James Gosling with his team. The main feature of Java, *the Platform independent*, is the intermediate code that can be recognized by all Java Virtual Machines (JVMs) running under different platforms. Due to the rapid growth, the Sun Microsystems released the second generation of Java with three major divisions: J2SE (Java 2 Platform Standard Edition), J2EE (Java 2 Platform Enterprise Edition) and J2ME (Java 2 Platform Micro Edition). The J2SE consists of Application Programming Interfaces (APIs) needed to build the Java applications and applets. The J2ME supports the development of Java applications for mobile/wireless devices. And, the J2EE is a replacement for the traditional CGI (Common Gateway Interface) technologies and is used to build dynamic and enterprise web applications. The J2EE components are modified and enhanced time to time, and released to the users. Due to maturity, stability, scalability, security and enhanced features, the generation indicator (the number "2" in J2EE) is removed and now J2EE is referred as JEE (Java Enterprise Edition). The latest version of this Java Enterprise Edition is Java EE 6.

Thus, JEE is one part of Java technologies, used for developing web and enterprise applications and acts as an alternative to CGI technologies.

1.2 COMPONENTS OF JEE

The core components of JEE include Java Servlets, Java Server Pages (JSP), and Enterprise Java Beans (EJB). JEE also consists of several significant APIs including the list given below.

Component Technologies

⇒ Java Servlets -Dynamic web-page development

⇒ Java Server Pages (JSP) –Dynamic web-page development

⇒ Enterprise JavaBeans (EJB) –Middleware component service

Service Technologies

⇒ Java Database Connectivity (JDBC) –Database Connectivity to Java applications

⇒ Java Message Service (JMS) –Asynchronous messaging service

⇒ Java Transaction API (JTA) –Distributed transaction management

⇒ Java Mail –e-Mail service

⇒ JavaBeans Activation Framework (JAF)

- Dynamically register / access the types of arbitrary data and actions on them. Used by Java Mail.

⇒ Java Authentication and Authorization Service (JAAS) –Java code based security

⇒ Java Naming and Directory Interface (JNDI)

- Access to Naming and Directory services (Windows registry, Lightweight Directory Access Protocol –LDAP, Novell Directory Services –NDS, CORBA, RMI, EJB, Database Connection Objects ...).

Integration Technologies

⇒ Java API for XML Processing (JAXP) –Java XML Programming API

⇒ Java Connector Architecture (JCA)

- Connecting application servers and Enterprise Information Systems (EIS)

⇒ Java Interface Definition Language (IDL) and Web Services

- Defining distributed objects. Implemented in Distributed Systems like CORBA.

Communication Technologies

⇒ RMI-IIOP

(**R**emote **M**ethod **I**nvocation and **I**nternet **I**nter **O**RB (Object Request Broker) **P**rotocol)

– Provides CORBA Capabilities to Java Platform

The following are important new / enhanced features added in Java EE over the time.

⇒ JPA (Java Persistence API) –Manipulating RDBMS in Java programs

⇒ JSF (Java Server Faces) –Web application framework

⇒ JSTL (Java Server Pages Standard Tag Library) –Provides additional tags to JSP tags

⇒ JAXR (Java API for XML Registries) –API to access to various kinds of metadata registries

⇒ JMX (Java Management Extensions) –Managed Beans (MBeans) for managing application, hardware devices, and service oriented networks ...

⇒ JAXB (Java Architecture for XML Binding) –Map Java objects to XML and vice versa.

Some of the JEE 6 supported technologies are given below with version number of each individual technology.

- Java Servlet 3.0
- Java Server Pages (JSP) 2.2
- JSP Standard Tag Library (JSTL) 1.2
- Java Server Faces (JSF) 2.0
- Enterprise Java Beans 3.1
- Java Message Service (JMS) 1.1
- Java Transaction API (JTA) 1.1
- Java Mail 1.4
- Web Beans 1.0 and Dependency Injection for Java 1.0
- Bean Validation 1.0
- Java EE Connector Architecture (JCA) 1.6
- Java Persistence API (JPA) 2.0
- Common Annotations for Java Platform 1.1
- Java EE Application Deployment 1.2a
- J2EE Management 1.1
- Java API for RESTful Web Services (JAX-RS) 2.2
- Java API for XML-Based Web Service (JAX-WS)
- Java API for XM_-Based RPC (JAX-RPC) 1.1
- Java Architecture for XML Binding (JAXB) 2.2
- Java APIs for XML Messaging 1.3
- Java API for XML Registries (JAXR) 1.0
- JEE 6 related specifications in JSE (Java Standard Edition).
- Java Database Connectivity (JDBC) 4.0
- Java API for XML Processing (JAXP) 1.3
- JavaBeans Activation Framework (JAF) 1.1
- Java Management Extensions (JMX) 2.0
- Streaming API for XML (StAX) 1.0

1.3 CLIENT-SERVER TECHNOLOGY

The Internet works on peer-to-peer technology, that is, all the machines are servers as well as clients. Data are stored at the servers; whatever a client request the server, then the server will respond.

If you are browsing a web-site, say *http://www.yahoo.com*, then your machine (the browser that you are using, if we say exactly) is a client that requests data from the server, which is in this example, yahoo machine (the web-server software running at the server, if we say exactly). The welcome file (normally *"index.html"* or *"default.html"*) will be invoked by default if you are not mentioned the file-name in the URL address. Actually, the domain name, *www.yahoo.com*, will be converted into its corresponding IP address with the help of Domain Name Server (DNS).

HTML is a HyperText Markup Language that provides GUI input and output elements, such as Text box, Check box, Radio groups, List, etc., for the web pages. But it does not have the capability to process the data which will be placed by the user. So, a programming language is required to process the data which are available with HTML forms and display the resultant information as response.

The process can be done at two places, either at the Client or at the Server. Any verification checks like whether the user filled the mandatory fields of the form can be done at the client, but any validation checks, like whether the user entered correct user-name and password, can not be performed at the clients, because it requires reference with a database which is available at server.

The technologies and programming used to process data at clients is called "*Client-side programming*", where as the programming used at the servers to process the data that were sent by the clients in requests is called "*Server-side Programming*". Some of the Client-side programming (scripting) include Java Script, VB Script and Java Applets, and some Server-side programming include Java Servlets, JSP, ASP and PHP.

1.3.1 Client/Server Logical Layering

An application software can be built-up with the following logical layers. Each layer is responsible for a specific task in the application.

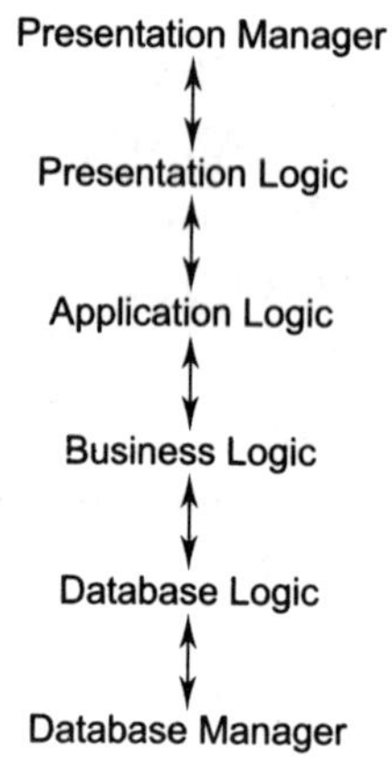

Presentation Manager: It is responsible for the look and feel of an application. It is independent of the applications. All the applications can use the same presentation manager. For example, Windows OS offers only one Presentation Manager, but Linux OS offers many Presentation Managers for the X-Window system like GNOME, KDE. (*i.e.*, the Desktop and appearance will vary).

Presentation Logic: It is application dependent layer, which is responsible for the content to display.

Application Layer: It is also application dependent layer, which defines the actual logic of the application.

Business Logic: This is not application dependent, but organization dependent layer, which defines the business rules of an organization.

Database Logic: This is actually an application dependent, even organization dependent layer which defines the data dictionary (table, columns, data types ...) for an application.

Database Manager: This layer may be dependent on the application or the organization, responsible for the storage of data.

1.3.2 Client/Server Physical Layering

While creating a client/server application, the logical layers can be divided, and each/group of layers may be implemented in one/many applications, which may run on single/multiple computers. These divisions of layers are called physical layers. A physical layer is called a tier.

1 **Tier Architecture:** The 1-tier applications implement all these six logical layers in a single physical layer. That tier is called *"Application tier"*. Actually 1-tier applications are not supporting distributed client-server technologies.

2 **Tier Architecture:** The 2–tier applications divide the 6 layers into two processes: Client tier and Server tier. For example, Visual Basic implements the client-tier and MS-Access implements the Server-tier.

3 **Tier Architecture:** The 3–tier applications divide the 6 layers into 3 processes: Client tier, Business tier and Data tier.

n-Tier Architecture: As the name implies, the n-tier applications divide the 6 layers into many number (n) of tiers.

1.4 JEE ARCHITECTURE

JEE is a multi-tiered (generally four-tier) architecture as shown below.

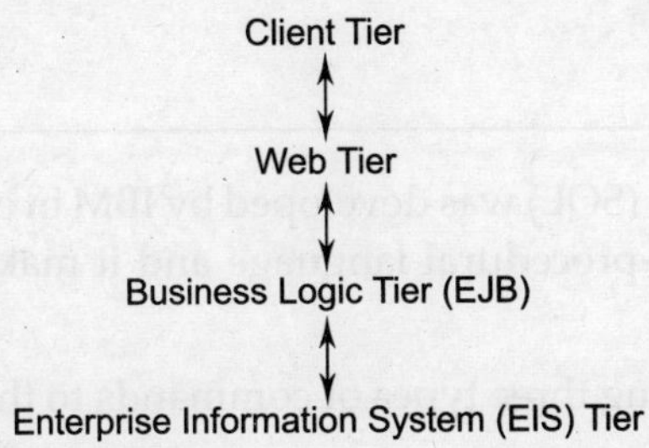

Client Tier: Depending on the application, a web-browser, an applet, or a Java application can act as a client (tier), who is responsible for the user interface.

Web Tier: This tier is responsible for the presentation and application logic. There are two main components on this tier: *Java Servlets* and *JSP,* those generate the appropriate HTML that contains the result (data) to be displayed on the browser (client tier).

Business Logic Tier: This tier is responsible for business logic; manages multiple distributive objects (For example, Enterprise Java Beans). The EJB class contains business logic and is callable from a *Servlet* or *JSP* (web-tier).

Enterprise Information Systems (EIS) Tier: This tier is the J2EE architecture's connectivity to resources that are not part of J2EE such as Databases, Legacy systems, and the systems like ERP that are accessible to the components of J2EE architecture.

SUMMARY

This chapter briefly introduced the basics of Java Enterprise Edition. The supported technologies and their latest version numbers are given for Java EE 6 platform. The client-server technology, most of the enterprise applications are based on this technology, is explained with its architecture. Finally, a high-level view of JEE architecture is given for quick understanding of a Java based Enterprise Application.

2

WORKING WITH ORACLE DATABASE

2.0 INTRODUCTION

This chapter briefly explains the simple SQL commands to work with Oracle database. Adequate examples and screen outputs are given for illustration to easily understand the concept.

2.1 SQL

The Structured Query Language (SQL) was developed by IBM in early 1970's and it is the database language for Oracle. It is a non-procedural language and it makes the user to interact with the database.

The SQL provides the following three types of commands to the user to communicate with the database.

- Data Definition Language (DDL) : create, alter, drop
- Data Manipulation Language (DML) : select, insert, delete, update
- Transaction Control Language (TCL) : commit, savepoint, rollback

2.2 DATA TYPES

A data type should be specified for each column of the table. The SQL allows the following data types.

char

It is used to store alphanumeric data. Its range is 1 – 255 bytes.

varchar2

It is used to store alphanumeric data. Its range us 1 – 2000 bytes.

If the user enters a value that is shorter than the specified length, then the database would blank-pad to the fixed length in *char* datatype, but in *varchar2* datatype, the column's length is assumed as the user entered datum's length.

long

It is used to store variable character length data.

number

It is used to store numbers.

```
number(d)
number(d,f)
```

were, 'd' is the number of digits in the number and 'f' is the number of digits after the decimal point in the case of floating point numbers.

date

It is used to store dates. (The default date type is dd-mon-yy).

raw(size)

It is used to store byte oriented (binary) data.

long raw

It is used to store variable length binary data.

2.3 DDL COMMANDS

The Data Definition Language (DDL) commands are used to create new tables, alter the structure of existing tables and drop tables.

2.3.1 create

This command creates a table.

General format:

```
create table <table-name> (column-name1 datatype, column-name2 datatype, ...)
```

Example:

```
SQL> create table student (rno number(5), sname varchar2(15), m1 number(3),
m2 number(3));
Table created.
```

2.3.2 alter

The alter command alters the structure of an existing table.

General format:

```
alter table <table-name> add (column-name datatype, column-name datatype, ...)
alter table <table-name> modify (column-name datatype, column-name datatype, ...)
```

Example:

```
SQL> desc student;
Name                            Null?    Type
------------------------------- -------- ---
RNO                                      NUMBER(5)
```

```
SNAME                              VARCHAR2(15)
M1                                 NUMBER(3)
M2                                 NUMBER(3)
SQL> alter table student add (m3 number(3), total number(3), result char(4));
Table altered.
SQL> desc student;
Name                      Null?    Type
- - - - - - - - - - - - - - - - - - - - - - -
RNO                                NUMBER(5)
SNAME                              VARCHAR2(15)
M1                                 NUMBER(3)
M2                                 NUMBER(3)
M3                                 NUMBER(3)
TOTAL                              NUMBER(3)
RESULT                             CHAR(4)
SQL> alter table student modify (result varchar2(4));
Table altered.
SQL> desc student;
Name                      Null?    Type
- - - - - - - - - - - - - - - - - - - - - - -
RNO                                NUMBER(5)
SNAME                              VARCHAR2(15)
M1                                 NUMBER(3)
M2                                 NUMBER(3)
M3                                 NUMBER(3)
TOTAL                              NUMBER(3)
RESULT                             VARCHAR2(4)
```

2.3.3 drop

This command drops (erase) the table from the database.

General format:

```
drop table <table-name>
```

Example:

```
SQL> desc student;
Name                      Null?    Type
- - - - - - - - - - - - - - - - - - - - - - -
RNO                                NUMBER(5)
SNAME                              VARCHAR2(15)
M1                                 NUMBER(3)
```

```
M2                                          NUMBER(3)
M3                                          NUMBER(3)
TOTAL                                       NUMBER(3)
RESULT                                      VARCHAR2(4)
SQL> drop table student;
Table dropped.
SQL> desc student;
Object does not exist.
```

Integrity constraints:

These constraints avoid invalid data entries into the table.

'not null' constraint:

Generally, all the columns may have *'null'* values. When a *'not null'* constraint is used on a column, then that column will not allow *null* values.

Example:

```
SQL> create table stud (rno number(5) not null, sname varchar2(15));
Table created.
SQL> insert into stud (rno) values (1001);
1 row created.
SQL> insert into stud (sname) values ('IBRAHIM');
insert into stud (sname) values ('IBRAHIM')
            *
ERROR at line 1:
ORA-01400: cannot insert NULL into ("ORCL"."STUD"."RNO")
```

The user must specify a value for *"rno"* in a row of the *stud* table; that column should not be *null*.

'primary key' constraint:

When it is set on a column, it avoids duplication value as well as *'null'* value to that column.

Example:

```
SQL> create table stud (rno number(5) Primary key, sname varchar2(15));
Table created.
SQL> insert into stud values (10001, 'Ibrahim');
1 row created.
SQL> insert into stud values (10002, null);
1 row created.
SQL> insert into stud values (null, 'Kannan');
 insert into stud values (null, 'Kannan')
                          *
```

```
ERROR at line 1:
ORA-01400: cannot insert NULL into ("ORCL"."STUD"."RNO")
SQL> insert into stud values (10001, 'Kannan');
 insert into stud values (10001, 'Kannan')
*
ERROR at line 1:
ORA-00001: unique constraint (ORCL.SYS_C002030) violated
```

The user must specify a unique value and not a *null value* to *rno* column in the table.

'check' constraint:

The given value will be stored on the column if and only if the specified condition is true.

Example:

```
SQL> create table stud (rno number(5),
                        mark number(3) check (mark >= 0 and mark <= 100) );
Table created.
SQL> insert into stud values (1001, 60);
1 row created.
SQL> insert into stud values (1001, -60);
insert into stud values (1001, -60)
*
ERROR at line 1:
ORA-02290: check constraint (ORCL.SYS_C002031) violated
SQL> insert into stud values (1001, 160);
insert into stud values (1001, 160)
*
ERROR at line 1:
ORA-02290: check constraint (ORCL.SYS_C002031) violated
```

The given mark is stored in the mark column, if and only if the mark is with in the range 0 and 100.

2.4 DML COMMANDS

The Date Manipulation Language (DML) commands are used to manipulate data on tables.

2.4.1 Insert

This command is used to insert one / more value(s) to column(s) of a table.

General format:

To insert values for all the columns of a table,

```
insert into <table-name> values (list of values)
```

To insert values for particular columns of a table,

```
insert into <table-name> (column-names) values (list of values)
```

If more than one values are to be inserted, then the values should be separated by commas and the values for the data types *char*, *varchar2* and *date* should be enclosed with in single quotes.

Example:

```
SQL> desc student;
Name                         Null?    Type
----------------------------- -------- ----
RNO                                    NUMBER(5)
SNAME                                  VARCHAR2(15)
M1                                     NUMBER(3)
M2                                     NUMBER(3)
M3                                     NUMBER(3)
TOTAL                                  NUMBER(3)
RESULT                                 VARCHAR2(4)
SQL> insert into student (rno, sname, m1, m2, m3) values
                         (1001, 'IBRAHIM', 60, 70, 80);
1 row created.
SQL> insert into student (rno, sname, m1, m2, m3) values
                         (&rno, '&sname', &m1, &m2, &m3);
Enter value for rno: 1002
Enter value for sname: KUMAR
Enter value for m1: 65
Enter value for m2: 86
Enter value for m3: 92
old 1: insert into student (rno, sname, m1, m2, m3) values
                         (&rno, '&sname', &m1, &m2, &m3)
new 1: insert into student (rno, sname, m1, m2, m3) values
                         (1002, 'KUMAR', 65, 86, 92)
1 row created.
SQL> insert into student (rno, sname, m1, m2, m3) values
                         (1003, 'RAHMAN', 49, 50, 55);
1 row created.
```

2.4.2 Select

This command selects the required rows from the specified tables.

General format:

```
select column-name1, column-name2, ... from table1, table2, ... where condition
```

The symbol '*' represents all two columns of a specified table.

Example:

```
SQL> select * from student;
   RNO  SNAME                 M1        M2        M3       TOTAL  RESU
  ---  ----------------  ------   ------   ------   ------  ---
  1001  IBRAHIM               60        70        80         210  PASS
  1002  KUMAR                 65        86        92         243  PASS
  1003  RAHMAN                49        50        55         154  FAIL
SQL> select rno, result from student;
 RNO RESU
 -----
1001 PASS
1002 PASS
1003 FAIL
SQL> select * from student where rno = 1002;
   RNO  SNAME                 M1        M2        M3       TOTAL  RESU
  ---  ----------------  ------   ------   ------   ------  ---
  1002  KUMAR                 65        86        92         243  PASS
SQL> select * from student where result='PASS';
   RNO  SNAME                 M1        M2        M3       TOTAL  RESU
  ---  ----------------  ------   ------   ------   ------  ---
  1001  IBRAHIM               60        70        80         210  PASS
  1002  KUMAR                 65        86        92         243  PASS
```

2.4.3 update

This command is used to update (change) the existing values in a table.

General format:

```
update <table-name> set column-name=value1, column-name2=value2, ...
                                                    where condition
```

Example:

```
SQL> select * from student;
   RNO  SNAME                 M1        M2        M3       TOTAL  RESU
  ---  ----------------  ------   ------   ------   ------  ---
  1001  IBRAHIM               60        70        80
  1002  KUMAR                 65        86        92
  1003  RAHMAN                49        50        55
SQL> update student set total=m1+m2+m3;
3 rows updated.
SQL> update student set result='PASS' where m1>=50 and m2>=50 and m3>=50;
2 rows updated.
```

```
SQL> update student set result='FAIL' where m1<50 or m2<50 or m3<50;
1 row updated.
SQL> select * from student;
   RNO  SNAME                M1          M2          M3      TOTAL  RESU
  ---  --------------------  ----------  ----------  ------  -----  ----
  1001  IBRAHIM              60          70          80      210    PASS
  1002  KUMAR                65          86          92      243    PASS
  1003  RAHMAN               49          50          55      154    FAIL
```

2.4.4 delete

This command is used to delete the specified rows of a table.

General format:

```
delete from <table-name> where condition
```

Example:

```
SQL> select * from student;
   RNO  SNAME                M1          M2          M3      TOTAL  RESU
  ---  --------------------  ----------  ----------  ------  -----  ----
  1001  IBRAHIM              60          70          80      210    PASS
  1002  KUMAR                65          86          92      243    PASS
  1003  RAHMAN               49          50          55      154    FAIL
SQL> delete from student where rno=1002;
1 row deleted.
SQL> select * from student;
   RNO  SNAME                M1          M2          M3      TOTAL  RESU
  ---  --------------------  ----------  ----------  ------  -----  ----
  1001  IBRAHIM              60          70          80      210    PASS
  1003  RAHMAN               49          50          55      154    FAIL
SQL> delete from student;
2 rows deleted.
SQL> select * from student;
no rows selected
```

2.5 TRANSACTION CONTROL LANGUAGE (TCL) COMMANDS

All the changes (operations) made to the database in between a *commit* and/or a *rollback* operation is refereed as a "*Transaction*".

2.5.1 commit

This command ends a transaction. The changes (made by transactions) are made permanent to the database.

General format:

```
commit
```

2.5.2 savepoint

A savepoint is a marker which represents a position in a transaction.

General format:

```
savepoint savepoint-id
```

2.5.3 rollback

This command is used to rollback (undo) the changes done in a table.

General format:

```
rollback to savepoint savepoint-id
```

Example:

```
SQL> create table stud (rno number(5), result varchar2(6));
Table created.
SQL> insert into stud values (1001, 'PASS');
1 row created.
SQL> insert into stud values (1002, 'FAIL');
1 row created.
SQL> insert into stud values (1003, 'PASS');
1 row created.
SQL> select * from stud;
      RNO  RESULT
- - - - -  - - - -
     1001  PASS
     1002  FAIL
     1003  PASS
SQL> commit;
Commit complete.
SQL> select * from stud;
      RNO  RESULT
- - - - -  - - - -
     1001  PASS
     1002  FAIL
     1003  PASS
SQL> update stud set result='PASS' where rno=1002;
1 row updated.
SQL> savepoint sp;
Savepoint created.
```

```
SQL> update stud set result='FAIL' where rno=1001;
1 row updated.
SQL> update stud set result='FAIL' where rno=1003;
1 row updated.
SQL> select * from stud;
      RNO  RESULT
- - - - -  - - - -
     1001  FAIL
     1002  PASS
     1003  FAIL
SQL> rollback to savepoint sp;
Rollback complete.
SQL> select * from stud;
      RNO  RESULT
- - - - -  - - - -
     1001  PASS
     1002  PASS
     1003  PASS
SQL> rollback;
Rollback complete.
SQL> select * from stud;
      RNO  RESULT
- - - - -  - - - -
     1001  PASS
     1002  FAIL
     1003  PASS
SQL> update stud set result='PASS' where rno=1002;
1 row updated.
SQL> select * from stud;
      RNO  RESULT
- - - - -  - - - -
     1001  PASS
     1002  PASS
     1003  PASS
SQL> commit;
Commit complete.
SQL> rollback;
Rollback complete.
```

```
SQL> select * from stud;
       RNO  RESULT
-----  ----
      1001  PASS
      1002  PASS
      1003  PASS
```

2.6 SET OPERATIONS ON DATABASE TABLES

The set operations can be used to combine the results of two queries into a single one.

General format:

```
SelectStatement1 SetOperator SelectStatement2 where Condition
```

The allowed set operators are union, intersect and minus.

2.6.1 union

This *union* operator returns all distinct rows selected by either query.

Example:

```
SQL> select * from stud1;
       RNO  RESULT
  -----  ----
      1001  Pass
      1002  Fail
      1003  Pass
SQL> select * from stud2;
       RNO  RESULT
  -----  ----
      1001  Pass
      1004  Fail
SQL> select * from stud1 union select * from stud2;
       RNO  RESULT
  -----  ----
      1001  Pass
      1002  Fail
      1003  Pass
      1004  Fail
```

2.6.2 intersect

This *intersect* operator returns only the rows that are retrieved by both queries.

Example:

```
SQL> select * from stud1 intersect select * from stud2;
      RNO   RESULT
  - - - - -  - - - -
     1001   Pass
```

2.6.3 minus

This *minus* operator returns all distinct rows selected only by the first query and not by the second; the rows returned by the second query are matched with the rows returned by the first query, then such kind of rows are eliminated in the resultant rows.

Example:

```
SQL> select * from stud1 minus select * from stud2;
      RNO   RESULT
  - - - - -  - - - -
     1002   Fail
     1003   Pass
```

2.7 JOIN OPERATIONS ON DATABASE TABLES

The join operations can be used to combine the data spread across the tables.

General format:

```
select column(s) from table(s) where condition
```

2.7.1 Simple Join

This retrieves the rows from two tables that are having a common column-name. Equi-join is based on equalities (only = symbol is used in condition). Non equi-join uses other relational operations such as <, <=, >, >=, <> in condition.

Example:

```
SQL> select * from st2;
      RNO          TOTAL   RESULT
  - - - - -     - - - - -   - - - -
     1000            234   Pass
     1001            123   Fail
     1002            290   Pass
SQL> select * from st1;
      RNO   RESULT
  - - - - -  - - - -
     1000   Ibrahim
     1001   Kannan
     1003   Navas
```

```
SQL> select * from st1, st2 where st1.rno=st2.rno;

   RNO  SNAME                     RNO        TOTAL  RESULT
  ---   -----   ---------   -----  -----
  1000  Ibrahim                  1000          234  Pass
  1001  Kannan                   1001          123  Fail
```

2.7.2 Self Join

It is used for joining of a table to itself, joins one row to another.

Example:

```
SQL> select s1.* from student s1, student s2
                                          where s1.m1>s2.m2 and s1.rno=s2.rno;
```

2.7.3 Outer Join

This will act as a simple join, and also retrieves rows from one table that do not match any row in other table. The symbol (+) represents outer joins.

Example:

```
SQL> select * from st1 , st2 where st1.rno (+)=st2.rno;
   RNO  SNAME                     RNO        TOTAL  RESULT
  ---   -----   ---------   -----  -----
  1000  Ibrahim                  1000          234  Pass
  1001  Kannan                   1001          123  Fail
                                 1002          290  Pass
```

This query retrieves the rows which has the same *rno* value in both tables and also retrieves rows which are unique to *st2*.

2.8 SUB-QUERIES

A query may contain another query for simplifying its operation, *i.e.*, nesting of such queries one with in another is called sub-query. The sub-queries are written with in parenthesis.

Example:

```
SQL> select rno from st2 where total = (select max(total) from st2);
      RNO
  -----
     1002
```

2.9 STORED PROCEDURES

Generally, these procedures are used to perform the actions which are required frequently.

General format for creating a stored procedure:

```
create procedure <procedure-name> (<parameter-list>) is
<local variable declarations>;
begin
 Procedure_body
end;
```

There are three types of modes for passing arguments.

- Passing values and do not return value from procedure (in mode)
- Passing no value but returning value (out mode)
- Passing initial value and returning the updated value (inout mode)

If the user does not specified any mode, then the 'in' mode is taken by default.

Example:

in Parameter

```
SQL> select * from stl;
     RNO   SNAME
  ----  --------
    1005   Ibrahim
    1001   Kannan
    1003   Navas
SQL> create procedure del (rollno in number) is
   2 begin
   3 delete from stl where stl.rno=rollno;
   4 end;
   5 /
Procedure created.
SQL> begin
   2 del(1001);
   3 end;
   4 /
PL/SQL procedure successfully completed.
SQL> select * from stl;
     RNO   SNAME
  ----  --------
    1005   Ibrahim
    1003   Navas
```

2.10 SOME BUILT-IN FUNCTIONS

Group functions:

`sum(x)`	Returns the summation of x in the group of records; The x is a column name.
`max(x)`	Returns the maximum of x in the group of records.
`min(x)`	Returns the minimum of x in the group of records.
`avg(x)`	Returns the average of x in the group of records.

`count(x)` It returns the number of values present in the column x with out including *'null'* values. The '*' may be given as argument to count all the rows of the table including duplicates and *'null'* values.

Examples:

```
SQL> select * from stud;
      RNO            MARK
  ----           -----
     1001              78
     1002              65
     1003              98
     1004              34
     1005              32
SQL> select sum(mark) from stud;
  SUM(MARK)
  ------
        307
SQL> select max(mark) from stud;
  MAX(MARK)
  ------
         98
SQL> select min(mark) from stud;
  MIN(MARK)
  ------
         32
SQL> select avg(mark) from stud;
  AVG(MARK)
  ------
       61.4
SQL> select count(*) from stud;
   COUNT(*)
  ------
          5
```

Data Conversion functions:

`to_char(date [,date-format])`	It converts *date* datatype value to *vachar2* datatype. The *'date-format'* specifies the format of the date in *varchar2*type.
`to_date(char [,date-format]`	It converts *char* or *varchar2* datatype into *date* datatype. The *'date-format'* specifies the format of the date in *date* type. The *[,date-format]* is optional.

Examples:

```
SQL> insert into emp values (50001, '12-DEC-2005');
1 row created.
SQL> insert into emp values (50002, '07-JAN-2006');
1 row created.
SQL> insert into emp values (50003,'11-FEB-2006');
1 row created.
SQL> select * from emp;
      ENO  DOJ
   ----  -----
    50001  12-DEC-05
    50002  07-JAN-06
    50003  11-FEB-06
SQL> select eno, to_char(doj,'dd/mm/yyyy') from emp;
      ENO  TO_CHAR(DO
   ----  ------
    50001  12/12/2005
    50002  07/01/2006
    50003  11/02/2006
SQL> insert into emp values (50004, to_date('01/01/2001','dd/mm/yyyy'));
1 row created.
SQL> select * from emp;
      ENO  DOJ
   ----  -----
    50001  12-DEC-05
    50002  07-JAN-06
    50003  11-FEB-06
    50004  01-JAN-01
```

SUMMARY

This chapter stated with listing supported data types in Oracle, and each type of SQL commands are explained with illustrations. Then, it explained important core concepts such as set operations, and join operations, and sub-queries. This chapter further introduced to the readers about how to write Stored Procedures and how to call them.

3

JDBC

3.0 INTRODUCTION

The Java Database Connectivity (JDBC) provides database programming API for Java programs. This API can be used to access any supported RDBMS software. In this chapter, important aspects of JDBC with Oracle database are demonstrated.

3.1 TYPICAL APPLICATION ARCHITECTURE

Java programs use JDBC to manipulate database operation with connected Database. The Driver acts as an intermediate between the Java application and the underlying database.

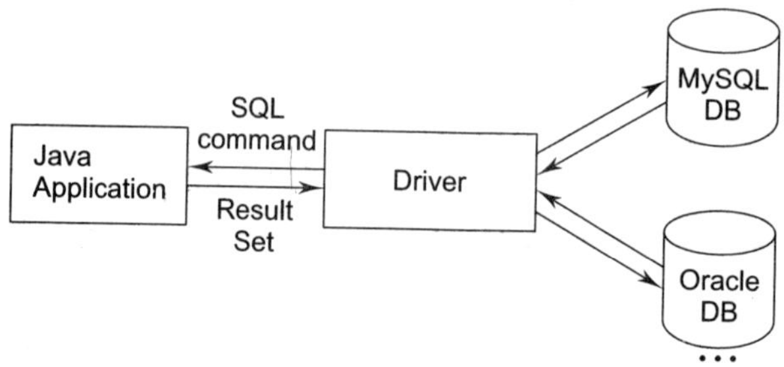

The JDBC driver specification classifies the JDBC drivers into four groups as follows.

Type 1: JDBC-ODBC Bridge: This driver is supplied by Sun Microsystems which provides a bridge between JDBC API and ODBC API *i.e.,* it converts all JDBC API calls into corresponding ODBC API calls (passed on the connected database) and vice-versa.

Type 2: Native API Partly- Java Driver: This driver converts all JDBC API calls into corresponding vendor-specific API calls (passed on the connected vendor's database) and vice-versa.

Type 3: JDBC- Net Pure Java Driver: These drivers provide three-tier solutions for database access model. This driver translates all the JDBC API calls into database independent network protocol. Then, this is sent to a middleware server, which translates its input into DBMS-specific protocol as output. Then this output is sent to a particular connected database and vice-versa.

Type 4: Native- Protocol Pure Java Driver: This driver directly communicates with the vendor's database engine via its native protocol. There are no any translations between the application and the database.

3.2 DATA TYPE COMPARISON

The SQL data types and their corresponding Java data types are given below.

SQL Data Type	Java Data Type
INTEGER	int
SAMLLINT	short
NUMERIC(M,N)	java.sql.Numeric
FLOAT(N), DOUBLE	double
REAL	float
CHAR(N), VARCHAR(N), LONGVARCHAR	String
BOOLEAN	boolean
DATE	java.sql.Date
TIME	java.sql.Time
BLOB	java.sql.Blob
CLOB	java.sql.Clob
ARRAY	java.sql.Array
DECIMAL	java.math.BigDecimal

3.3 ESTABLISHING CONNECTION WITH DATABASE

The JDBC driver must be loaded before connecting to the database by a Java program.

The class name for the JDBC-ODBC Bridge Driver (Type 1 Driver, and it is available with JDK) is **sun.jdbc.odbc.JdbcOdbcDriver**

A driver can be loaded by calling the *Class.forName()* method with the driver name as its argument.

Example:

```
Class.forName("sun.jdbc.odbc.JdbcOdbcDriver");
```

It creates an instance of the driver (JdbcOdbcDriver) and registers it with the *DriverManager*.

We can use JDBC drivers provided database vendors (Type 4 drivers), for that the class for the driver (jar file) should be in CLASSPATH. Generally these drivers are supplied in jar file format by database vendors and many of them can be downloaded from Internet.

Oracle Thin Client:

```
Class.forName("oracle.jdbc.driver.OracleDriver ");
```

MySQL:

```
Class.forName("com.mysql.jdbc.Driver");
```

Establishing a Database Connection

The get Connection() static method available in DriverManager class is used to get (open) a database connection.

JDBC-ODBC Bridge:

```
Connection c = DriverManager.getConnection("JDBC URL","username","password");
```

The statement will establish a connection to the given database. Here, "JDBC URL" specifies the data source name, which has the following syntax,

Protocol:Subprotocol:DSN

The Protocol always be "jdbc" and Subprotocol generally be "odbc"; the subprotocol specifies which kind of database connectivity being requested such as *odbc, oracle*; and the DSN is the Data Source Name which is created in ODBC Connection. The "username" and "password" specify the username and password to connect the required database.

Oracle Thin Client:

```
Connection c= DriverManager.getConnection ("jdbc:oracle:thin: <HOST>:<PORT>:
                                  <DATABASE_SID>", "username", "password");
```

MySQL:

```
Connection c = DriverManager.getConnection("jdbc:mysql://<HOST>:<PORT>/<DATABASE>",
                                          "username", "password");
```

3.4 JDBC API

The important and frequently used APIs for JDBC are briefed below.

3.4.1 Method under `DriverManager` class

`static Connection getConnection(String url, String username, String password)`

It establishes a connection to the specified database and returns a Connection object.

3.4.2 Methods under `Connection` Interface

`Statement createStatement()`

It returns a Statement object that can be used to execute SQL commands without parameters (and, necessary SQL statements are specified later in this case).

`PreparedStatement prepareStatement(String sqlcommand)`

It returns a PreparedStatement object containing the precompiled statement. The SQL statement that can contain one or more parameter placeholders denoted by ? characters (And, necessary SQL statements are specified here in this case).

`void close()`

It closes the current connection with the database.

3.4.3 Methods under Statement Interface

`ResultSet executeQuery(String sqlselectcommand)`

It executes the specified SQL select command and returns a ResultSet to view the query result.

`int executeUpdate(String sqlcommand)`

It executes all the SQL statements other than SQL SELECT and returns the number of records affected, or returns -1 if the records are not affected.

`boolean execute(String sqlcommand)`

It executes all type of the SQL statements specified as its parameter and returns true if the statement returns a ResultSet (if SQL SELECT statement is specified), false otherwise. Use the getResultSet() or getUpdateCount() method to obtain the Statement outcome.

`ResultSet getResultSet()`

It retrieves the current ResultSet object. *i.e.*, it returns the ResultSet of the preceding query Statement (normally, that query is executed through *execute()* method), or *null* if the preceding Statement did not have a result set. Call this method only once per executed statement.

`int getUpdateCount()`

It returns the number of records affected by the preceding update statement (normally, executed through *execute()* method), or -1 if the preceding statement was a statement without an update count. Call this method only once per executed statement.

Example:

Using JDBC-ODBC Bridge,

```
Class.forName("sun.jdbc.odbc.JdbcOdbcDriver");
Connection c = DriverManager.getConnection("jdbc:odbc:ibrahim","scott","tiger");
```

Note that *ibrahim* is the DSN to the Oracle database which is created earlier (using Start → Control Panel → Administrative Tools → Data Sources). The *username* and *password* for connecting the Oracle database are specified as the second and third parameters.

```
Statement st = c.createStatement();
st.executeUpdate("CREATE TABLE STUDENT (RNO NUMBER(5),
                  SNAME VARCHAR2(15), M1 NUMBER(3),
                  M2 NUMBER(3), M3 NUMBER(3), TOTAL NUMBER(3),
                  AVERAGE NUMBER(5,2), RESULT VARCHAR2(4))" );

ResultSet r = st.executeQuery("SELECT * FROM STUDENT");
```

The create statement is specified for Oracle database. If you are connected other databases, then modify the create statement with the data types that are supported by the connected database. For example, if MS Access database is connected, then use the following statement.

```
st.executeUpdate("CREATE TABLE STUDENT (RNO INTEGER,
                  SNAME TEXT, M1 INTEGER,
                  M2 INTEGER, M3 INTEGER, TOTAL INTEGER,
                  AVERAGE DOUBLE, RESULT TEXT)" );
ResultSet r = st.executeQuery("SELECT * FROM STUDENT");
```

3.4.4 Methods under PreparedStatement Interface

`ResultSet executeQuery()`

It executes a prepared SQL SELECT query (specified in *prepareStatement()* method) and returns a ResultSet.

`int executeUpdate()`

It executes all the prepared SQL statements other than SQL SELECT and returns the number of rows affected or returns 0 for DDL statements.

`void clearParameters()`

It clears all the current parameter values associated with the PreparedStatement.

`void setXXX(int n, XXX x)`

It sets the value of the nth parameter to x for the SQL statement specified in prepareStatement() method. The parameters start with the index 1. Here, XXX represents the type of the data such as Boolean, Int, Long.

For example,

```
void setBoolean(int n, boolean x)
void setByte(int n, byte x)
void setShort(int n, short x)
void setInt(int n, int x)
void setLong(int n, long x)
void setFloat(int n, float x)
void setDouble(int n, double x)
void setDate(int n, java.sql.Date x)
void setTime(int n, java.sql.Time x)
void setBlob(int n, java.sql.Blob x)
void setClob(int n, java.sql.Clob x)
```

`int findColumn(String columnname)`

It returns the column index associated with a column name.

`void close()`

It closes the current result set.

3.4.5 Scrollable and Updatable ResultSet

As you know, the *next()* method of the ResultSet only moves down the rows in a result set. But, the scrolling result set in the latest version of JDBC lets you to move forward and backward through a result set or even positioned at a specific row. And the new version provides interesting facilities: Updateable result set, through which, you can simply update the result set entries, then the database will automatically updated (CONCUR_UPDATABLE), and the result set is updated autcmatically when ever the database has been modified by the same process or by another concurrent process that use the same database (SCROLL_SENSITIVE).

To obtain scrollable and/or updatable result set, you have to use different Statement / PreparedStatement objects. They can be obtained using the following methods.

To obtain Statement object,

```
Statement createStatement(int resultSetType, int resultSetConcurrency)
```

To obtain PreparedStatement object,

```
PreparedStatement prepareStatement(String sqlCommand,
                                   int resultSetType,
                                   int resultSetConcurrency)
```

where, the *resultSetType* can be any one of the following static constants available in the ResultSet interface.

TYPE_FORWARD_ONLY	The result set is not scrollable.
TYPE_SCROLL_INSENSITIVE	The result set is scrollable, but not sensitive to the database changes (If the database is updated, then the updation will not be reflected in the current relevant ResultSet).
TYPE_SCROLL_SENSITIVE	The result set is scrollable and also sensitive to database changes.

And, the *resultSet Concurrency* can be any one of the following static constants available in the Result Set interface.

CONCUR_READ_ONLY	The result set cannot be used to update the database.
CONCUR_UPDATABLE	The result set can be used to update the database.

Examples:

```
Statement st = c.createStatement(
                        ResultSet.TYPE_SCROLL_INSENSITIVE,
                        ResultSet.CONCUR_UPDATABLE);
ResultSet rs = s.executeQuery("SELECT * FROM STUDENT");
PreparedStatement ps = c.prepareStatement(
                        "SELECT * FROM STUDENT",
                        ResultSet.TYPE_SCROLL_INSENSITIVE,
                        ResultSet.CONCUR_UPDATABLE);
ResultSet rs = ps.executeQuery();
```

The methods of ResultSet interface for Scrollable and Updatable Result Sets:

`boolean previous()`

It moves the virtual cursor to the preceding row of the current result set and returns *true* if the cursor is positioned on a row, otherwise returns *false.*

`boolean first()`

It moves the virtual cursor to the first row of the current result set and returns *true* if the cursor is positioned on a row, otherwise returns *false.*

`boolean last()`

It moves the cursor to the last row of the current result set and returns *true* if the cursor is positioned on a row, otherwise returns *false*.

`boolean absolute(int r)`

It moves the cursor to the row 'r' of the current result set and returns *true* if the cursor is positioned on a row, otherwise returns *false*.

`boolean relative(int r)`

It moves the virtual cursor by 'd' rows from the current row of the current result set and returns *true* if the cursor is positioned on a row, otherwise returns *false*. If d is negative, then the cursor is moved backward.

```
void updateXXX(int ColumnNumber, XXX data)
void updateXXX(String ColumnName, XXX data)
```

where, XXX is the required data type (as in *setXXX()* and *getXXX()* methods). These methods update the specified column in the current row of the result set. The index starts with 1. (Note that if the result set is set as CONCUR_UPDATABLE, then the updation will take place on the database automatically.)

`void moveToInsertRow()`

It moves the virtual; cursor to a specified row called "*insert*" row. We can update data for this "insert" row using the updateXXX() methods and a insertRow() method. Then a new row is inserted to the current result set. (Note that if the result set is CONCUR_UPDATABLE, then this new row is also inserted in the database automatically).

`void moveToCurrentRow()`

It moves the cursor back from the "*insert*" row to the row that it occupied when the moveToInsertRow() method was called.

`void insertRow()`

It inserts the contents of the "insert" row in to the result set. (If the result set is set as CONCUR_UPDATABLE, then the row is inserted also to the database).

`void deleteRow()`

It deletes the current row from the result set. (If the result set is CONCUR_UPDATABLE, then also deleted from the database).

`void updateRow()`

It updates the current row changes. It sends the current row updates to the database if CONCUR_UPDATABLE is set.

`void cancelRowUpdates()`

It cancels the current row updates.

`boolean rowInserted()`

It returns *true* if the row has been inserted, otherwise returns *false*.

`boolean rowUpdated()`

It returns *true* if the row has been updated, otherwise returns *false*.

`boolean rowDeleted()`

It returns *true* if the row is deleted, otherwise returns *false*.

3.4.6 Accessing Metadata

If we want to access the information about the selected data (data about data such as number of columns, column names, etc). We can use the *ResultSetMetaData* interface.

Obtain *ResultSetMetaData* object from the *ResultSet* using *getMetaData()* method.

ResultSetMetaData getMetaData()

Methods under `ResultSetMetaData` interface

`int getColumnCount()`

It returns the number of columns in the current result set.

`String getColumnName(int columnindex)`

It returns the column name associated with the specified column index of the current result set. (Column index starts with 1).

`int getPrecision(int columnindex)`

It returns the specified column's precision (length).

3.4.7 Handling Transactions

In JDBC, by default, a database connection is in auto commit mode (makes all changes in the database permanent), and each SQL command is committed to the database as soon as it is executed. Once a command is committed, you cannot roll it back.

A group of SQL statements for a particular task is called a transaction. We may want to execute all the statements in a transaction or none of them. Such kinds of transaction oriented methods are available at Connection interface.

`void commit()`

It makes the changes on the database permanent *i.e.*, it commits all the statements that were issued since the last commit.

`boolean getAutoCommit()`

It returns the status of the auto commit mode of the invoking Connection.

`void setAutoCommit(boolean mode)`

It sets the auto commit mode of Connection.

`void rollback()`

It undoes the effects of all the statements that were issued since the last commit. You typically issue a rollback when your transaction was interrupted by a SQLException.

`Savepoint setSavepoint()`

It creates a named savepoint (a location in the transaction)

`void rollback(Savepoint spname)`

It undoes the effects of all the statements that were issued since the specified *savepoint* was set.

`void releaseSavepoint(Savepoint spname)`

It removes the *Savepoint* object.

Example:

```
try
{
    Class.forName("sun.jdbc.odbc.JdbcOdbcDriver");
    Connection c = DriverManager.getConnection("jdbc:odbc:ibrahim","scott","tiger");
}
catch(Exception e)
{
    System.out.println("Unable to load the driver." + e);
}
try
{
    boolean b = c.getAutoCommit();
    c.setAutoCommit(false);
    Statement st = c.createStatement();
    st.executeUpdate("UPDATE SBACCOUNT SET AMOUNT = AMOUNT-500 WHERE ACNO=1000");
    st.executeUpdate("UPDATE SBACCOUNT SET AMOUNT = AMOUNT+500 WHERE ACNO=2000");
    c.commit();
    c.setAutoCommit(b);
}
catch(SQLException e)
{
    c.rollback();
}
```

If there is no runtime error occurred during the transaction of Amount updation, then *rollback()* will not be executed so that the row updates will done successfully. If a runtime error occurred due to SQL operation during the transaction, then the SQLException is thrown so that the transaction is rolled back, hence no updation will take place int the database.

Example:

```
...
...
Savepoint sp = c.setSavepoint();
...
...
...
c.rollback(sp);
```

The statements after the setting of the Savepoint *sp* will be rolled back (undone).

3.4.8 Batch Updates

In a batch update, a sequence of SQL commands (in a transaction) are included in a batch using addBatch() method; and a batch can be executed using the executeBatch() method. This executeBatch() method returns an array that contains the number of SQL statements that were executed successfully.

However, you can not add SQL SELECT statements to a batch since executing a SELECT query returns a ResultSet.

Set AutoCommit to false before executing a batch and call commit() method after the execution of a batch to make the changes permanent with the database.

```
try
{
    c.setAutoCommit(false);
    Statement st = c.createStatement();
    st.addBatch("UPDATE SBACCOUNT SET AMOUNT = AMOUNT-500 WHERE ACNO=1000");
    st.addBatch("UPDATE SBACCOUNT SET AMOUNT = AMOUNT+500 WHERE ACNO=2000");
    st.executeBatch();
    c.commit();
    c.setAutoCommit(true);
}
catch(Exception e)
{
   System.out.println(e);
}
```

3.4.9 Manipulation with Stored Procedures

A stored procedure in database refers a group of statements like methods in Java.

Use prepareCall() method of Connection by specifying the procedure call statement enclosed by braces as its parameter to obtain a CallableStatement object. Then, call the execute() method with the associated CallableStatement object.

We can create stored procedures in a database through JDBC using the executeUpdate() method like creating tables. Note that the exact syntax for the stored procedures differs among databases and also some databases do not support the stored procedures.

Example: Stored procedure without parameters

Creating a stored procedure:

```
Statement st = c.createStatement();
st.executeUpdate("create procedure DISPSTUDENT as SELECT * FROM STUDENT");
```

Calling a stored procedure:

```
CallableStatement cs = c.prepareCall("{call DISPSTUDENT}");
ResultSet r = cs.executeQuery();
```

Example: Stored procedure with a parameter

Creating a stored procedure:

```
Statement st = c.createStatement();
```

```
st.executeUpdate(" create procedure del(rollno in number) is " +
                 " begin                                      " +
                 " delete from STUDENT where STUDENT.RNO = rollno;" +
                 "end");
```

Calling a stored procedure:

```
CallableStatement cs = c.prepareCall("{call del(?)}");
cs.setInt(1,1000);
cs.execute();
```

3.5 SAMPLE PROGRAMS

The following sample programs illustrate how to manipulate data in database through Java applications with JDBC. All of the programs use JDBC-ODBC Bridge Driver (Type 1 Deriver) to establish connection with database, and Oracle is used as database. The readers are advised to alter the connection settings in the programs to use other types of JDBC drivers, and alter SQL statements if other database (other than Oracle) is used.

Write a program to create a table named STUDENT with the following fields.

Roll number

Student name

Marks in three subjects

Total

Average and

Result

Program:

Program: Program to create a table in connected Oracle database.

Concept: Illustrating Statement interface and executeUpdate() method

```
import java.sql.*;
public class JdbcCreate
{
    public static void main(String args[])
    {
        try
        {
          Class.forName("sun.jdbc.odbc.JdbcOdbcDriver");
        }
        catch(Exception e)
        {
          System.out.println("Error on loading JDBC-ODBC Driver : " + e);
        }
        try
```

```
{
    Connection c =
    DriverManager.getConnection ("jdbc:odbc:ibrahim","scott","tiger");
    Statement st = c.createStatement();
    st.executeUpdate("CREATE TABLE STUDENT (RNO NUMBER(5),
                     SNAME VARCHAR2(15)," +
                     "M1 NUMBER(3), M2 NUMBER(3),
                     M3 NUMBER(3), TOTAL NUMBER(3)," +
                     "AVERAGE
                     NUMBER(5,2), RESULT VARCHAR2(4))" );
    System.out.println("Table is created successfully.");
}
catch(SQLException e)
{
    System.out.println("Error in creating the table. " + e);
}
    }
}
```

Output:

Creating a DSN:

Before executing this program, create a user DSN named *"ibrahim"* for Oracle database as follows.

(In Windows OS) Choose, Start → Settings → Control Panel → Administrative Tools → Data Sources (ODBC).

Then, the following window is displayed.

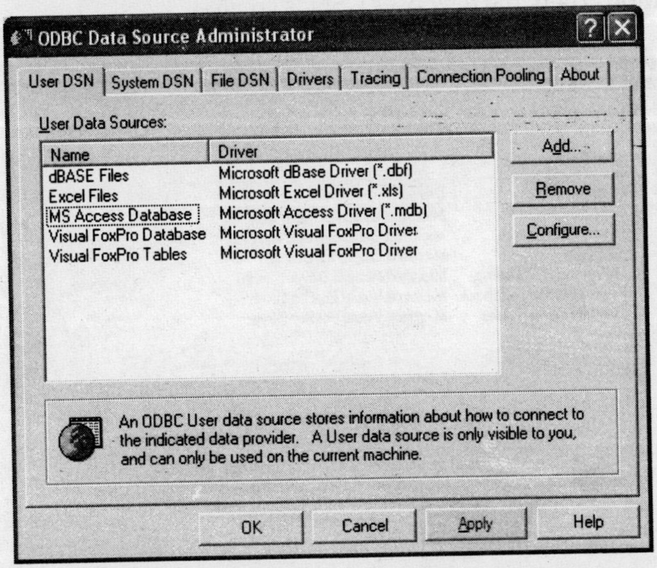

Click on *"Add…"* button. Then, a *"Create New Data Source"* window is opened. Select *"Microsoft ODBC for Oracle"* in the Name list box and click "Finish" button.

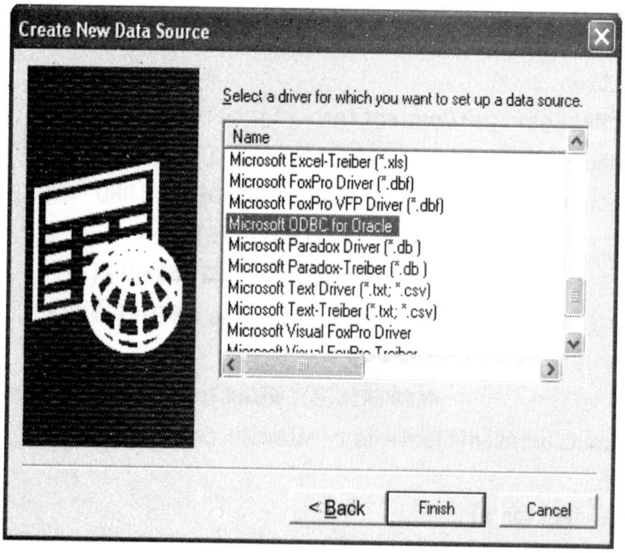

Then, the "*Microsoft ODBC for Oracle Setup*" window is opened. Here, type "*ibrahim*" for Data Source Name, type user-name of Oracle in User Name text box, and type server connecting string in Server text box. Note that I am using "*scott*" as user-name and "*jmcl*" as Server connecting string. Specify these two parameters according to your system setting.

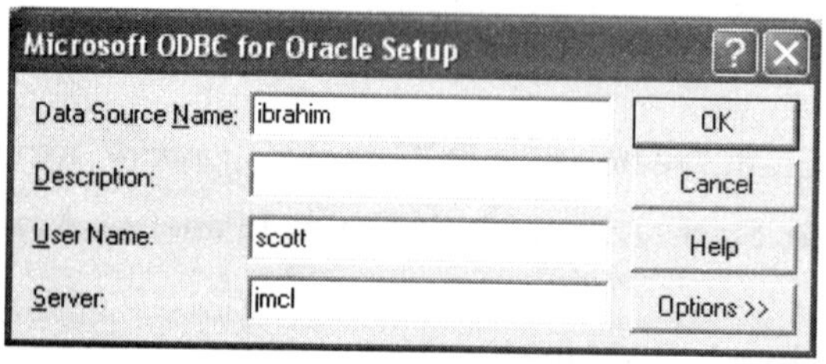

Click the "*OK*" button. Then, the new user DSN is created.

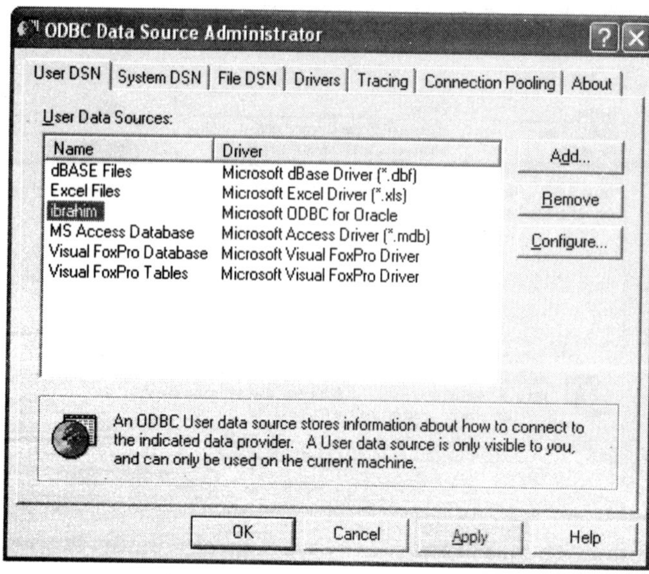

Compiling and Running the Java Program: Assumed that the Java files are stored in D:\Ibrahim directory and JDK bin directory is on PATH. And required libraries (JDBC driver jar files if other types of drivers are used ...) and current directory is on CLASSPATH.

```
D:\IBRAHIM> javac JdbcCreate.java
D:\IBRAHIM> java JdbcCreate
Table is created successfully.
```

Test with the Database:

Open the Oracle SQL prompt and give the *desc student* command to test whether the table is created or not.

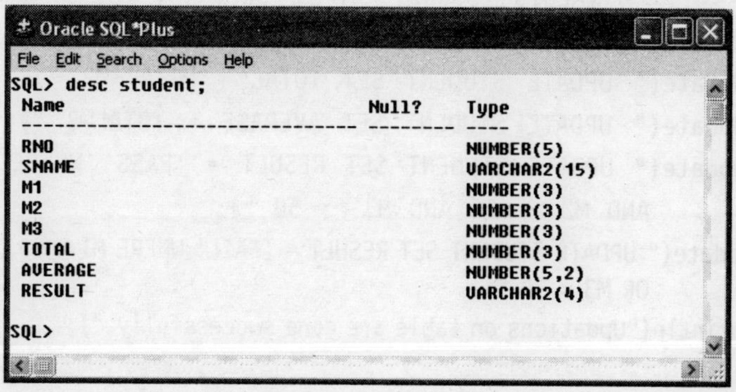

```
Oracle SQL*Plus
File Edit Search Options Help
SQL> desc student;
 Name                                      Null?    Type
 ----------------------------------------- -------- ------------
 RNO                                                NUMBER(5)
 SNAME                                              VARCHAR2(15)
 M1                                                 NUMBER(3)
 M2                                                 NUMBER(3)
 M3                                                 NUMBER(3)
 TOTAL                                              NUMBER(3)
 AVERAGE                                            NUMBER(5,2)
 RESULT                                             VARCHAR2(4)

SQL>
```

Write a program to insert five different values for the fields, Roll number, Student name, and Marks in three subjects of the table STUDENT. Update the table for the fields, Total, Average, and Result.

Program:

```
import java.sql.*;
public class JdbcInsertUpdate
{
 public static void main(String args[])
 {
  try
  {
    Class.forName("sun.jdbc.odbc.JdbcOdbcDriver");
  }
  catch(Exception e)
  {
    System.out.println("Error on loading JDBC-ODBC Driver : " + e);
  }
  try
  {
    Connection c = DriverManager.getConnection("jdbc:odbc:ibrahim","scott","tiger");
    Statement st = c.createStatement();
```

```
        st.executeUpdate(" INSERT INTO STUDENT (RNO,SNAME,M1,M2,M3) " +
                         " VALUES (50001, 'MOHAMED IBRAHIM', 100, 90, 80) ");
        st.executeUpdate(" INSERT INTO STUDENT (RNO,SNAME,M1,M2,M3) " +
                         " VALUES (50002, 'JOIN PEETER', 65, 98, 49) ");
        st.executeUpdate(" INSERT INTO STUDENT (RNO,SNAME,M1,M2,M3) " +
                         " VALUES (50003, 'RAMESH KANNA', 50, 51, 72) ");
        st.executeUpdate(" INSERT INTO STUDENT (RNO,SNAME,M1,M2,M3) " +
                         " VALUES (50004, 'SHEIK ABDULLAH', 12, 50, 34) ");
        st.executeUpdate(" INSERT INTO STUDENT (RNO,SNAME,M1,M2,M3) " +
                         " VALUES (50005, 'TAMIL SELVAN', 78,56, 61) ");
        System.out.println("Five rows are inserted successfully.");
        st.executeUpdate(" UPDATE STUDENT SET TOTAL = M1+M1+M2 ");
        st.executeUpdate(" UPDATE STUDENT SET AVERAGE = TOTAL/3 ");
        st.executeUpdate(" UPDATE STUDENT SET RESULT = 'PASS' WHERE M1 >= 50
                        AND M2 >= 50 AND M3 >= 50 ");
        st.executeUpdate(" UPDATE STUDENT SET RESULT = 'FAIL' WHERE M1 < 50 OR M2 < 50
                        OR M3 < 50 ");
        System.out.println("Updations on table are done successfully.");
      }
      catch(SQLException e)
      {
        System.out.println("Error: " + e);
      }
    }
  }
```

Output:

```
D:\IBRAHIM> javac JdbcInsertUpdate.java
D:\IBRAHIM> java JdbcInsertUpdate
Five rows are inserted successfully.
Updations on table are done successfully.
```

Test with the Database

Open the Oracle SQL prompt and give the command as shown below.

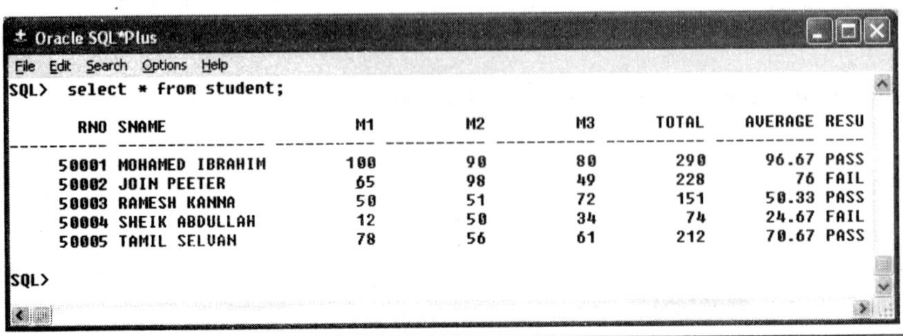

```
SQL> select * from student;

       RNO SNAME                   M1         M2         M3      TOTAL    AVERAGE RESU
---------- --------------- ---------- ---------- ---------- ---------- ---------- ----
     50001 MOHAMED IBRAHIM        100         90         80        290      96.67 PASS
     50002 JOIN PEETER             65         98         49        228         76 FAIL
     50003 RAMESH KANNA            50         51         72        151      50.33 PASS
     50004 SHEIK ABDULLAH          12         50         34         74      24.67 FAIL
     50005 TAMIL SELVAN            78         56         61        212      70.67 PASS

SQL>
```

Write a program to select the rows of the STUDENT table and display them on the screen.

Program:

```
import java.sql.*;
public class JdbcSelect
{
public static void main(String args[])
{
  try
  {
    Class.forName("sun.jdbc.odbc.JdbcOdbcDriver");
  }
  catch(Exception e)
  {
    System.out.println("Error on loading JDBC-ODBC Driver : " + e);
  }
  try
  {
   Connection c = DriverManager.getConnection("jdbc:odbc:ibrahim","scott","tiger");
   Statement st = c.createStatement();
   ResultSet r = st.executeQuery("SELECT * FROM STUDENT");
   System.out.println("\n ROLL No. SNAME \t M1 M2 M3 TOTAL AVERAGE RESULT ");
   for (int i=1; i<=60; i++)
   System.out.print("=");
  while( r.next() )
  {
   int rollno = r.getInt("RNO");
   String sname = r.getString("SNAME");
   int mark1 = r.getInt("M1");
   int mark2 = r.getInt("M2");
   int mark3 = r.getInt("M3");
   int total = r.getInt("TOTAL");
   double aver = r.getDouble("AVERAGE");
   String result = r.getString("RESULT");
   System.out.printf("\n %6d %-16s %3d %3d %3d %3d %6.2f %4s",
                   rollno, sname, mark1, mark2, mark3, total, aver, result);
  }
  System.out.println();
  for (int i=1; i<=60; i++)
    System.out.print("=");
```

```
    }
    catch(Exception e)
    {
    System.out.println("Error: " + e);
    }
  }
}
```

Output:

```
D:\IBRAHIM> javac JdbcSelect.java
D:\IBRAHIM> java JdbcSelect
ROLL No.   SNAME              M1     M2     M3    TOTAL   AVERAGE RESULT
=======================================================================
50001 MOHAMED IBRAHIM        100     90     80     290      96.67 PASS
50002 JOIN PEETER             65     98     49     228      76.00 FAIL
50003 RAMESH KANNA            50     51     72     151      50.33 PASS
50004 SHEIK ABDULLAH          12     50     34      74      24.67 FAIL
50005 TAMIL SELVAN            78     56     61     212      70.67 PASS
=======================================================================
```

Write a program to insert and update five rows to the existing STUDENT table using PreparedStatement.

Program:

```
import java.sql.*;
public class PreparedSt
{
  public static void main(String args[])
  {
    int rno[] = {50006, 50007, 50008, 50009, 50010};
    String sname[] = {"RAVI KUMAR", "MAC ANTANY", "KRISHNA KUMAR",
                      "MOHAMED YASIN", "VIJAYA KUMAR" };
    int m1[] = {90,67,65,72,75};
    int m2[] = {93,90,41,80,46};
    int m3[] = {85,59,82,85,32};
    try
    {
      Class.forName("sun.jdbc.odbc.JdbcOdbcDriver");
      Connection c = Driver Manager.getConnection ("jdbc:odbc:ibrahim","scott","tiger");
      Statement st = c.createStatement();
      PreparedStatement ps = c.prepareStatement(
                            "INSERT INTO STUDENT (RNO,SNAME,M1,M2,M3)
```

```
                          VALUES(?,?,?,?,?)");
     for (int i=0;i<rno.length;i++)
      {
         ps.setInt(1,rno[i]);
         ps.setString(2,sname[i]);
         ps.setInt(3,m1[i]);
         ps.setInt(4,m2[i]);
         ps.setInt(5,m3[i]);
         ps.executeUpdate();
      }
      System.out.println("Five rows are inserted successfully.");
      st.executeUpdate(" UPDATE STUDENT SET TOTAL = M1+M1+M2 ");
      st.executeUpdate(" UPDATE STUDENT SET AVERAGE = TOTAL/3.0 ");
      st.executeUpdate(" UPDATE STUDENT SET RESULT = 'PASS' WHERE M1 >= 50
                  AND M2 >= 50 AND M3 >= 50 ");
      st.executeUpdate(" UPDATE STUDENT SET RESULT = 'FAIL' WHERE M1 < 50
                  OR M2 < 50 OR M3 < 50 ");
      System.out.println("Updations on table are done successfully.");
    }
    catch(Exception e)
    {
     System.out.println(e);
    }
  }
}
```

Output:

```
D:\IBRAHIM> javac PreparedSt.java
D:\IBRAHIM> java PreparedSt
Five rows are inserted successfully.
Updations on table are done successfully.
```

Test with the Database:

Open the Oracle SQL prompt and give the command as shown below.

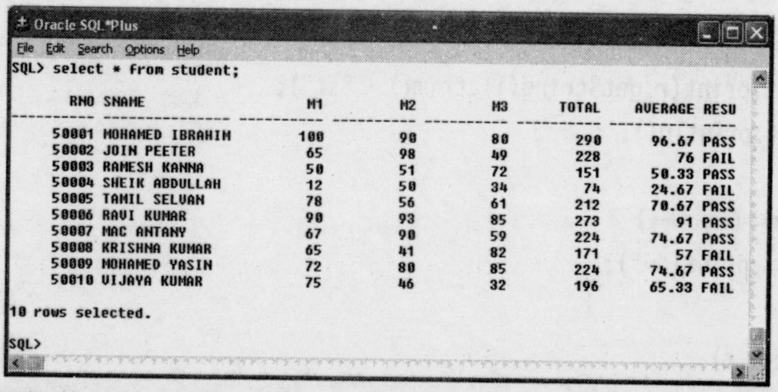

```
Oracle SQL*Plus
File Edit Search Options Help
SQL> select * from student;

       RNO SNAME                   M1         M2         M3      TOTAL    AVERAGE RESU
---------- --------------- ---------- ---------- ---------- ---------- ---------- ----
     50001 MOHAMED IBRAHIM        100         90         80        290      96.67 PASS
     50002 JOIN PEETER             65         98         49        228         76 FAIL
     50003 RAMESH KANNA            50         51         72        151      50.33 PASS
     50004 SHEIK ABDULLAH          12         50         34         74      24.67 FAIL
     50005 TAMIL SELVAN            78         56         61        212      70.67 PASS
     50006 RAVI KUMAR              90         93         85        273         91 PASS
     50007 MAC ANTANY              67         90         59        224      74.67 PASS
     50008 KRISHNA KUMAR           65         41         82        171         57 FAIL
     50009 MOHAMED YASIN           72         80         85        224      74.67 PASS
     50010 VIJAYA KUMAR            75         46         32        196      65.33 FAIL

10 rows selected.

SQL>
```

Write a program to retrieve the rows of the STUDENT table and its Metadata information such as Number of columns and the names of the Columns. Display them on the Screen in a neat format.

Program:

```
import java.sql.*;
public class MetaData
{
   public static void main(String args[])
   {
    int i;
    try
    {
     Class.forName("sun.jdbc.odbc.JdbcOdbcDriver");
    }
    catch(Exception e)
    {
     System.out.println("Error on loading JDBC-ODBC Driver : " + e);
    }
    try
    {
     Connection c = DriverManager.getConnection("jdbc:odbc:ibrahim","scott","tiger");
     Statement st = c.createStatement();
     ResultSet r = st.executeQuery("SELECT * FROM STUDENT");
     ResultSetMetaData rsmd = r.getMetaData();
     int noofcolumns = rsmd.getColumnCount();
     for (i=1; i<=noofcolumns; i++)
      System.out.print(rsmd.getColumnName(i) + " \t");
     System.out.println();
     for (i=1;i<=65;i++)
     System.out.print("=");
      System.out.println();
     while( r.next() )
      {
      for (i=1; i<=noofcolumns; i++)
       System.out.print(r.getString(i).trim() + "\t");
       System.out.println();
      }
      for (i=1; i<=65; i++)
       System.out.print("=");
    }
    catch(Exception e)
```

```
    {
      System.out.println(e);
    }
  }
}
```

Output:

```
D:\IBRAHIM> javac MetaData.java
D:\IBRAHIM> java MetaData
RNO      SNAME   M1          M2      M3    TOTAL    AVERAGE    RESULT
=======================================================================
50001    MOHAMED IBRAHIM    100     90     80      290     96.67    PASS
50002    JOIN PEETER         65     98     49      228     76.00    FAIL
50003    RAMESH KANNA        50     51     72      151     50.33    PASS
50004    SHEIK ABDULLAH      12     50     34       74     24.67    FAIL
50005    TAMIL SELVAN        78     56     61      212     70.67    PASS
50006    RAVI KUMAR          90     93     85      273     91.00    PASS
50007    MAC ANTANY          67     90     59      224     74.67    PASS
50008    KRISHNA KUMAR       65     41     82      171     57.00    FAIL
50009    MOHAMED YASIN       72     80     85      224     74.67    PASS
50010    VIJAYA KUMAR        75     46     32      196     65.33    FAIL
=======================================================================
```

Write a program to insert and update rows to the STUDENT table. Get the required data from the user. (Use Statement interface)

Program:

```
import java.sql.*;
import java.util.*;
public class InteractiveInsert
{
  public static void main(String args[])
  {
    char cho;
    try
    {
      Class.forName("sun.jdbc.odbc.JdbcOdbcDriver");
    }
    catch(Exception e)
    {
      System.out.println("Error on loading JDBC-ODBC Driver : " + e);
```

```
    }
    try
    {
     Connection c = DriverManager.getConnection("jdbc:odbc:ibrahim","scott","tiger");
     Statement st = c.createStatement();
     Scanner s = new Scanner(System.in);
     do
     {
      System.out.print("Enter Roll number ===> ");
      int rollno = s.nextInt();
      s.nextLine(); // Clearing the new-line character.
      System.out.print("Enter Student Name ===> ");
      String sname = s.nextLine();
      System.out.print("Enter Mark in Subject 1 ===> ");
      int mark1 = s.nextInt();
      System.out.print("Enter Mark in Subject 2 ===> ");
      int mark2 = s.nextInt();
      System.out.print("Enter Mark in Subject 3 ===> ");
      int mark3 = s.nextInt();
      String smt = "INSERT INTO STUDENT (RNO,SNAME,M1,M2,M3) VALUES ("
                 + rollno + ",'" + sname + "'," + mark1 + ","
                 + mark2 + "," + mark3 + ")" ;
    st.executeUpdate(smt);
    st.executeUpdate(" UPDATE STUDENT SET TOTAL = M1+M1+M2 ");
    st.executeUpdate(" UPDATE STUDENT SET AVERAGE = TOTAL/3 ");
    st.executeUpdate(" UPDATE STUDENT SET RESULT = 'PASS' WHERE M1 >= 50
                    AND M2 >= 50 AND M3 >= 50 ");
    st.executeUpdate(" UPDATE STUDENT SET RESULT = 'FAIL' WHERE M1 < 50
                    OR M2 < 50 OR M3 < 50 ");
    System.out.println("A Row is inserted and updated successfully.");
    System.out.print("Do you want to continue ? [Y|N] ");
    cho = (char) System.in.read();
   } while (cho == 'Y');
  }
  catch(Exception e)
  {
    System.out.println("Error: " + e);
  }
 }
}
```

Output:

```
D:\IBRAHIM> javac InteractiveInsert.java
D:\IBRAHIM> java InteractiveInsert
Enter Roll number ===> 60001
Enter Student Name ===> RAHMAN
Enter Mark in Subject 1 ===> 78
Enter Mark in Subject 2 ===> 98
Enter Mark in Subject 3 ===> 58
A Row is inserted and updated successfully.
Do you want to continue ? [Y|N] Y
Enter Roll number ===> 60002
Enter Student Name ===> NIZAM
Enter Mark in Subject 1 ===> 50
Enter Mark in Subject 2 ===> 49
Enter Mark in Subject 3 ===> 62
A Row is inserted and updated successfully.
Do you want to continue ? [Y|N] N
```

Test with the Database:

Open the Oracle SQL prompt and give the command as shown below.

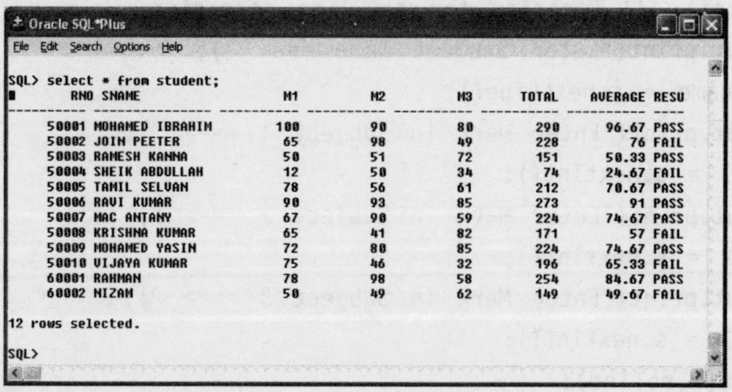

```
SQL> select * from student;

      RNO SNAME                  M1         M2         M3      TOTAL    AVERAGE RESU
--------- --------------- ---------- ---------- ---------- ---------- ---------- ----
    50001 MOHAMED IBRAHIM       100         90         80        290      96.67 PASS
    50002 JOIN PEETER            65         98         49        228         76 FAIL
    50003 RAMESH KANNA           50         51         72        151      50.33 PASS
    50004 SHEIK ABDULLAH         12         50         34         74      24.67 FAIL
    50005 TAMIL SELVAN           78         56         61        212      70.67 PASS
    50006 RAVI KUMAR             90         93         85        273         91 PASS
    50007 MAC ANTANY             67         90         59        224      74.67 PASS
    50008 KRISHNA KUMAR          65         41         82        171         57 FAIL
    50009 MOHAMED YASIN          72         80         85        224      74.67 PASS
    50010 VIJAYA KUMAR           75         46         32        196      65.33 FAIL
    60001 RAHMAN                 78         98         58        254      84.67 PASS
    60002 NIZAM                  50         49         62        149      49.67 FAIL

12 rows selected.

SQL>
```

Write a program to insert and update rows to the STUDENT table. Get the required data from the user. (Use PreparedStatement interface and Batch Update)

Program:

```
import java.sql.*;
import java.util.*;
public class IntInsertPreSt
{
   public static void main(String args[])
   {
     char cho;
```

```
try
{
  Class.forName("sun.jdbc.odbc.JdbcOdbcDriver");
}
catch(Exception e)
{
  System.out.println("Error on loading JDBC-ODBC Driver : " + e);
}
try
{
 Connection c = DriverManager.getConnection("jdbc:odbc:ibrahim","scott","tiger");
 Statement st = c.createStatement();
 PreparedStatement ps = c.prepareStatement(
                "INSERT INTO STUDENT (RNO,SNAME,M1,M2,M3) VALUES (?,?,?,?,?)"
);
 Scanner s = new Scanner(System.in);
 do
 {
  System.out.print("Enter Roll number ===> ");
  int rollno = s.nextInt();
  s.nextLine(); // Clearing the new-line character.
  System.out.print("Enter Student Name ===> ");
  String sname = s.nextLine();
  System.out.print("Enter Mark in Subject 1 ===> ");
  int mark1 = s.nextInt();
  System.out.print("Enter Mark in Subject 2 ===> ");
  int mark2 = s.nextInt();
  System.out.print("Enter Mark in Subject 3 ===> ");
  int mark3 = s.nextInt();
  ps.setInt(1,rollno);
  ps.setString(2,sname);
  ps.setInt(3,mark1);
  ps.setInt(4,mark2);
  ps.setInt(5,mark3);
  ps.executeUpdate();
  st.addBatch(" UPDATE STUDENT SET TOTAL = M1+M1+M2 ");
  st.addBatch(" UPDATE STUDENT SET AVERAGE = TOTAL/3 ");
  st.addBatch(" UPDATE STUDENT SET RESULT = 'PASS' WHERE M1>=50 AND M2>=50
          AND M3>=50 ");
  st.addBatch(" UPDATE STUDENT SET RESULT = 'FAIL' WHERE M1<50 OR M2<50
          OR M3<50 ");
```

```
            st.executeBatch();
            System.out.println("A Row is inserted and updated successfully.");
            System.out.print("Do you want to continue ? [Y|N] ");
            cho = (char) System.in.read();
         } while (cho == 'Y');
      }
      catch(Exception e)
      {
         System.out.println("Error: " + e);
      }
   }
}
```

Output:

```
D:\IBRAHIM> javac IntInsertPreSt.java
D:\IBRAHIM> java IntInsertPreSt
Enter Roll number ===> 80001
Enter Student Name ===> PREM
Enter Mark in Subject 1 ===> 89
Enter Mark in Subject 2 ===> 45
Enter Mark in Subject 3 ===> 65
A Row is inserted and updated successfully.
Do you want to continue ? [Y|N] Y
Enter Roll number ===> 80002
Enter Student Name ===> NAVAS
Enter Mark in Subject 1 ===> 89
Enter Mark in Subject 2 ===> 97
Enter Mark in Subject 3 ===> 67
A Row is inserted and updated successfully.
Do you want to continue ? [Y|N] N
```

Test with the Database:

Open the Oracle SQL prompt and give the command as shown below.

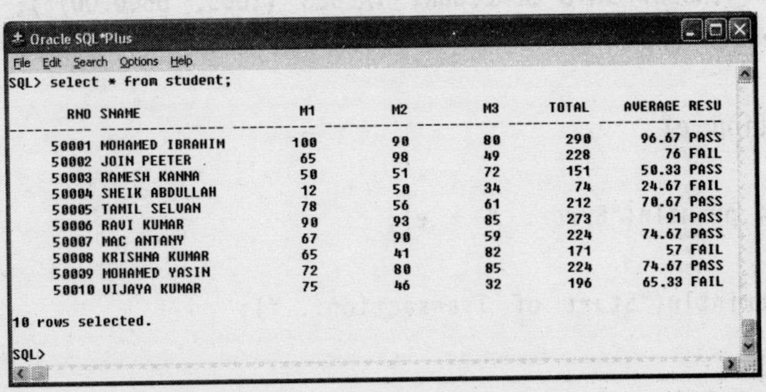

```
SQL> select * from student;

       RNO SNAME                  M1         M2         M3      TOTAL    AVERAGE RESU
---------- --------------- ---------- ---------- ---------- ---------- ---------- ----
     50001 MOHAMED IBRAHIM       100         90         80        290      96.67 PASS
     50002 JOIN PEETER            65         98         49        228         76 FAIL
     50003 RAMESH KANNA           50         51         72        151      50.33 PASS
     50004 SHEIK ABDULLAH         12         50         34         74      24.67 FAIL
     50005 TAMIL SELVAN           78         56         61        212      70.67 PASS
     50006 RAVI KUMAR             90         93         85        273         91 PASS
     50007 MAC ANTANY             67         90         59        224      74.67 PASS
     50008 KRISHNA KUMAR          65         41         82        171         57 FAIL
     50039 MOHAMED YASIN          72         80         85        224      74.67 PASS
     50010 VIJAYA KUMAR           75         46         32        196      65.33 FAIL

10 rows selected.

SQL>
```

Write a program to create a table named SBACCOUNT with two fields: Acc.No. and Balance. Insert five rows as a Batch. Debit a sum of Rs. 500 from the A/c 1002 and credit the same in the A/c 1005. The condition is these two statements should be executed or not at all.

Program:

```
import java.sql.*;
import java.util.*;
public class Transaction
{
  public static void main(String args[]) throws Exception
  {
  Connection c = null;
  Statement st = null;
  try
  {
    Class.forName("sun.jdbc.odbc.JdbcOdbcDriver");
  }
  catch(Exception e)
  {
    System.out.println("Error on loading JDBC-ODBC Driver : " + e);
  }
  try
  {
   c = DriverManager.getConnection("jdbc:odbc:ibrahim","scott","tiger");
   st = c.createStatement();
   st.executeUpdate("CREATE TABLE SBACCOUNT (ACNO NUMBER(4), BALANCE NUMBER(8,2))" );
   st.addBatch("INSERT INTO SBACCOUNT VALUES (1001, 10000.00)");
   st.addBatch("INSERT INTO SBACCOUNT VALUES (1002, 12000.00)");
   st.addBatch("INSERT INTO SBACCOUNT VALUES (1003, 15000.00)");
   st.addBatch("INSERT INTO SBACCOUNT VALUES (1004, 7000.00)");
   st.addBatch("INSERT INTO SBACCOUNT VALUES (1005, 6500.00)");
   st.executeBatch();
  }
  catch(Exception e)
  {
   System.out.println("Error: " + e);
  }
  System.out.println("Start of Transaction...");
  try
```

```
    {
      boolean b = c.getAutoCommit();
      c.setAutoCommit(false);
      st.executeUpdate("UPDATE SBACCOUNT SET BALANCE=BALANCE-500 WHERE ACNO=1002");
      st.executeUpdate("UPDATE SBACCOUNT SET BALANCE=BALANCE+500 WHERE ACNO=1005");
      c.commit();
      c.setAutoCommit(b);
      }
      catch (SQLException e)
      {
      c.rollback();
      }
      System.out.println("...End of Transaction");
    }
  }
```

Output:

```
D:\IBRAHIM> javac Transaction.java
D:\IBRAHIM> java Transaction
Start of Transaction...
...End of Transaction
```

Test with the Database:

Open the Oracle SQL prompt and give the command as shown below.

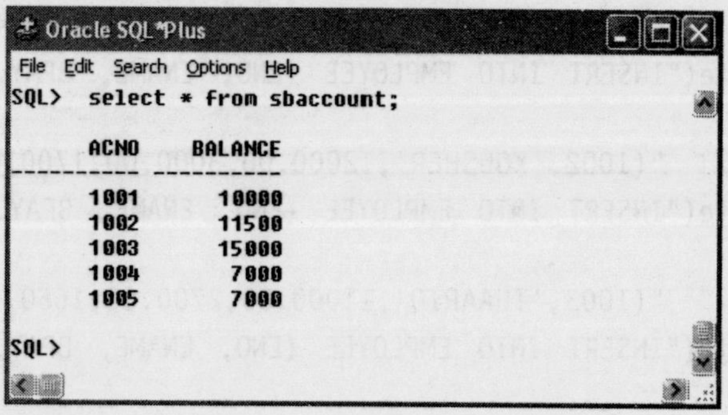

Write a program to create a table named EMPLOYEE with the following fields.

Employee number

Employee name

Basic pay

Allowance

Deduction

Net pay

Insert and update five rows, select the rows and display them on the screen.

Program:

```
import java.sql.*;
public class JdbcEmployee
{
  public static void main(String args[])
  {
  try
  {
    Class.forName("sun.jdbc.odbc.JdbcOdbcDriver");
  }
  catch(Exception e)
  {
    System.out.println("Error on loading JDBC-ODBC Driver : " + e);
  }
  try
  {
    Connection c = DriverManager.getConnection("jdbc:odbc:ibrahim","scott","tiger");
    Statement st = c.createStatement();
    st.executeUpdate("CREATE TABLE EMPLOYEE (ENO NUMBER(4), ENAME VARCHAR2(15)," +
          "BPAY NUMBER(8,2), ALLOW NUMBER(8,2), DEDUCT NUMBER(8,2), NPAY
          NUMBER(8,2))");
    st.executeUpdate("INSERT INTO EMPLOYEE (ENO, ENAME, BPAY, ALLOW, DEDUCT)
    VALUES " +
               "(1001,'IBRAHIM',15000.00,4000.00,2500.00)");
    st.executeUpdate("INSERT INTO EMPLOYEE (ENO, ENAME, BPAY, ALLOW, DEDUCT)
    VALUES " +
               "(1002,'KOUSHER',12000.00,3000.00,1700.00)");
    st.executeUpdate("INSERT INTO EMPLOYEE (ENO, ENAME, BPAY, ALLOW, DEDUCT)
    VALUES " +
               "(1003,'THAARIQ',11000.00,2700.00,1650.00)");
    st.executeUpdate("INSERT INTO EMPLOYEE (ENO, ENAME, BPAY, ALLOW, DEDUCT)
    VALUES " +
               "(1004,'MUSTAFA',13500.00,3680.00,2380.00)");
    st.executeUpdate("INSERT INTO EMPLOYEE (ENO, ENAME, BPAY, ALLOW, DEDUCT)
    VALUES " +
               "(1005,'ABDULLA',10500,2300.00,1350.00)");
    st.executeUpdate("UPDATE EMPLOYEE SET NPAY=BPAY+ALLOW-DEDUCT");
    ResultSet r = st.executeQuery("SELECT * FROM EMPLOYEE");
    System.out.println("\n EMP.NO. ENAME BASIC_PAY ALLOWANCES DEDUCTIONS NETPAY ");
System.out.println("========================================================================");
    while( r.next() )
```

```
    {
        int empno = r.getInt("ENO");
        String ename = r.getString("ENAME");
        float basic = r.getFloat("BPAY");
        float allow = r.getFloat("ALLOW");
        float deduct = r.getFloat("DEDUCT");
        float netpay = r.getFloat("NPAY");
        System.out.println(" " + empno + " " + ename + " " + basic +
                          " " + allow + "\t" + deduct + "\t " + netpay);

    }
    System.out.println("==================================================");
  }
  catch(Exception e)
  {
   System.out.println(e);
  }
 }
}
```

Output:

```
D:\IBRAHIM> javac JdbcEmployee.java
D:\IBRAHIM> java JdbcEmployee
EMP.NO.  ENAME      BASIC_PAY   ALLOWANCES   DEDUCTIONS   NETPAY
=================================================================
1001    IBRAHIM     15000.0     4000.0       2500.0       16500.0
1002    KOUSHER     12000.0     3000.0       1700.0       13300.0
1003    THAARIQ     11000.0     2700.0       1650.0       12050.0
1004    MUSTAFA     13500.0     3680.0       2380.0       14800.0
1005    ABDULLA     10500.0     2300.0       1350.0       11450.0
=================================================================
```

Test with the Database:

Open the Oracle SQL prompt and give the command as shown below.

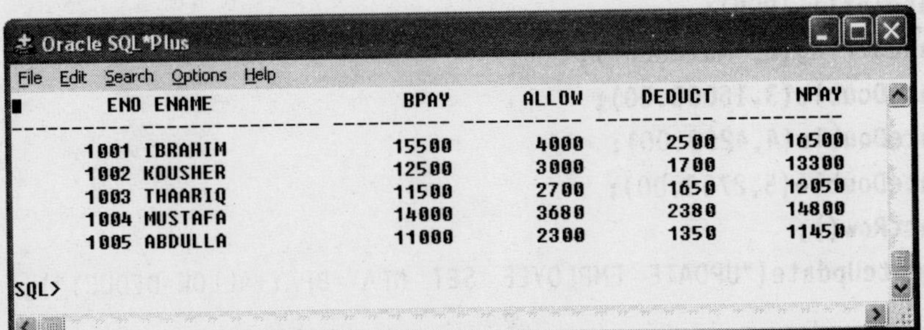

ENO	ENAME	BPAY	ALLOW	DEDUCT	NPAY
1001	IBRAHIM	15500	4000	2500	16500
1002	KOUSHER	12500	3000	1700	13300
1003	THAARIQ	11500	2700	1650	12050
1004	MUSTAFA	14000	3680	2380	14800
1005	ABDULLA	11000	2300	1350	11450

SQL>

Write a program to make changes with the database when you change the result set. (ResultSet.CONCUR_UPDATABLE)

Program:

```
import java.sql.*;
public class JdbcConcurUpdate
{
 public static void main(String args[])
 {
 try
 {
   Class.forName("sun.jdbc.odbc.JdbcOdbcDriver");
 }
 catch(Exception e)
 {
   System.out.println("Error on loading JDBC-ODBC Driver : " + e);
 }
 try
 {
   Connection c = DriverManager.getConnection("jdbc:odbc:ibrahim","scott","tiger");
   Statement st = c.createStatement(ResultSet.TYPE_SCROLL_INSENSITIVE,
                                    ResultSet.CONCUR_UPDATABLE);
   ResultSet r = st.executeQuery("SELECT * FROM EMPLOYEE");
   System.out.println("Updating the third row");
   r.absolute(3);
   r.updateString(2,"Ismail");
   r.updateDouble(3,11500.00);
   r.updateRow();
   System.out.println("Deleting the second row");
   r.relative(-1);
   r.deleteRow();
   System.out.println("Inserting a row at the last");
   r.moveToInsertRow();
   r.updateInt(1,1009);
   r.updateString(2,"Maideen");
   r.updateDouble(3,16000.00);
   r.updateDouble(4,4250.00);
   r.updateDouble(5,2750.00);
   r.insertRow();
   st.executeUpdate("UPDATE EMPLOYEE SET NPAY=BPAY+ALLOW-DEDUCT");
 }
 catch(Exception e)
```

```
    {
       System.out.println(e);
    }
  }
}
```

Output:

```
D:\IBRAHIM> javac JdbcConcurUpdate.java
D:\IBRAHIM> java JdbcConcurUpdate
Updating the third row
Deleting the second row
Inserting a row at the last
```

Test with the Database:

Open the Oracle SQL prompt and give the command as shown below.

Table before running the program.

```
Oracle SQL*Plus
File Edit Search Options Help
SQL> select * from employee;
       ENO ENAME                BPAY      ALLOW     DEDUCT       NPAY
---------- --------------- ---------- ---------- ---------- ----------
      1001 IBRAHIM              15000       4000       2500      16500
      1002 KOUSHER              12000       3000       1700      13300
      1003 THAARIQ              11000       2700       1650      12050
      1004 MUSTAFA              13500       3680       2380      14800
      1005 ABDULLA              10500       2300       1350      11450

SQL>
```

Table after running the program.

```
Oracle SQL*Plus
File Edit Search Options Help
SQL> select * from employee;
       ENO ENAME                BPAY      ALLOW     DEDUCT       NPAY
---------- --------------- ---------- ---------- ---------- ----------
      1001 IBRAHIM              15000       4000       2500      16500
      1003 Ismail               11500       2700       1650      12550
      1004 MUSTAFA              13500       3680       2380      14800
      1005 ABDULLA              10500       2300       1350      11450
      1009 Maideen              16000       4250       2750      17500

SQL>
```

Write a program to make changes with the current result set when you change the database. (ResultSet.TYPE_SCROLL_SENSITIVE)

Program:

```
import java.sql.*;
public class JdbcScrollSensitive
{
```

```
public static void main(String args[])
{
 try
 {
   Class.forName("sun.jdbc.odbc.JdbcOdbcDriver");
 }
 catch(Exception e)
 {
   System.out.println("Error on loading JDBC-ODBC Driver : " + e);
 }
 try
 {
   Connection c = DriverManager.getConnection("jdbc:odbc:ibrahim","scott","tiger");
   Statement st = c.createStatement(ResultSet.TYPE_SCROLL_SENSITIVE,
                                    ResultSet.CONCUR_UPDATABLE);
   ResultSet r = st.executeQuery("SELECT * FROM EMPLOYEE");
   display(r);
   System.out.println("Do modification on the Database");
   System.out.println("Then, Press [Enter] key.");
   System.in.read();
   r.beforeFirst();
   display(r);
 }
 catch(Exception e)
 {
   System.out.println(e);
 }
}
static void display(ResultSet rs)
{
 line();
try
{
 while( rs.next() )
 {
  int empno = rs.getInt("ENO");
  String ename = rs.getString("ENAME");
  float basic = rs.getFloat("BPAY");
  float allow = rs.getFloat("ALLOW");
  float deduct = rs.getFloat("DEDUCT");
```

```
    float netpay = rs.getFloat("NPAY");
    System.out.println(" " + empno + " \t " + ename + " \t" + basic +
                        " \t" + allow + "\t" + deduct + "\t " + netpay);
  }
 }
 catch(SQLException e)
 {
   System.out.println(e);
 }
 line();
}
static void line()
 {
for (int i=1; i<=65; i++)
  System.out.print("=");
System.out.println();
 }
}
```

Output:

```
D:\IBRAHIM> javac JdbcScrollSensitive.java
```

Test with the Database:

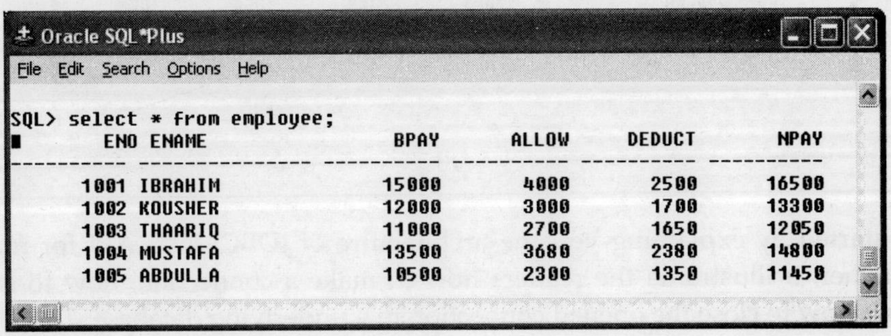


```
D:\IBRAHIM> java JdbcScrollSensitive
=================================================================
1001   IBRAHIM    15000.0     4000.0    2500.0    16500.0
1002   KOUSHER    12000.0     3000.0    1700.0    13300.0
1003   THAARIQ    11000.0     2700.0    1650.0    12050.0
1004   MUSTAFA    13500.0     3680.0    2380.0    14800.0
1005   ABDULLA    10500.0     2300.0    1350.0    11450.0
=================================================================
```

Do modification on the Database

Open the SQL prompt and do modification with the database and give *commit* command as follows.

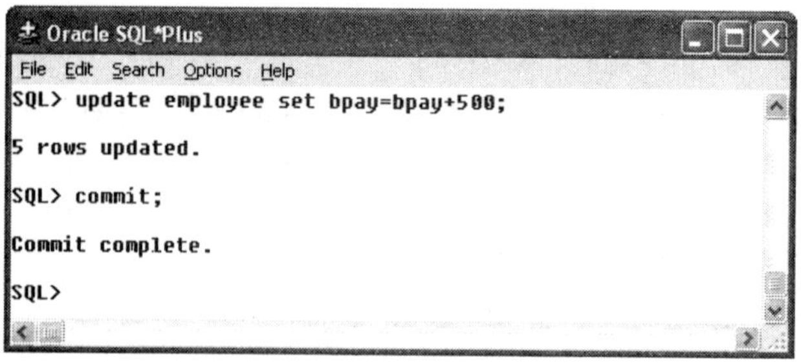

Press *[Enter]* key

```
==========================================================================
1001    IBRAHIM     15500.0     4000.0     2500.0     16500.0
1002    KOUSHER     12500.0     3000.0     1700.0     13300.0
1003    THAARIQ     11500.0     2700.0     1650.0     12050.0
1004    MUSTAFA     14000.0     3680.0     2380.0     14800.0
1005    ABDULLA     11000.0     2300.0     1350.0     11450.0
```

Test with the Database:

Open the Oracle SQL prompt and give the command as shown below.

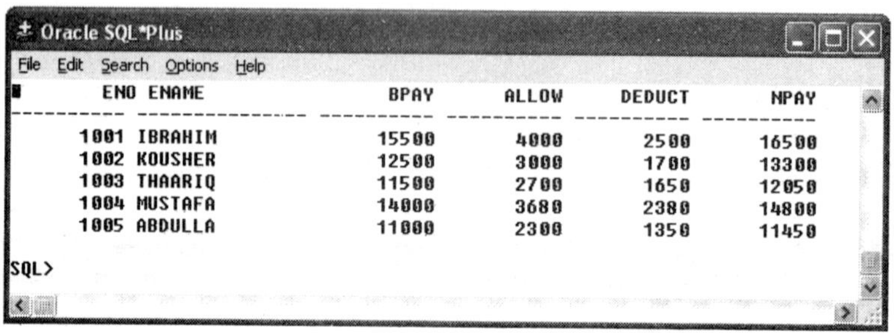

SUMMARY

This chapter started by explaining you the architecture of JDBC, Java API for manipulating Databases. Further, it illustrated the readers how to make a connection, how to execute SQL commands, and how to close the opened connection in a underlying database. This chapter used Oracle database for illustration examples, and sufficient examples are given to make easy understanding of accessing database with Java code.

4

UNDERSTANDING HTML FORM ELEMENTS

4.0 INTRODUCTION

The HTML (Hyper Text Mark-up Language) is a mark-up documentation language, primarily designed by Tim Berners-Lee. It is a universal language to design static web pages and it is machine independent; all the web-browsers running at different platforms understand the HTML code. This chapter introduces the HTML and some of its important tags, but for depth.

4.1 GENERAL FORMAT OF A HTML PROGRAM

Each HRML document has two parts: HEAD and BODY.

```
<html>
  <head>
    Head Section
  </head>
  <body>
    Body Information
  </body>
</html>
```

Here, the <head> describes information such as Title, Meta information (used by search engines) and Scripts (client-side code). It is optional one. The body section describes the information to be displayed on the user-area of the browser and it is essential for all HTML pages except those which use frameset.

4.2 SOME BASIC HTML TAGS

HTML tags are standardised by W3C (World Wide Web Consortium) and almost all the tags are implemented by the browser vendors. Some of the frequently used HTML tags are given below.

4.2.1 Heading

```
<h1> Heading </h1>    Biggest heading
<h6> Heading </h6>    Smallest heading
```

4.2.2 Paragraph

```
<p align="left | right | center | justify"> Paragraph Text </p>
```

The paragraphs are always starts with a new line. The *align* attribute specifies the alignment of the paragraph and it may have any one of the values: *left, right, center* and *justify*. Default is *left* alignment.

4.2.3 Formatting

```
<b> Text </b>                          Bold
<i> Text </i>                          Italic
<u> Text </u>                          Underline
<strike> Text </strike>                Strike through
<sub> subscript Text </sub>            Subscript
<sup> superscript Text </sup>          Superscript
```

4.2.4 Setting Fonts

```
<font face="font-name" size="size" color="#RRGGBB"> Text </font>
```

The *face* attribute specifies the name of the font in which the Text is to be displayed on the browser. The *size* attribute specifies the size of the characters in the specified font. The *color* attribute specifies the colour of the text to be displayed. The RR, GG, and BB are the hexadecimal numbers specifying RGB values of the text colour, and they can have values from 00 to FF. For example, the value #FF0000 gives full red.

4.2.5 Displaying Images

```
<img src="image file-name" width="width of the image"
                          height="height of the image"
</img>
```

4.2.6 Unordered List

```
<UL type="disc | circle | square">
<LI> List Index 1 </LI>
<LI> List Index 2 </LI>
<LI> List Index 3 </LI>
...
</UL>
```

The *type* attribute specifies the bullet to be displayed in front of the list indices.

4.2.7 Ordered List

```
<OL type="1 | A | a | I | i" start="starting index">
```

```
<LI> List Index 1 </LI>
<LI> List Index 2 </LI>
<LI> List Index 3 </LI>
...
</OL>
```

The *type* attribute specifies the index types such as `1 2 3 …`, `A B C …`, `I II III`, or `i ii iii` … . And the *start* attribute specifies the starting number for the list indices.

4.2.8 Hyperlink

When the hyper text is clicked, then the specified page is navigated and displayed.

```
<a href="file-name"> Hyper text </a>
```

4.2.9 Table

Tables are to display data in rows and columns format. Tables are also very much used to arrange the input / output form elements in a neat format.

```
<table>
  <tr>
     <td> Cell 1 of row 1 </td>
     <td> Cell 2 of row 1 </td>
     ...
  </tr>
  <tr>
     <td> Cell 1 of row 2 </td>
     <td> Cell 2 of row 2 </td>
     ...
  </tr>
  ...
</table>
```

4.3 FRAMES AND FRAMESETS

```
<frameset rows|cols="frame-sizes">
  <frame name="frame-name" src="source-filename">
  <frame name="frame-name" src="source-filename">
  ...
</frameset>
```

4.4 HTML FORM AND FORM ELEMENTS

The HTML forms are used to get input from the users and those inputs will be processed by client-side or server-side programs. The *action* attribute informs the browser the location of the server-side program to which the form is to be submitted. The *method* attribute determines the type of the request method to be used to ransfer the form data. If the GET method is specified, then the form data are appended at the end of the URL and sent to the server. If POST method is used, then a new line is added to the body of the request content to send the form data. The default is GET. Since the GET method ransfers data by appending with the end of the URL of the server program (specified in *action* attribute), it is simpler and fast. But, the data are displayed at the browser's address bar as well as it restricts the size of the data. Since the POST method inserts the data with the request, we can send huge data and the data will not be displayed on the browser's address bar so that the data becomes confidential.

```
<form name="form-name" action="action-URL" method="GET|POST">
        Form elements embedded with HTML data
</form>
```

4.4.1 TextBox

```
<input type="text" name="object-name"
         size="number of characters visible" value="default-value">
```

4.4.2 Password

It is similar to text box, but the characters are displayed as asterisks. But, the original characters are sent to action scripts.

```
<input type="password" name="object-name" value="default-value">
```

4.4.3 Check Box

```
<input type="checkbox" name="object-name" value="datum" checked>
```

If you specified the "*checked*" option, then the checkbox will be checked by default.

4.4.4 Radio Buttons

```
<input type="radio" name="object-name" value="datum">
<input type="radio" name="object-name" value="datum">
...
```

When you are creating a radio group (*i.e.*, if you select an radio button in a radio group, then the already selected radio button in the group will be deselected automatically), then use the same object-name for all the radio buttons.

4.4.5 Combo Box

```
<select name="object-name">
 <option value="datum" selected> Option1 </option>
 <option value="datum"> Option2 </option>
 ...
</select>
```

It will create a Combo box, *i.e.*, only one item is displayed, if you click a combo option button, other items can be viewed and the necessary item can be selected.

4.4.6 List Box

If you specify *size* or *multiple* attribute to the above *select* tag, then it will act as List box. The *size* attribute specifies the number of items visible (It must have a value greater than one for list boxes) and the *multiple* attribute allows you to select multiple items from the list box.

```
<select name="object-name" size="No. of items visible" multiple>
  <option value="datum" selected> Option1 </option>
  <option value="datum"> Option2 </option>
  ...
</select>
```

4.4.7 Text Area

```
<textarea name="object-name" rows="number of rows visible"
                        cols="number of columns visible">
  Default text
</textarea>
```

This will create a text area (we can enter multiple lines of text) in which (rows X cols) number of characters visible, but we can enter more characters.

4.4.8 Hidden

```
<input type="hidden" name="object-name" value="datum">
```

This field is not displayed on the browser, but its name along with its value will be sent to the action script for processing when the form is submitted.

4.4.9 File

```
<input type="file" name="object-name" size="size">
```

This will create a text box with "*Browse...*" button, if you click his button, then a file dialog will be displayed to choose a file, then the chosen file is placed in the text box.

4.4.10 Reset Button

When it is clicked, then it resets (bring the form elements to default state) the corresponding form elements.

```
<input type="reset" value="caption">
```

4.4.11 Submit Button

When it is clicked, then it submits the corresponding form data to the server for further processing.

```
<input type="submit" value="caption">
```

4.5 SAMPLE PROGRAMS

Heading

Store the following content in the file named "heading.html" in C:\bmi (for example).

```
<html>
 <head>
  <title> Different types of headings </title>
</head>
<body>
  <h1> Heading1 </h1>
  <h2> Heading1 </h2>
  <h3> Heading1 </h3>
  <h4> Heading1 </h4>
  <h5> Heading1 </h5>
  <h6> Heading1 </h6>
 </body>
</html>
```

Invoke the browser (for example, MS Internet Explorer) and open the "heading.html" file.

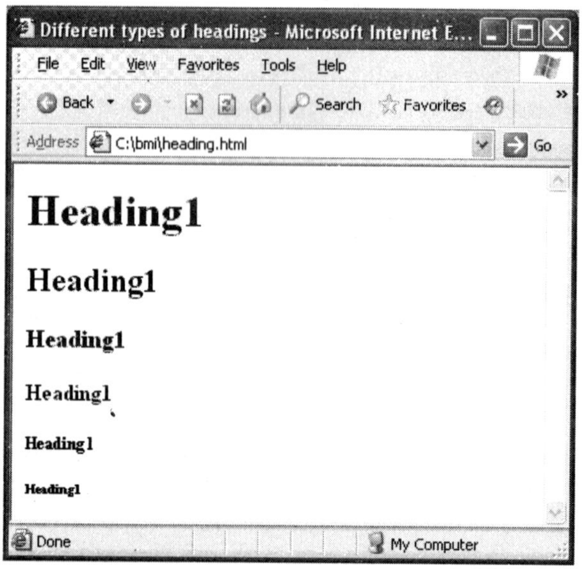

Paragraph

File Name: para.html

```
<html>
 <head>
  <title> Paragraph </title>
</head>
<body>
<p> this is left alignment </p>
<p align="right"> this is right alignment </p>
<p align="center"> this is center alignment </p>
```

```
<p align="justify"> his is justified alignment in a paragraph </p>
 </body>
</html>
```

Output:

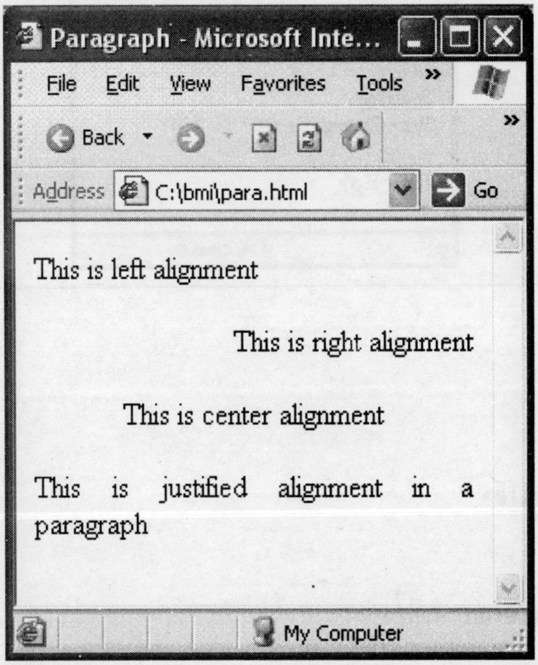

Text Formatting

File Name: format.html

```
<html>
 <head>
  <title> Formatting </title>
 </head>
 <body>
  <b> Bold </b> <br>
  <i> Italic </i> <br>
  <u> Underline </u> <br>
  <strike> Strike hrough Rs. 250</strike> Rs. 150<br>
  3<sup>2</sup> = 8 <br>
  Water H<sub>2</sub>0
 </body>
</html>
```

Output:

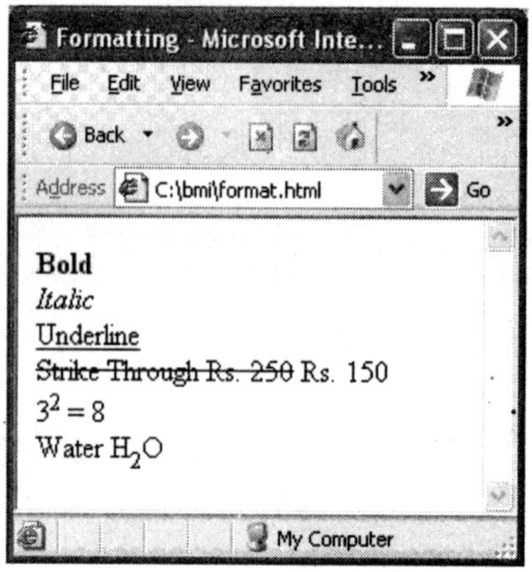

Lists

File Name: list.html

```
<html>
 <head>
  <title> List </title>
</head>
<body>
    <h2> Courses offered </h2>
    <UL>
        <LI> Post Graduates </LI>
        <OL>
            <LI> MCA </LI>
            <LI> MBA </LI>
            <LI> M.Sc </LI>
            <LI> MA </LI>
        </OL>
        <LI> Under Graduates </LI>
        <OL type="A">
            <LI> BCA </LI>
            <LI> BBA </LI>
            <LI> B.Sc </LI>
            <LI> BA </LI>
        </OL>
    </UL>
 </body>
</html>
```

Output:

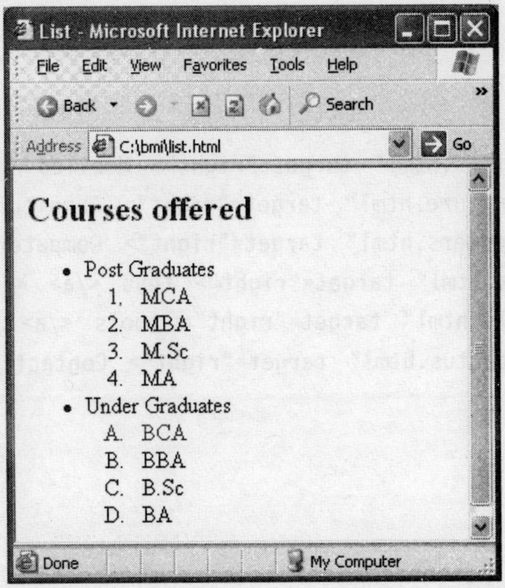

Frames and Frame Set

File Name: frames.html

```
<html>
 <head>
  <title> Frames and Frameset </title>
 </head>
       <frameset rows="20%,80%">
             <frame src="top.html" scrolling="no">
             <frameset cols="25%,75%">
                   <frame src="left.html"">
                   <frame name="right" src="right.html">
             </frameset>
       </frameset>
 </html>
```

File Name: top.html

```
<html>
 <body>
  <center>
  <font face="Courier New" color="#FF0000" size="35">
   XYZ Pvt Ltd
  </font>
  </center>
 </body>
</html>
```

File Name: left.html

```
<html>
 <body>
  <ul>
   <li> <a href="mobiles.html" target="right"> Mobiles </a> </li>
   <li> <a href="furniture.html" target="right"> Furniture </a> </li>
   <li> <a href="computers.html" target="right"> Computers </a> </li>
   <li> <a href="toys.html" target="right"> toys </a> </li>
   <li> <a href="tools.html" target="right"> tools </a> </li>
   <li> <a href="contactus.html" target="right"> Contact us </a> </li>
  </ul>
 </body>
</html>
```

File Name: right.html

```
<html>
 <body>
  <h1> Welcome to eCommerce site </h1>
 </body>
</html>
```

Develop contents for missing HTML files such as mobiles.html, furniture.html ..., if you click any of the link in the left-side frame, then the resultant page will be displayed in the right-side frame.

Output:

Form Elements

File Name: Biodata.html

```
<html>
 <head>
  <title> Bio-Data </title>
 </head>
```

```
<body>
 <center>
 <h1> BIO-DATA </h1>
 <FORM NAME="Form1" ACTION="http://localhost/BioData.jsp" METHOD="POST">
 <table>
  <tr>
   <td> Employee number: </td>
   <td> <input type="text" name="txteno" size="6"> </td>
  </tr>
  <tr>
   <td> Employee Name: </td>
   <td> <input type="text" name="txtname" size="10"> </td>
  </tr>
  <tr>
   <td> Sex: </td>
   <td> <input type="radio" name="rasex" value="Male" checked> Male
        <input type="radio" name="rasex" value="Female"> Female </td>
  </tr>
  <tr>
   <td> Languages Known: </td>
   <td> <input type="checkbox" name="chklan1" value="Tamil" checked> amil
        <input type="checkbox" name="chklan2" value="English"> English
   </td>
  </tr>
  <tr>
   <td> Specialization: </td>
   <td> <select name="listspecial" size="3" multiple>
          <option value="Web Designing"> Web Designing </option>
          <option value="System Programming"> System Programming </option>
          <option value="Linux Administration">
              Linux Administration
          </option>
          <option value="Windows NT Administration">
              Windows NT Administration
          </option>
          <option value="Object Oriented Programming System">
              OOPS
          </option>
          <option value="Database Administration"> DBA </option>
        </select>
   <td>
```

```
    </tr>
    <tr>
     <td> Nationality: </td>
     <td>
       <select name="chonation">
        <option value="India"> India </option>
        <option value="America"> America </option>
        <option value="Singapore"> Singapore </option>
        <option value="Malaysia"> Malaisia </option>
        <option value="UAE"> United Arab Embreds </option>
        <option value="Others"> Others </option>
       </select> </td>
      </tr>
      <tr>
       <td> Address: </td>
       <td> <textarea name="txtaddress" rows="5" cols="30">
              Type your address here </textarea> </td>
      </tr>
     </table>
     <input type="hidden" name="sno" value="1">
     <input type="submit" value="SUBMIT"> <input type="reset" value="RESET">
   </form>
  </body>
</html>
```

Output:

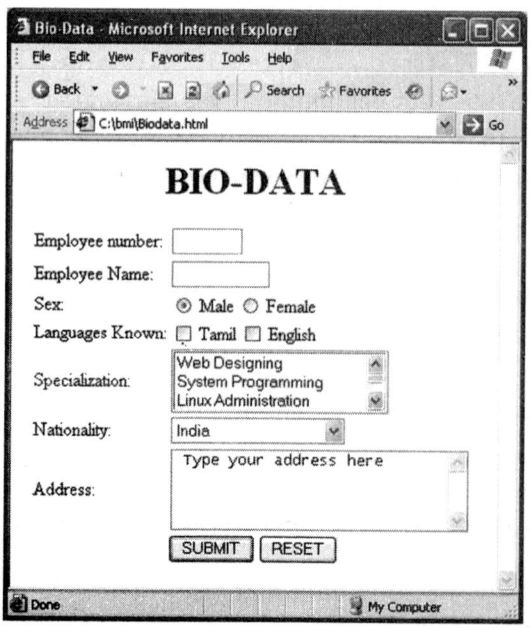

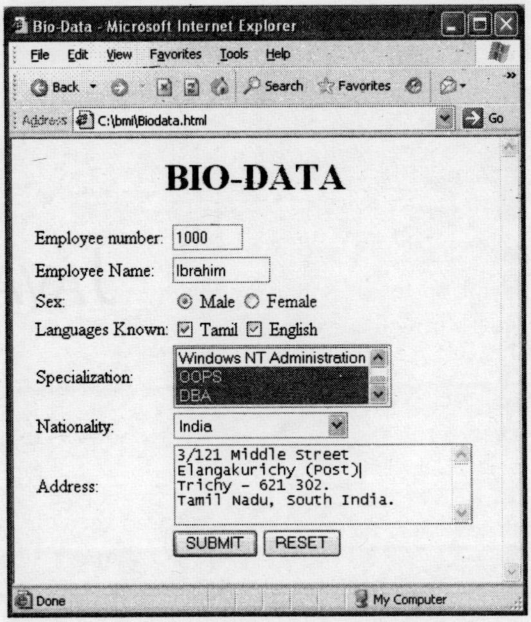

SUMMARY

HTML is a mark-up language, used to develop web-pages. This chapter stated with the structure of a HTML document. And further introduced the readers some of the basic HTML tags for formatting, dividing screen areas into frames, and finally with HTML input elements which form User Interface for dynamic web applications.

5

JAVA SERVLETS

5.0 INTRODUCTION

This chapter explains the important concepts of Java Servlet, one of the core components of Java Enterprise Edition. It is an alternative to traditional GCI approach for developing dynamic web-pages. This chapter list important classes and interfaces of Servlet API and illustrating examples.

5.1 JAVA SERVLETS AND DYNAMIC WEBPAGE DEVELOPMENT

The Java Servlet is a Server-side program that adds dynamic features to HTML forms. Even though the traditional CGI (Common Gateway Interface) technologies are also used for server-side programming, the Servlets have a number of advantages over CGI such as Platform Independence (They can be run on any of the Servlet enabled web-servers which are running at different platforms), Performance (The traditional CGI creates a new process to serve the client, but Servlet creates only a new thread to serve a client), extensibility (Java is robust so that Servlets take all the advantages of Java, and Servlets can be easily extended to suit the application's needs), Safe and Secure (Since Java provides excellent safety features like dynamic memory allocation / deallocation, Exception Handling, etc., Servlets can take these advantages and since the Servlets are running at servers, they are protected by web-servers).

5.2 LIFE-CYCLE OF A SERVLET

The following three methods are called automatically by the server in a life-cycle of a Servlet program.

```
public void init(ServletConfig config) throws ServletException
```

This method will be called by the server immediately after the servlet is first loaded into memory. It is used for initialisation purpose.

```
public void service(ServletRequest request, ServletResponse response)
                                        throws ServletException, IOException
```

This method is used to handle one of more client requests (this method will be executed when HTML form is submitted by the client)

```
public void destroy()
```

This method will be called by the Server just before the Servlet is unloaded from the memory. This is used to release any resources that are used by the Servlet program.

5.3 SERVLET API

This section lists some important Servlet API. Examples using these API are given at the end of this chapter.

5.3.1 javax.servlet Package

This package supports basic Servlet functionalities.

5.3.1.1 Important Interfaces in javax.servlet Package

Servlet Interface: All Servlets should implement this interface directly or indirectly (by extending a class that implements this interface).

Important Methods:

```
public void init(ServletConfig sc) throws ServletException
```

This method is called when the Servlet is initialised (loaded).

```
public void service(ServletRequest request, ServletResponse response)
                                        throws ServletException, IOException
```

This method is called to process the requests from clients.

```
public void destroy()
```

This method is called when the Servlet is unloaded (Servlet is being taken out of service).

```
public ServletConfig getServletConfig()
```

This method returns an object of *ServletConfig* interface which contains the initialisation parameters.

```
public String getServletInfo()
```

This method returns information about the associated servlet (version, copyright, etc.)

ServletConfig Interface: This interface is used to get initialisation parameters by Servlets.

Important Methods

```
public String getInitParameter(String param)
```

It returns the value of the initialisation parameter specified in *param*, or *null* if the parameter does not exist.

```
public Enumeration getInitParameterNames()
```

It returns all the initialisation parameter names as an Enumeration of Strings, or an empty Enumeration if the servlet has no initialisation parameters. (Initialisation parameters are specified in the deployment descriptor file – *web.xml* – for the servlets)

```
public ServletContext getServletContext()
```

It returns a reference to the *ServletContext* interface in which the servlet is executing.

```
public String getServletName()
```

It returns the name of servlet instance as a string (defined in the deployment descriptor file).

5.3.1.2 Important Classes in javax.servlet Package

GenericServlet class: It implements the *Servlet* and *ServletConfig* interfaces and overrides all the methods declared on those interfaces.

ServletRequest class: This is mainly used to get the request information from a client.

Important Methods:

`public String getParameter(String pname)`

It returns the value of the request parameter (form elements from client) specified in its argument as a string, or returns *null* if the request parameter does not exist.

`public Enumeration getParameterNames()`

It returns the request parameter names as an Enumeration of Strings, or an empty Enumeration if no request parameters.

`public String[] getParameterValues()`

It returns the parameter values of the request as a String array.

`public int getContentLength()`

It returns the number of bytes (length) of the request body from the client.

`public String getContentType()`

It returns the MIME type of the body of the request, or *null* if the type is not known.

`public String getServerName()`

It returns the name of the server that receives the client request.

`public int getServerPort()`

Returns the port number on which the client request was received.

`public String getRemoteHost()`

It returns the domain name of the client which makes the request.

`public String getRemoteAddr()`

It returns the IP address of the client which makes the request.

ServletResponse class: This is used to send response (usually in HTML format) to the client.

Important Methods:

`public void setContentType(Sting type)`

It sets the content type (MIME type such as *text/html*) as specified in its argument for sending response data.

`public PrintWriter getWriter() throws IOException`

It returns the *PrintWriter* object that can be used to write character data (such as HTML, WML programs) in the response. (Note that the *PrintWriter* class provides *print()* and *println()* methods in order to write character data for client). Either this method (character stream) or `getOutputStream()` (byte stream) may be used to write data to the client, but not both.

`public ServletOutputStream getOutputStream() throws IOException`

It returns the *ServletOutputStream* object that can be used to write binary data in the response. Either this method (byte stream) or get Writer() (character stream) may be used to write data to the client, but not both.

`public void setBufferSize(int bytes)`

It sets the size of the output buffer for the body of the response. The response content will be sent to the client only if the buffer is full or if the servlet finishes its operation.

```
public int getBufferSize()
```

It returns the actual output buffer size used for the response.

```
public void flushBuffer() throws IOException
```

It forces any content in the output buffer to be sent to the client.

5.3.2 javax.servlet.http Package

In addition to the features of `javax.servlet` package, this package provides some important features such as *Session-tracking* and *Cookies*. It is also used to handle GET and POST requests individually. For example, in Generic Servlets, the *service()* method will be invoked whether the GET or the POST method is used in FORM element of HTML for submitting data. But, in the case of Http Servlets, if GET method is used in the HTML FORM element, then the *doGet()* method of the Http Servlet will be invoked. Likewise, if POST method is used in HTML FORM element, then the *doPost()* method of the Http Servlet will be invoked. So, the programmer can write his code based on the method in which the data arrive.

5.3.2.1 Important Interfaces in javax.servlet.http package

`HttpServletRequest` interface: This is mainly used to get request data from the HTTP clients. This interface inherits *javax.servlet.ServletRequest* interface. So that we can use all the methods available in *ServletRequest* through the object that implements this *HttpServletRequest*.

Important Methods under HttpServletRequest:

```
public Cookie[] getCookies()
```

It returns an array of the Cookie objects that the client sent to the server with the request. (Cookie is a server-side object stored at client. It generally stores the state information at the client machine for session tracking.)

```
public String getMethod()
```

It returns the name of the HTTP request method (GET, POST).

```
public String getQueryString()
```

Returns the query string from the URL when GET method is used. (Query String starts after the question mark symbol in the URL)

```
public string getServletPath()
```

It returns the path to the servlet (does not include query string) as string (taken from the request URL).

```
public HttpSession getSession(boolean new_session)
```

It returns the current *HttpSession* if the HTTP session is available. If there is no session and the parameter is *true*, then a new session is created and returned. If there is no session and the parameter is *false*, then it returns *null*.

`HttpServletResponse` interface: This is used to send data to client as HTTP response. This interface inherits *javax.servlet.ServletResponse* interface. So that we can use all the methods available in *ServletZResponse* through the object that implements this *HttpServletResponse*.

Important Methods under HttpServletResponse:

```
public void addCookie(Cookie cookie)
```

It adds a Cookie specified in the argument to the HTTP response.

`public void sendRedirect(String url) throws IOException`

It redirects the current page to the location specified in its argument.

HttpSession interface: This is used to read/write session data between client requests. A session usually corresponds to one user, who may access the server many times for accessing pages.

Important Methods:

`public void setAttribute(Sting name, Object attribute)`

Binds the object specified in its second parameter to a name specified in its first parameter in the Session.

`public Object getAttribute(String name)`

It returns the object associated with the attribute *name,* or returns *null* if the attribute name is not found in the Session.

`public void removeAttribute(String name)`

It removes the object reference associated with the attribute *name* from the Session.

`public long getCreationTime()`

It returns the time of the initiation of the session (The time is represented in milliseconds since midnight January 1, 1970 GMT. Pass this value to the constructor of *Date* class for display purpose).

`long getLastAccessedTime()`

It returns the time (in milliseconds) the session was last accessed.

5.3.2.2 Important Class in javax.servlet.http package

Cookie class: A Cookie is a small amount of data that is stored on the client's machine and can be created and accessed by Servers. Generally, Cookies contain state information. A cookie is composed of two values: *cookie-name* and *cookie-value.*

The constructor of Cookie class is,

`Cookie(String name, String value)`

Important Methods:

`public String getName()`

It returns the name of the invoking Cookie.

`public String getValue()`

It returns the value associated with the invoking Cookie.

`public void setValue(String value)`

Sets a new value associated with the invoking Cookie.

`public void setDomain(String url)`

It specifies the domain in which the Cookie is to be stored.

`public void setMaxAge(int seconds)`

It set s the maximum age of the Cookie to live in seconds.

`public void setComment(String comment)`

Sets the specified comment with an invoking Cookie object.

`public String getComment()`

Returns the comment associated with the invoking Cookie object.

5.4 DEPLOYMENT DESCRIPTOR FOR WEB APPLICATIONS

The descriptor (*web.xml* file) provides the configuration information for a Servlet container to properly load and initialize the web applications. The appearance of the *web.xml* file (stored at WEB-INF directories, for example, G:\jakarta-tomcat-5.5.11\webapps\bmi\WEB-INF) is shown below.

```
<?xml version="1.0" encoding="ISO-8859-1"?>
<!DOCTYPE web-app
    PUBLIC "-//Sun Microsystems, Inc.//DTD Web Application 2.3//EN"
    "http://java.sun.com/dtd/web-app_2_3.dtd">
<web-app>
 ...
</web-app>
```

With in the *web-app* tag, we have to describe various aspects of the web application. For accessing every Servlet, we have to add two entries (*servlet* and *servlet-mapping*) in this *web.xml* file.

The *servlet* tag mainly describes the location and the initialization parameters of a Servlet.

```
<servlet>
 <servlet-name> Name of the Servlet </servlet-name>
 <servlet-class> Servlet Class Name </servlet-class>
 <init-param>
   <param-name> Initialisation Parameter 1 </param-name>
   <param-value> Value for Initialisation Parameter 1 </param-value>
   ...
 </init-param>
 <init-param>
  <param-name> Initialisation Parameter 2 </param-name>
  <param-value> Value for Initialisation Parameter 2 </param-value>
  ...
 </init-param>
  ...
</servlet>
```

These initialisation parameters are accessed through `getInitParameter()` method of `ServletConfig` class in a Servlet program (Possibly in *init()* method).

The *servlet-mapping* tag mainly describes how to call Servlet in a browser (or on the *action* attribute of the HTML FORM tag).

```
<servlet-mapping>
   <servlet-name> Name of the Servlet </servlet-name>
   <url-pattern> /label </url-pattern>
</servlet-mapping>
```

We can invoke the specified Servlet using the URL - *<server-domain>*/`label`.

Example:

```
<?xml version="1.0" encoding="ISO-8859-1"?>
<!DOCTYPE web-app
   PUBLIC "-//Sun Microsystems, Inc.//DTD Web Application 2.3//EN"
   "http://java.sun.com/dtd/web-app_2_3.dtd">
<web-app>
  <display-name>Servlet Examples</display-name>
  <description>
      Servlet Examples
  </description>
  <servlet>
      <servlet-name> yn </servlet-name>
      <servlet-class> YourName </servlet-class>
  </servlet>
  <servlet-mapping>
      <servlet-name> yn </servlet-name>
      <url-pattern> /yname </url-pattern>
  </servlet-mapping>
</web-app>
```

We can call the Servlet (whose class file is `YourName.class`) through the URL- http://<server-domain>/yname.

5.5 DEPLOYING WEB APPLICATION IN APACHE TOMCAT

Download the latest version of Tomcat from *http://jakarta.apache.org* in Zip format. Unzip the file and extract the contents and store them on your favourite drive. Then the directory structure becomes as follows.

The *bin* directory contains batch files for starting and stopping the Tomcat web-server.

The *common* directory contains jar files (containing built-in classes including *javax* package) that are common to all Tomcat servers.

The *conf* directory contains configuration information of the Tomcat server such as listening port, Invoker Servlet, etc.

The *server* directory contains jar files (containing built-in classes) that are common to all web-applications in the Tomcat web-server.

The *webapps* contains example web applications and this is the place where your web applications reside.

The *work* is temporary working directory used by web applications. It contains the auto-generated Servlet class files and source files for all the invoked JSP files. Note that all the JSP files are converted into corresponding Servlets before execution.

Actually, Tomcat is a web server and also acts as a light-weight application server because it has a built-in servlet engine named ***Catalina*** and a JSP engine named ***Jasper***.

Starting and Stopping Tomcat

I am assuming that the tomcat is installed in *G:\jakarta-tomcat-5.5.11* directory and JDK 1.5 is installed in *G:\jdk1.5.0_01* directory. We have to assign path to the environmental variables: CATALINA_HOME, JAVA_HOME, PATH, and CLASSPATH. To set values for these variables permanently (common for all the DOS windows that are opened by the users, so that the user need not set values for these variables for every opened DOS windows).

Right click on *MyComputer* icon on the Desktop and select *Properties* menu-item from the displayed pop-up window. Then, the "*System Properties*" window will be displayed. Choose "*Advanced*" tab and then click "*Environment Variables*" button. The "*Environment Variables*" window is displayed.

Click the "*New*" button, and type as follows in the displayed dialog window.

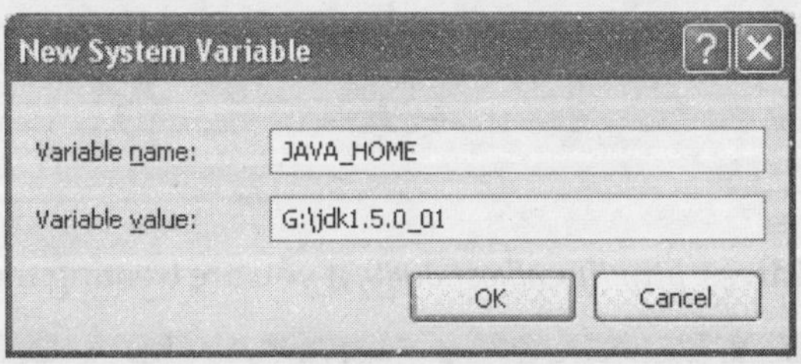

Click the "*OK*" button. Again click the "*New*" button on the "*Environment Variables*" window, and type as follows in the displayed dialog window.

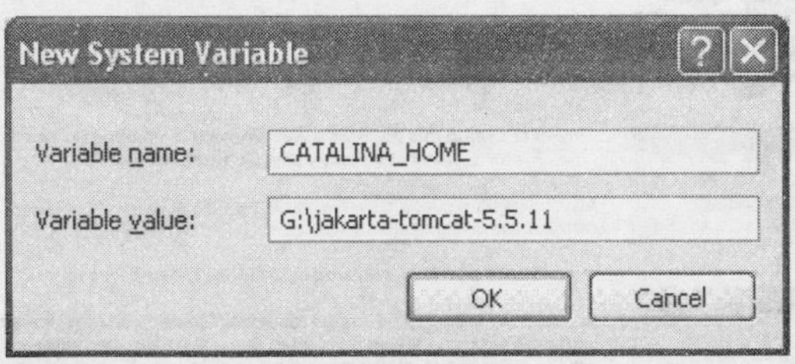

Click the "*OK*" button. Again click the "*New*" button on the "*Environment Variables*" window, and type as follows in the displayed dialog window.

Variable_name: `CLASSPATH`

Variable_value:

```
G:\jdk1.5.0_01\lib;G:\jakarta-tomcat-5.5.11\common\lib\servlet-api.jar;
G:\jakarta-tomcat-5.5.11\common\lib\jsp-api.jar;
G:\jakarta-tomcat-5.5.11\common\lib\jasper-runtime.jar;.;
```

Click the "*OK*" button. Select the "*Path*" environmental variable from the displayed list box and click "*Edit*" button, and append the text "*G:\jdk1.5.0_01\bin*" in the *Variable value* text box.

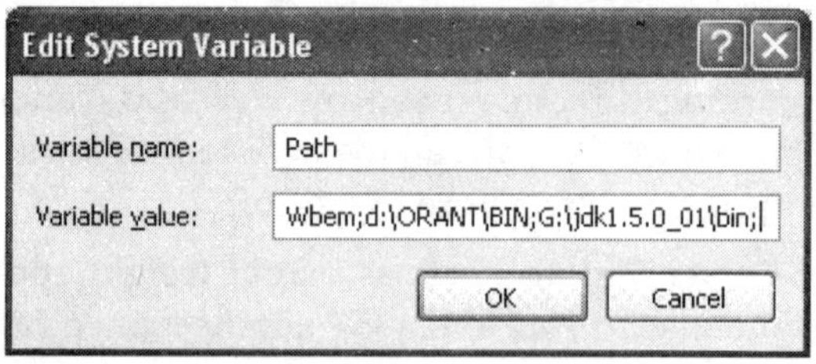

Click the "*OK*" buttons on the displayed three windows.

To start the Tomcat Server

Go to the bin directory of the Tomcat, *G:\jakarta-tomcat-5.5.11\bin*, and invoke the *startup.bat* file by double-clicking on it.

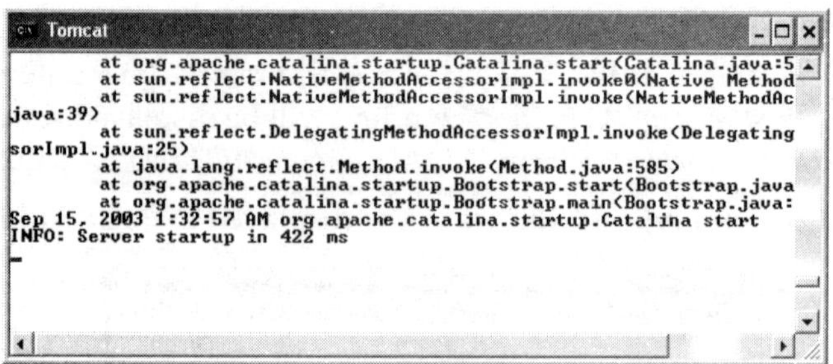

Testing the Server

Invoke a browser with the address: *http://localhost:8080*, if you are treating the same computer as client.

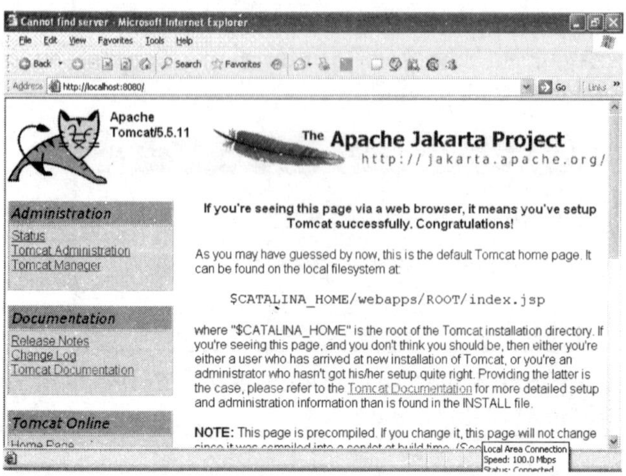

Specify the domain name or IP address of the server instead of *localhost* if you are using other computer as client. To know the IP address of a computer, use *ipconfig* command in the DOS command prompt.

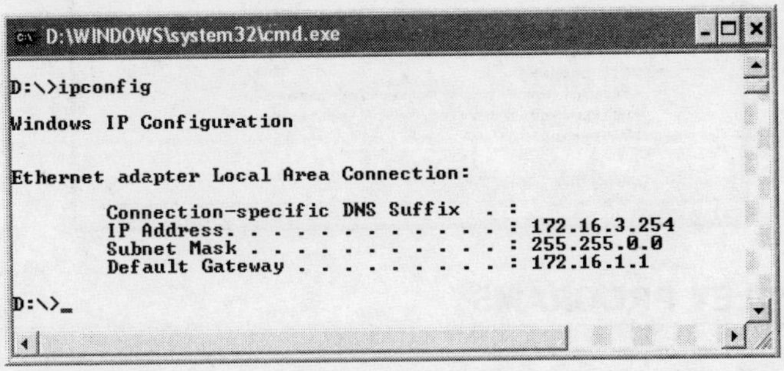

To stop the Tomcat Server

Go to the bin directory of the Tomcat, *G:\jakarta-tomcat-5.5.11\bin*, and invoke the *shutdown.bat* file by double-clicking on it.

Configuring Tomcat for running Servlets

Open the *server.xml* file that is stored in *G:\jakarta-tomcat-5.5.11\conf* directory in an editor (For example, in Wordpad).

Change the value of the *port* attribute of *Connector* tag to *"80"*.

```
<!-- Define a non-SSL HTTP/1.1 Connector on port 8080 -->
    <Connector port="80" maxHttpHeaderSize="8192"
    maxThreads="150" minSpareThreads="25" maxSpareThreads="75"
    enableLookups="false" redirectPort="8443" acceptCount="100"
    connectionTimeout="20000" disableUploadTimeout="true" />
```

And save the file. Open the *web.xml* file that is stored in G:*jakarta-tomcat-5.5.11\conf* directory in Wordpad.

Release the comment to *servlet* tag and *servlet-mapping* for the InvokerServlet, if you want to call the servlets using the */servlet* logical directory.) and save the file.

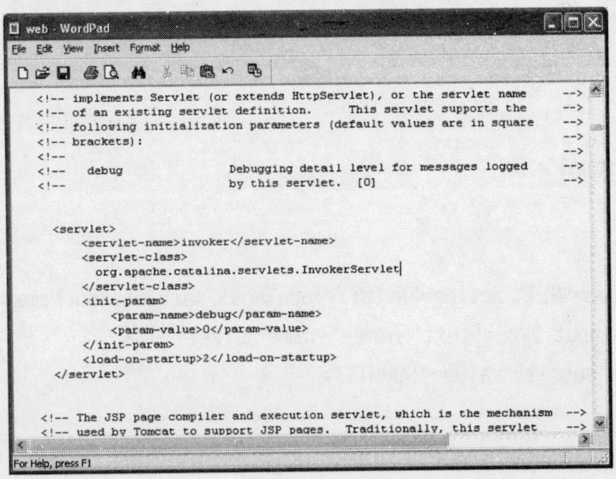

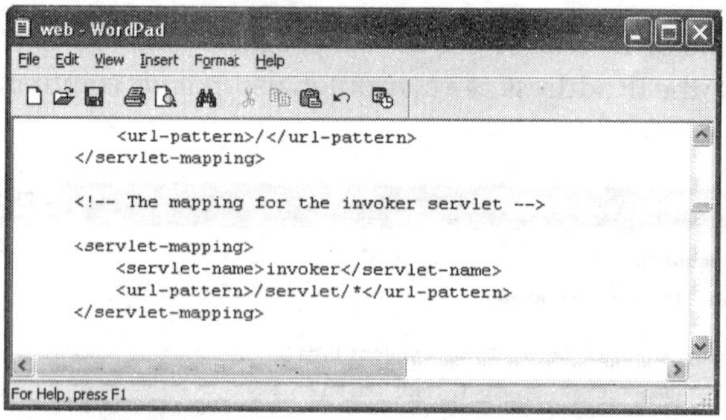

5.6 SAMPLE SERVLET PROGRAMS

The following section list some sample Servlet programs which uses important Servlet API.

Executing a Servlet program using InvokerServlet

Compile the following *YourName.java* and store its class in the directory - *G:\jakarta-tomcat-5.5.11\webapps\ROOT\WEB-INF\classes* and the *YName.html* file in the directory - *G:\jakarta-tomcat-5.5.11\webapps\ROOT.*

File Name: YourName.java

```
import java.io.*;
import javax.servlet.*;
public class YourName extends GenericServlet
{
 public void service(ServletRequest request, ServletResponse response)
                                        throws ServletException,IOException
 {
  response.setContentType("text/html");
  PrintWriter out = response.getWriter();
  out.println("<html><body> Your name is " + request.getParameter("yname"));
  out.println("</body></html>");
  out.close();
 }
}
```

File Name: YName.html

```
<html>
<body>
 <form name="f1" method="GET" action="http://localhost/servlet/YourName">
   Enter your name <input type="text" name="yname" size="20">
   <br> <input type="submit" value="SUBMIT">
 </form>
</body>
```

```
</html>
```

Start the server and invoke the browser with the address: *http://localhost/YName.html*.

Type your name the Textbox and click on SUBMIT button.

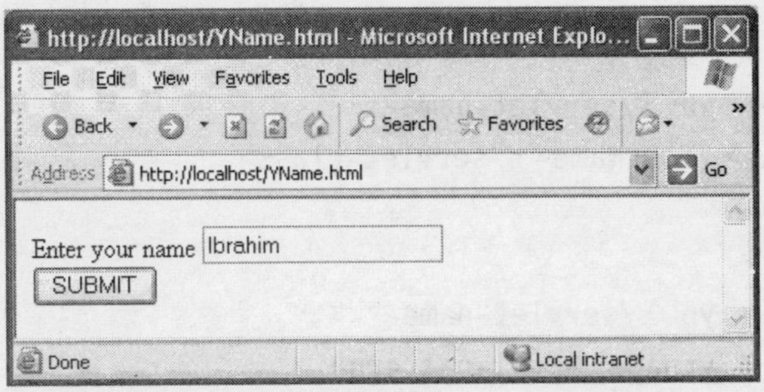

Then, the servlet is invoked, as the result the client has the following response.

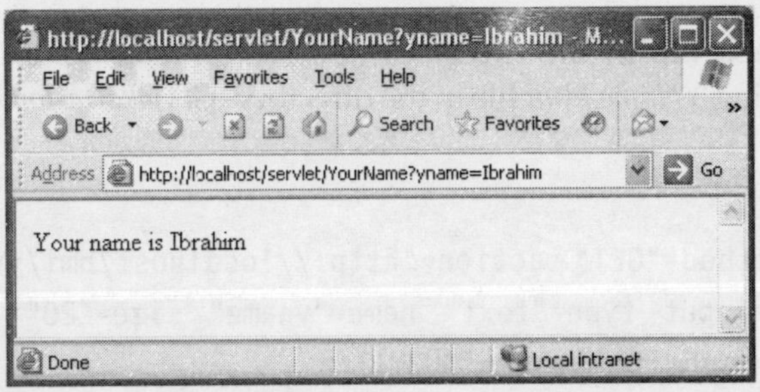

We should only use this InvokerServlet facility for testing the servlet programs. It is not a proper method for building web application. So you should create a logical directory and work with it as illustrated below.

Create a Sub-directory named *bmi* under the directory *G:\jakarta-tomcat-5.5.11\webapps*. In *bmi*, create a sub-directory named *WEB-INF* and this *WEB-INF* directory should contain two subdirectories: *classes* and *lib*. The *classes* directory contains all servlet *.class* files and the *lib* directory contains jar files which can be used by *.class* files that are stored in *classes* directory.

The directory structure is as follows.

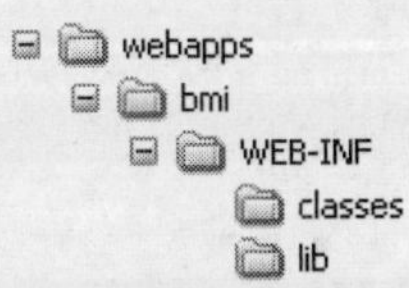

A deployment descriptor file named *web.xml* should be stored in the directory- *G:\jakarta-tomcat-5.5.11\webapps\bmi\WEB-INF*.

It has two entries *<servlet>* and *<servlet-mapping>* for every servlet. The following are the *web.xml* file content for out *YourName* servlet class.

```
<?xml version="1.0" encoding="ISO-8859-1"?>
<!DOCTYPE web-app
        PUBLIC "-//Sun Microsystems, Inc.//DTD Web Application 2.3//EN"
        "http://java.sun.com/dtd/web-app_2_3.dtd">
<web-app>
```

```
    <display-name> Servlet Examples </display-name>
    <description>
      Servlet Examples
    </description>
    <servlet>
       <servlet-name> yn </servlet-name>
       <servlet-class> YourName </servlet-class>
    </servlet>
    <servlet-mapping>
       <servlet-name> yn </servlet-name>
       <url-pattern> /yrname </url-pattern>
    </servlet-mapping>
</web-app>
```

Store the *YourName.class* file in the directory- *G:\jakarta-tomcat-5.5.11\webapps\bmi\WEB-INF\classes* and the following *YName.html* file in the directory- *G:\jakarta-tomcat-5.5.11\webapps\bmi.*

```
<html>
<body>
 <form name="f1" method="GET" action="http://localhost/bmi/yrname">
  Enter your name <input type="text" name="yname" size="20">
  <br> <input type="submit" value="SUBMIT">
 </form>
</body>
</html>
```

Testing the application

Start the Tomcat server. If you are using Windows XP, then the IIS server will be started during start-up operation. So, you should stop this IIS server. Select Start → Settings → Control Panel → Administrative Tools → Services. From the list of services, select *IIS Admin* and click on "stop service" button.

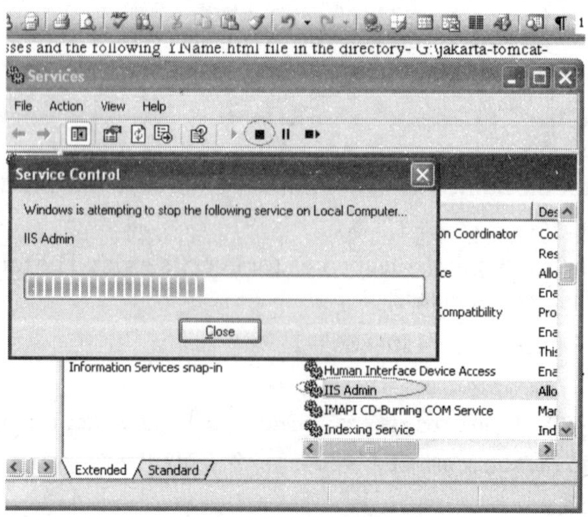

Invoke the browser with the address: *http://localhost/bmi/YName.html*.

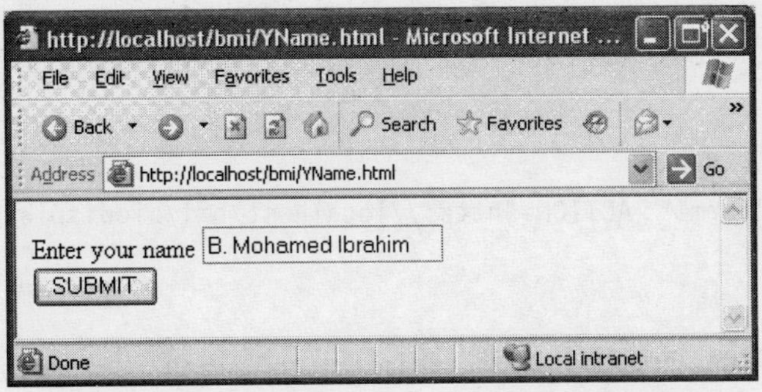

Enter your name in the text box and click on the "SUBMIT" button.

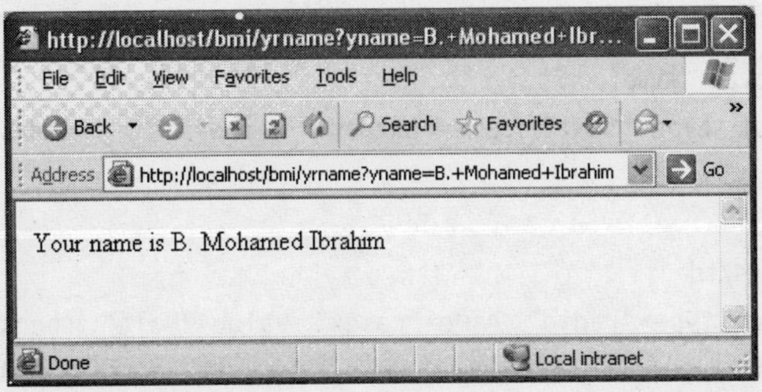

Change the server-name (localhost) if you invoke the application from other computer.

Handling request data

Store the "*Biodata.html*" file in the directory- G:\jakarta-tomcat-5.5.11\webapps\bmi.

Store the "*BioData.class*" file in the directory- G:\jakarta-tomcat-5.5.11\webapps\bmi\WEB-INF\classes.

Add the following two entries in the *web.xml* file stored in the directory- G:\jakarta-tomcat-5.5.11\webapps\bmi\WEB-INF.

```
<servlet>
  <servlet-name> bio </servlet-name>
  <servlet-class> BioData </servlet-class>
</servlet>
<servlet-mapping>
  <servlet-name> yn </servlet-name>
  <url-pattern> /yrname </url-pattern>
</servlet-mapping>
```

File Name: Biodata.html

```
<html>
 <head>
```

```
    <title> Bio-Data </title>
   </head>
  <body>
    <center>
    <h1> BIO-DATA </h1>
    <FORM NAME="form1" ACTION="http://localhost/bmi/biodisplay" METHOD="POST">
    <table>
     <tr>
      <td> Employee number: </td>
      <td> <input type="text" name="txteno" size="6"> </td>
     </tr>
     <tr>
      <td> Employee Name: </td>
      <td> <input type="text" name="txtname" size="10"> </td>
     </tr>
     <tr>
      <td> Sex: </td>
      <td> <input type="radio" name="rasex" value="Male" checked> Male
          <input type="radio" name="rasex" value="Female"> Female </td>
      </tr>
     <tr>
     <td> Languages Known: </td>
     <td> <input type="checkbox" name="chklan1" value="Tamil" checked> Tamil
          <input type="checkbox" name="chklan2" value="English"> English
     </td>
    </tr>
    <tr>
     <td> Specialization: </td>
     <td> <select name="listspecial" size="3">
           <option value="Web Designing"> Web Designing </option>
           <option value="System Programming"> System Programming </option>
           <option value="Linux Administration"> Linux Administration
           </option>
           <option value="Windows NT Administration">
                Windows NT Administration </option>
           <option value="Object Oriented Programming System">
                OOPS </option>
           <option value="Database Administration"> DBA </option>
          </select>
```

```
<td>
</tr>
<tr>
<td> Nationality: </td>
<td>
  <select name="chonation" size="1">
  <option value="India"> India </option>
  <option value="America"> America </option>
  <option value="Singapore"> Singapore </option>
  <option value="Malaysia"> Malaisia </option>
  <option value="UAE"> Unted Arab Embreds </option>
  <option value="Others"> Others </option>
 </select> </td>
</tr>
<tr>
 <td> Address: </td>
 <td> <textarea name="txtaddress" rows="5" cols="30">
              Type your address here </textarea> </td>
 </tr>
</table>
<input type="hidden" name="sno" value="1">
<input type="submit" value="SUBMIT"> <input type="reset" value="RESET">
</form>
</body>
</html>
```

File Name: BioData.java

```
import java.io.*;
import java.util.*;
import javax.servlet.*;
public class BioData extends GenericServlet
 {
  public void service (ServletRequest request, ServletResponse response)
                  throws ServletException, IOException
 {
  response.setContentType("text/html");
  PrintWriter pw = response.getWriter();
  pw.println("<html> <head> <title> Bio-Data </title> </head>");
  pw.println("<body> <b><u> BIO-DATA </u></b> <br><br>");
```

```
    Enumeration e = request.getParameterNames();
    while (e.hasMoreElements())
     {
      String pname = (String) e.nextElement();
      String pvalue = request.getParameter(pname);
      pw.print(pname + " = " + pvalue + "<br>");
     }
    pw.println("</body></html>");
    pw.close();
   }
}
```

Start the Tomcat server.

Invoke the browser with the address: *http://localhost/bmi/Biodata.html.*

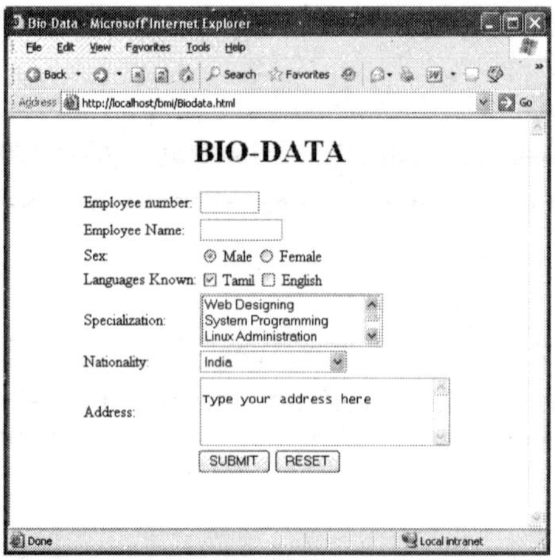

Fill the form and click on "SUBMIT" button.

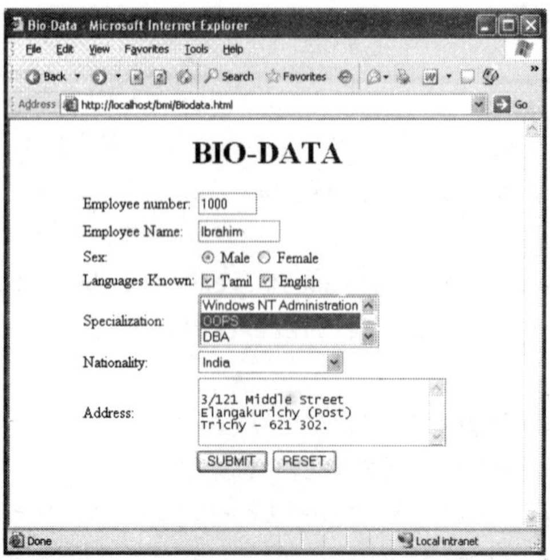

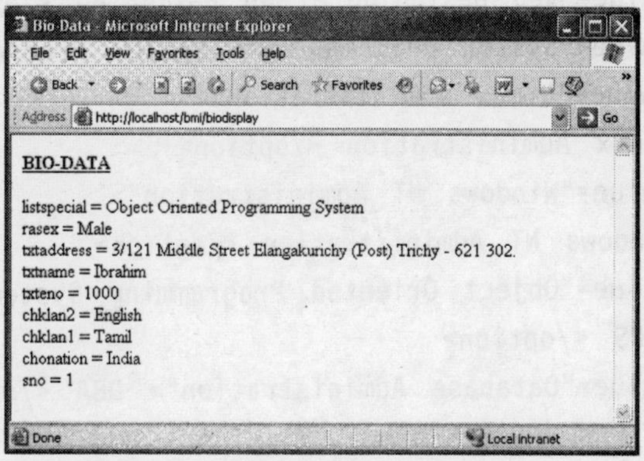

Handling Multi-selection List box

More than one item can be selected in a Multi-selection list box.

Store the *"Multilist.html"* file in the directory- G:\jakarta-tomcat-5.5.11\webapps\bmi.

Store the *"MultiListBox.class"* file in the directory-

G:\jakarta-tomcat-5.5.11\webapps\bmi\WEB-INF\classes.

Add the following two entries in the *web.xml* file stored in the directory-

G:\jakarta-tomcat-5.5.11\webapps\bmi\WEB-INF.

```
<servlet>
    <servlet-name> multilist </servlet-name>
    <servlet-class> MultiListBox </servlet-class>
</servlet>
<servlet-mapping>
    <servlet-name> multilist </servlet-name>
    <url-pattern> /mlist </url-pattern>
</servlet-mapping>
```

File Name: Multilist.html

```
<html>
 <head>
  <title> List box with Multiple Selection </title>
 </head>
 <body>
  <center>
  <h1> Specialization </h1>
  <form name="form1" action="http://localhost/bmi/mlist" method="POST">
  <table>
   <tr>
    <td> Specialization: </td>
    <td> <select name="listspecial" size="3" multiple="true">
```

```
            <option value="Web Designing"> Web Designing </option>
            <option value="System Programming"> System Programming </option>
            <option value="Linux Administration">
                    Linux Administration </option>
            <option value="Windows NT Administration">
                    Windows NT Administration </option>
            <option value="Object Oriented Programming System">
                    OOPS </option>
            <option value="Database Administration"> DBA </option>
          </select>
     <td>
    </tr>
   </table>
    <input type="submit" value="SUBMIT"> <input type="reset" value="RESET">
   </form>
  </body>
 </html>
```

File Name: MultiListBox.java

```
import java.io.*;
import java.util.*;
import javax.servlet.*;
public class MultiListBox extends GenericServlet
 {
 public void service (ServletRequest request, ServletResponse response)
                    throws ServletException, IOException
  {
   response.setContentType("text/html");
   PrintWriter pw = response.getWriter();
   pw.println("<html> <head> <title> Specialization </title> </head>");
   pw.println("<body> Your Specialization subjects are <br><br>");
   String values[] = request.getParameterValues("listspecial");
   for (int i=0;i<values.length;i++)
    {
   if (i>0) pw.print(" , ");
   pw.print(values[i]);
    }
  pw.println("</body></html>");
  pw.close();
```

```
 }
}
```

Start the Tomcat server and invoke the browser with the address:

http:// localhost/bmi/Multilist.html.

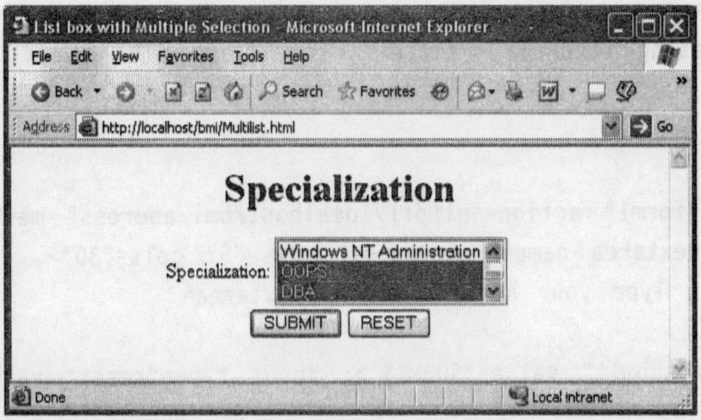

Select your specialization and click on "SUBMIT" button.

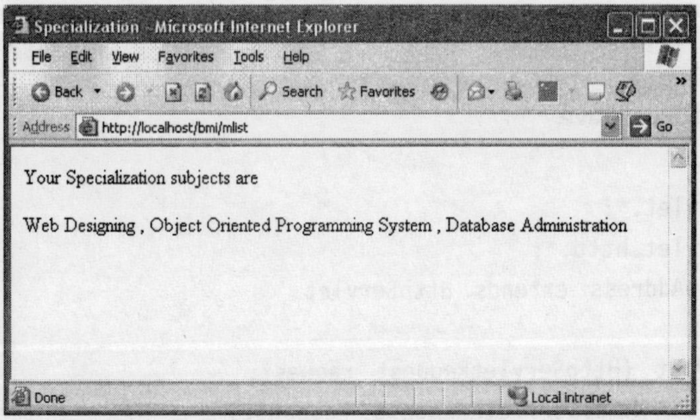

Accessing TextArea data, Use HTTP Servlet

Store the "*Address.html*" file in the directory- G:\jakarta-tomcat-5.5.11\webapps\bmi.

Store the "*DispAddress.class*" file in the directory-

G:\jakarta-tomcat-5.5.11\webapps\bmi\WEB-INF\classes.

Add the following two entries in the *web.xml* file stored in the directory-

G:\jakarta-tomcat-5.5.11\webapps\bmi\WEB-INF.

```
<servlet>
   <servlet-name> tarea </servlet-name>
   <servlet-class> DispAddress </servlet-class>
</servlet>
<servlet>
   <servlet-name> tarea </servlet-name>
```

```
    <servlet-class> DispAddress </servlet-class>
  </servlet>
```

File Name: Address.html

```
<html>
 <head>
   <title> Accessing TextArea </title>
  </head>
 <body>
   <center>
    <form name="form1" action="http://localhost/bmi/address" method="post">
     Address: <textarea name="txtaddress" rows="5" cols="30">
                Type your address here </textarea>
    <br>
    <input type="submit" value="SUBMIT"> <input type="reset" value="RESET">
   </form>
  </center>
 </body>
</html>
```

File Name: DispAddress.java

```
import java.io.*;
import javax.servlet.*;
import javax.servlet.http.*;
public class DispAddress extends HttpServlet
{
 public void doPost (HttpServletRequest request,
                    HttpServletResponse response)
                              throws ServletException, IOException
  {
    response.setContentType("text/html");
    PrintWriter out = response.getWriter();
    out.println("<html> <head> <title> Accessing Data from TextArea </title>
                                                          </head>");
    out.println("<body> Your Address is, <br><br> <b> ");
    String s = request.getParameter("txtaddress");
    String s1 = s.replaceAll("\n","<BR>");
    out.println(s1);
    out.println("</body></html>");
    out.close();
  }
```

```
}
```

Start the Tomcat server and invoke the browser with the address:

http:// localhost/bmi/Address.html.

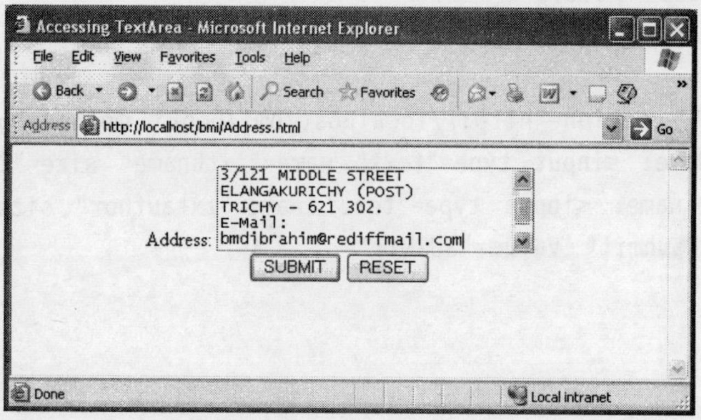

Type your address and click on "SUBMIT" button.

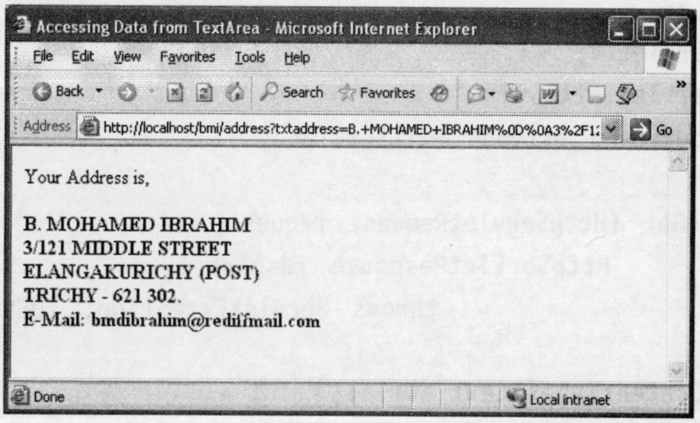

Cookies

Store the *"Book.html"* in the directory- G:\jakarta-tomcat-5.5.11\webapps\bmi.

Store the *"CookiesEg.class"* in the directory-

G:\jakarta-tomcat-5.5.11\webapps\bmi\WEB-INF\classes.

Add the following two entries in the *web.xml* file stored in the directory-

G:\jakarta-tomcat-5.5.11\webapps\bmi\WEB-INF.

```
<servlet>
   <servlet-name> sebook </servlet-name>
   <servlet-class> CookiesEg </servlet-class>
</servlet>
<servlet-mapping>
   <servlet-name> sebook </servlet-name>
   <url-pattern> /book </url-pattern>
</servlet-mapping>
```

File Name: Book.html

```
<html>
<head>
 <title> Cookies </title>
</head>
<body>
 <form name="f1" action="http://localhost/bmi/book" method="get">
  Enter Book Name: <input type="text" name="txtbname" size="20"> <br>
  Enter Author name: <input type="text" name="txtauthor" size="20"> <br>
  <input type="submit" value="SUBMIT">
 </form>
</body>
</html>
```

File Name: CookiesEg.java

```
import java.io.*;
import javax.servlet.*;
import javax.servlet.http.*;
public class CookiesEg extends HttpServlet
{
 public void doGet (HttpServletRequest request,
                 HttpServletResponse response)
                         throws ServletException, IOException
 {
  response.setContentType("text/html");
  PrintWriter out = response.getWriter();
  out.println("<html> <head> <title> Session Tracking using Cookies
                                         </title> </head>");
  out.println("<body> Cookies Data: <br> <br>");
  out.println("<table border=1> <tr> <td> Cookie Name </td>
                              <td> Cookie Value </td> </tr>");
  Cookie c[] = request.getCookies();
  if (c != null)
   for (int i=0;i<c.length;i++)
    out.println("<tr> <td>" + c[i].getName() + "</td> <td>" +
                         c[i].getValue() + "</td> </tr>");
    out.println("</table>");
    String cname = request.getParameter("txtbname");
    String cvalue = request.getParameter("txtauthor");
    Cookie co = new Cookie(cname,cvalue);
```

```
        response.addCookie(co);
        out.println("</body></html>");
        out.close();
    }
}
```

Start the Tomcat server and invoke the browser with the address:

http:// localhost/bmi/Book.html.

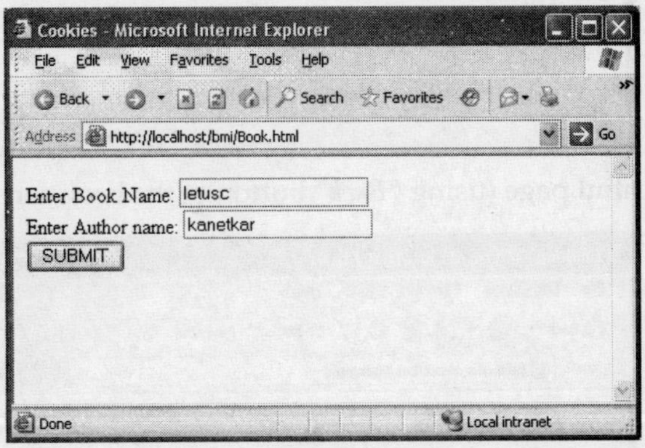

Fill the text boxes and press "SUBMIT" button.

Go back to the Book.html page (using "*Back*" button ⊕ Back of the browser).

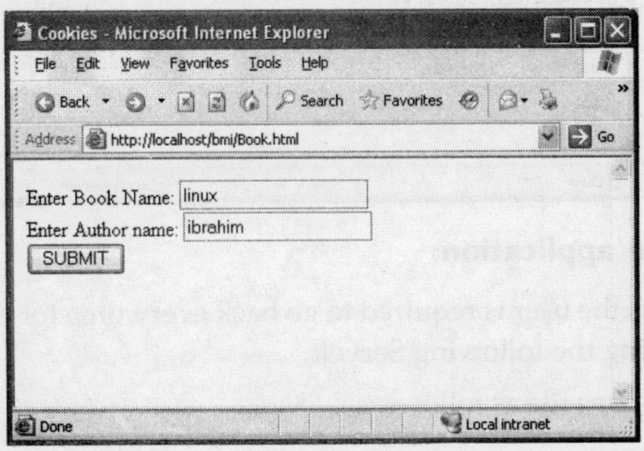

Fill the text boxes and press "SUBMIT" button.

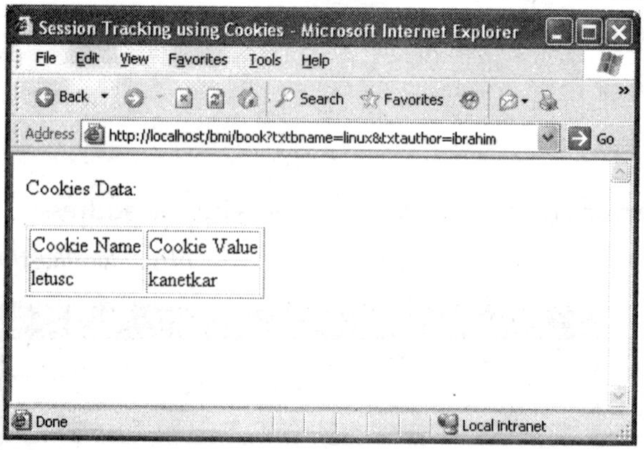

Go back to the Book.html page (using "*Back*" button of the browser).

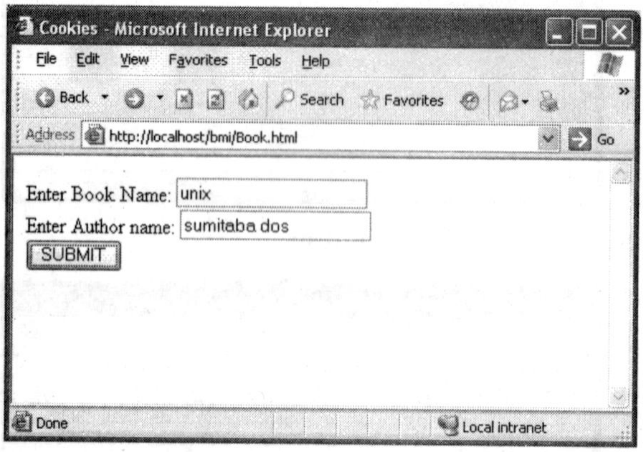

Fill the text boxes and press "SUBMIT" button.

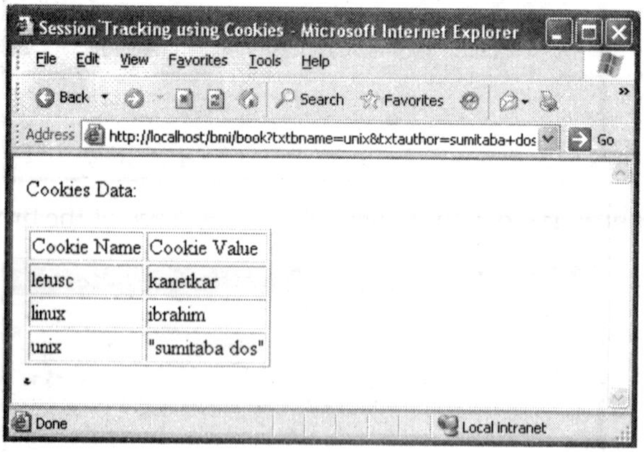

Enhancing the above application:

In the above application, the user is required to go back every time for entering data. This process can be simplified by using the following Servelt.

Change the *CookiesEg.java* file as follows.

```
import java.io.*;
import javax.servlet.*;
import javax.servlet.http.*;
public class CookiesEg extends HttpServlet
{
  public void doGet (HttpServletRequest request,
                     HttpServletResponse response)
                          throws ServletException, IOException
   {
    response.setContentType("text/html");
    PrintWriter out = response.getWriter();
    out.println("<html> <head> <title> Session Tracking using Cookies
                                                  </title> </head>");
    out.println("<body> Cookies Data: <br> <br>");
    out.println("<table border=1> <tr> <td> Cookie Name </td>
                                 <td> Cookie Value </td> </tr>");
    Cookie c[] = request.getCookies();
    if (c != null)
     for (int i=0;i<c.length;i++)
      out.println("<tr> <td>" + c[i].getName() + "</td> <td>" +
                                c[i].getValue() + "</td> </tr>");
    out.println("</table>");
    out.println
         ("<form name=f1 action=http://localhost/bmi/book2 method=get>");
    out.println
         ("Enter Book Name: <input type=text name=txtbname size=20> <br>");
    out.println
         ("Enter Author name: <input type=text name=txtauthor size=20>");
    out.println("<br> <input type=submit value=SUBMIT>");
    out.println("</form>");
    String cname = request.getParameter("txtbname");
    String cvalue = request.getParameter("txtauthor");
    if ((cname!=null))
       Cookie co = new Cookie(cname,cvalue);
    response.addCookie(co);
    out.println("</body></html>");
    out.close();
  }
}
```

Start the Tomcat server and invoke the browser with the address:

http:// localhost/bmi/Book.html.

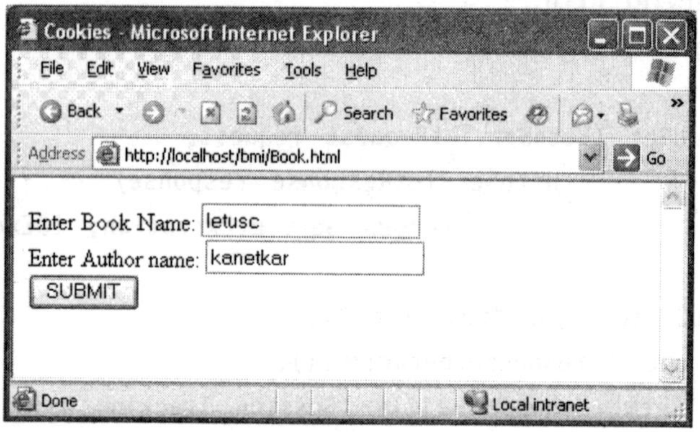

Fill the text boxes and press "SUBMIT" button.

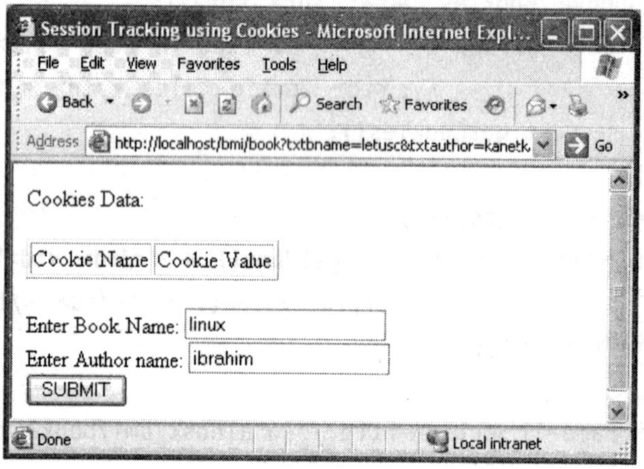

Fill the text boxes and press "SUBMIT" button.

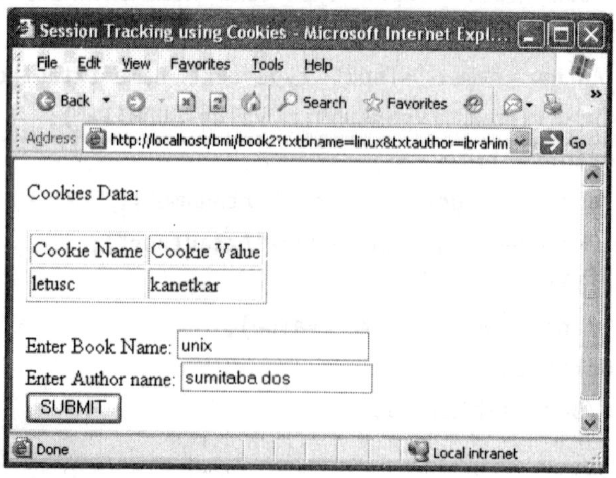

Fill the text boxes and press "SUBMIT" button.

Accessing Initialization Parameters

Store the "*Qualification.class*" in the directory-

G:\jakarta-tomcat-5.5.11\webapps\bmi\WEB-INF\classes.

Add the following two entries in the *web.xml* file stored in the directory-

G:\jakarta-tomcat-5.5.11\webapps\bmi\WEB-INF.

```
<servlet>
  <servlet-name> qualification </servlet-name>
  <servlet-class> Qualification </servlet-class>
  <init-param>
   <param-name> name </param-name>
   <param-value> B. Mohamed Ibrahim </param-value>
  </init-param>
  <init-param>
   <param-name> name </param-name>
   <param-value> B. Mohamed Ibrahim </param-value>
  </init-param>
  <init-param>
   <param-name> qualification </param-name>
   <param-value> MCA </param-value>
  </init-param>
</servlet>
<servlet-mapping>
   <servlet-name> qualification </servlet-name>
   <url-pattern> /initptr </url-pattern>
</servlet-mapping>
```

File Name: Qualification.java

```
import java.io.*;
import javax.servlet.*;
public class Qualification extends HttpServlet
{
public void service (ServletRequest request, ServletResponse response)
                        throws ServletException, IOException
 {
  ServletConfig sc = getServletConfig();
  response.setContentType("text/html");
  PrintWriter pw = response.getWriter();
  pw.println("<html> <head> <title> Designation </title> </head> <body>");
  pw.println("<b> Name: " + sc.getInitParameter("name") + "<br>");
  pw.println("Qualification: " + sc.getInitParameter("qualification") +
                                   "</b></body></html>");

  pw.close();
 }
}
```

Start the Tomcat server and invoke the browser with the address:

http:// localhost/bmi/initptr.

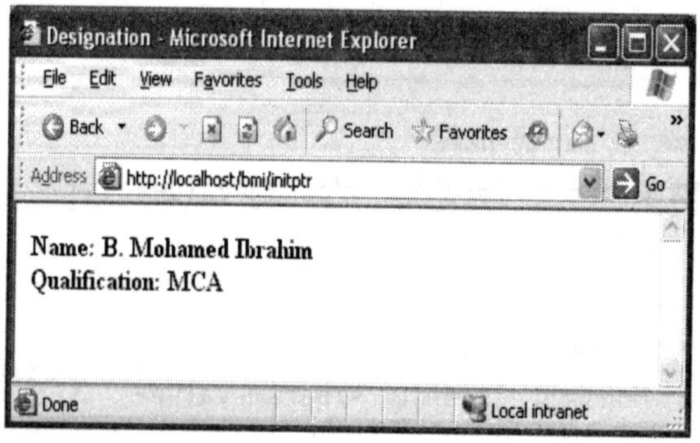

SUMMARY

This chapter started with the need and features of Servlets in dynamic web development. Further, listed the important APIs in both Generic and HTTP Servlets with difference among them. Apache Tomcat Application server is used as Servlet Container for testing example programs. However, the readers may deploy and test the given example programs with any other application server which supports Servlet API.

6

JAVA SERVLER PAGES (JSP)

6.0 INTRODUCTION

Java Server Pages (JSP) is one of the core components of JEE and it simplifies the use of Servets and supports almost all the features of Java Servlet technology, and is a server-side program provides dynamic support to the web pages. This chapter explores the concepts of JSP in detail with adequate illustrating examples.

6.1 ASPECTS OF JSP

JSP provides programmers a simple means to embed Java code in HTML code, whereas Java Servets outputs HTML code. And all JSP code will be converted into Servlet code by the Servlet container at the time of executing (invoking) JSP files.

JSP and Servlets: Even though all JSP files are converted into Servlets; the JSP file is easy to deploy because the JSP engine performs the recompilation for the Java code automatically. In Servlet, the response (the HTML content) is written using Stream's *println()* method, i.e., HTML program is written within Java code. But in JSP, the Java logic is embedded within HTML content.

JSP and ASP: The main difference is, the JSP is a product that provides platform independent so that it can run on any JVM-enabled Operating Systems including Windows and Linux. But the ASP, a Microsoft product, is not supporting platform independence so that it only runs under Windows platform.

The main components of the JSP are given below.

JSP Tags

Comments	<%--	--%>
Scripting Elements	<%	%>
Declarations	<%!	%>
Expressions	<%=	%>
Scriptlets	<%	%>

Directives <%@ %>

```
page
include
taglib
```

Implicit Objects

```
request
response
out
page
session
application
pageContext
config
```

Standard Actions

```
jsp:useBean
   jsp:setProperty
   jsp:getProperty
jsp:forward
   jsp:param
jsp:include
jsp:plugin
```

6.2 LIFE CYCLE OF A JSP PROGRAM

A JSP page is executed by a JSP engine (JSP Container), generally available on all Java based application servers (eg. Bea Weblogic) and web servers (Appche Tomcat). All the JSP files are converted into corresponding Servlet code automatically by web/application server before the execution.

There are three methods that are automatically called when a JSP page is requested and when that page terminates normally.

```
public void jspInit()
```

This method is invoked by the JSP container when the JSP is requested; and it is used to initialize objects and variables. This method is similar to the init() method in a Java Servlet.

```
public void jspDestroy()
```

This method is invoked by the JSP container when the JSP terminates normally; and it is used to provide clean up code for releasing the resources used during the execution of the JSP, such as disconnecting from a database. This method is similar to the `destroy()` method in a Java Servlet.

```
public void _jspService(HttpServletRequest request,
                        HttpServletResponse response)
                throws ServletException, IOException
```

This method is similar to service() method in a Servlet; it is automatically called and retrieves a connection to HTTP whenever a JSP page is requested from a Client. The developer can write code in this method to process requests which come from clients and send appropriate responses to them.

When the client requests a particular JSP page, the Server sends a request to the JSP engine / JSP container for generating a Servlet *.class* file corresponding to the JSP. Then the Servlet sends back the response to the client, from which the request was received.

6.3 JSP TAGS

These JSP tags are embedded with in HTML tags.

These tags are further divided as follows.

Comments	<%--	--%>
Scripting Elements	<%	%>
Declarations	<%!	%>
Expressions	<%=	%>
Scriptlets	<%	%>
Directives	<%@	%>

```
page
include
taglib
```

6.3.1 Comments

Comments in JSP are enclosed within <%— and —%> tags. One can also use the following regular HTML comment tags in a JSP file.

```
<!-- comments -->
```

Example:

```
<%-- This is a Comment --%>
```

6.3.2 Scripting Elements

We can use Java Code in the JSP document using these scripting elements.

6.3.2.1 Declarations

Declaration statements are written within <%! and %> tags and must be terminated with the semicolon.

Example:

```
<%! int n; %>
<%! int n=10; %>
```

```
<%! int n; double x;
    java.util.Date d; String s;
%>
<%! int n=0; double x=3.1415;
    java.uil.Date d = new java.util.Date();
    String s = "Ibrahim";
%>
```

We can also define methods as shown below.

```
<%!
   public int add (int n1, int n2)
   {
   int r = n1+n2;
   return r;
   }
%>
```

6.3.2.2 Expression

The expression returns the evaluated value of the specified Java expression back to the client. A expression must be written within the <%= and %> tags.

Examples:

```
<%= 5+2 %>
```

The expression is evaluated at the Server and the result 7 is sent to the client for display.

```
<%! int n1=5, n2=10; %>
<%= n1+n2 %>
```

Then, the values of n1 and n2 are added and then the result is sent to the client.

```
<%= new java.util.Date() %>
```

This statement sends the current date and time (in the server) to the client for display.

6.3.2.3 Scriptlets

A Scriptlet is a block of Java code enclosed within the <% and %> tags. They are executed when the page is requested.

Example:

```
<%
   int n1, n2, n3;
   n1 = 10;
   n2 = 20;
   n3 = n1 + n2;
%>
<%= n3 %>
```

The above code can also be written as,

```
<%
  int n1, n2, n3;
  n1 = 10;
  n2 = 20;
  n3 = n1 + n2;
  out.println(n3);
%>
```

Here, *out* is a built-in object used to send data to the client.

```
<%
 public int add(int n1, int n2)
 {
  return (n1+n2);
 }
%>
<%= add(10,20) %>
```

6.4 IMPLICIT OBJECTS

JSP supports the following implicit objects.

`request, response, out, page, session,`

`application, pageContext, config`

Implicit objects in JSP are based on the Servlet API and are implemented from Servlet classes and interfaces.

The developer can use these objects directly without writing any extra code. All these objects are used in JSP scriptlets and expressions. The methods that are accessible with these objects can be invoked using the syntax,

```
objectname.methodname(parameters_if_any)
```

6.4.1 Request Object

This is the object of `HttpServletRequest`, used to access the request information such as HTML forms' data that are sent from the clients through HTTP request.

Important methods accessible with request object:

`String getParameter(String pname)`

Returns the value of the specified parameter (from client's HTML form)

`String getServerName()`

Returns the name of the Server computer.

`Enumeration getPatrameterNames()`

Returns the parameter names of the request as Enumeration type.

`String[] getParameterValues()`

Returns the parameter values of the request as String array.

`String getServerPort()`

Returns the listening port of the server.

`String getMethod()`

Returns the HTTP method name used in HTML FORM element's METHOD attribute (such as `GET`, `POST`,...)

`String getQueryString()`

Returns the query string from the URL when GET method is used. (Query String starts after the question mark symbol in the URL)

6.4.2 Response Object

This is the object of `HttpServletResponse` class, used to send HTML output to clients.

Important methods accessible with response object:

`PrintWriter getWriter()`

Returns PrintWriter object used to send data to the clients.

`void sendRedirect(Strring url)`

Redirects the current page to specified URL.

`void setContentType(String type)`

Set the MIME type for the response content.

The Multipurpose Internet mail Extension (MIME) is a method of encoding a file for delivery over the Internet.

Commonly used MIME types and their corresponding file types are given below.

`text/plain`	Plain text
`text/html`	HTML
`text/xml`	XML
`text/css`	Cascading Style Sheet
`application/msword`	Microsoft Word content
`application/vnd.ms-excel`	Microsoft Excel content
`application/vnd.ms-powerpoint`	Microsoft PowerPoint content
`application/pdf`	Acrobat Portable Document format
`application/post-script`	Post-Script document
`application/x-java-archive`	Java Archive (JAR) file
`application/x-java-vm`	Java byte code (.class) file
`image/jpeg`	JPEG (Joint Photographic Experts Group) image
`image/gif`	GIF (Graphics Interchange Format) image
`image/png`	PNG (Portable Network Graphics) image
`audio/midi`	MIDI (Musical Instrument Digital Interface) Audio clip
`video/mpeg`	MPEG (Motion Pictures Experts Group) Video clip
`text/vnd.wap.wml`	WML

6.4.3 Out Object

It is the reference to the JSPWriter, used to send back data to the client.

Example:

```
<%
    out.println("<b> welcome </b>");
    int x = 10;
    out.println("<i> The value of x is " + x + "</i>" );
%>
```

6.4.4 Application Object

It is the object of ServletContext, and it represents the attributes of the entire application. So that all pages of the application can access it as long as the JSP engine is running.

Data can be set and get through the following methods with this application objects.

`void setAttribute(Sting name, Object object)`

Registers a name associated with an object.

`Object getAttribute(String name)`

Returns an object associated with the specified name.

`void removeAttribute(String name)`

Deletes an object reference associated with the specified name.

6.4.5 Session Object

It is the object of HttpSession, used to store objects between client requests. A session is created automatically when a client makes a request. This session object is available throughout the user's session, unless set to false.

`void setAttribute(Sting name, Object attribute)`

Registers a name associated with an object.

`Object getAttribute(String name)`

Returns an object associated with the name.

`void removeAttribute(String name)`

Deletes an object reference associated with a name.

`long getCreationTime()`

Returns the time (in milliseconds) of the initiation of the session.

`long getLastAcccessedTime()`

Returns the time (in milliseconds) the session was last accessed.

`void invalidate()`

Marks the session as being inactive and unbinds all the objects bound to it. (For example, this concept is applied in e-mail login/logout process. After a user logged out from his e-mail account, he can not view the previously accessed e-mail pages using the *Back* button of the browser. But, it is possible if the user is logged on. When the user logs on, his user information are stored on as *session* data and when he logs out, his corresponding session data are cleared using the *invalidate()* method.)

6.4.6 PageContext Object

It is the object of `PageContext`. It is used to access multiple page attributes that can be used to store shared data.

void setAttribute(Sting name, Object attribute)

Registers a name associated with an object.

`Object getAttribute(String name)`

Returns an object associated with the name.

`void removeAttribute(String name)`

Deletes an object reference associated with a name.

6.4.7 Config Object

It is the object of `ServletConfig`. This object is automatically generated by the Servlet engine. It contains configuration information to the Servlet during startup.

`String getInitParameter(String name)`

Returns the value of the initialization parameter specified in name.

`Enumeration getInitParameterNames()`

Returns the enumeration of all the initialization parameter names.

6.4.8 Page Object

This is the reference (to the current instance of the JSP page) that is used to refer the current instance of the generated servlet (like *this* keyword in a class). So, this object is not available to any included JSPs.

6.5 JSP DIRECTIVES

These directives are used to provide page-specific global information about JSP pages to the JSP engine before compilation.

The general format of using these directives is,

```
<%@directivename attribute1="value1" attribute2="value2" ... %>
```

The available directives are,

```
page
include
taglib
```

6.5.1 Page Directive

This directive is used for general settings of a JSP page.

Its attributes include `contentType`, `import`, `extends`, `errorPage`, `isErrorPage`, `session`, `isThreadSafe`, `language`, `autoFlash` and `info`.

General format of this *page* directive is,

```
<%@page contentType = "MIMI Type"
        import = "package list separated by Semicolon"
        isErrorPage = "true|false"
        errorPage = "errorpage URL"
        extends = "packagename.classname"
        language = "scripting language"
        session = "true|false"
        isThreadSafe = "true|false"
        buffer = "buffer size in bytes"
        info = "message text"
        autoFlash = "true" %>
```

contentType attribute:

This attribute is used to set the MIME type for the response, which is used to send data to the client.

Example:

```
<%@page contentType="text/html" %>
```

This directive sets "`text/html`" as the response content type. (The type of the data-content which will be sent to the client as response).

```
<%@page contentType="text/xml" %>
```

This directive sets xml as the response content type.

The default value for this attribute is "`text/html`".

import attribute:

This attribute is used to import packages to a JSP page. A semicolon must be used to separate package specifications.

Examples:

```
<%@page import="java.util.*" %>
<%@page import="java.util.Date;java.io.*;javax.sql.*" %>
```

errorPage attribute:

If an uncaught exception is thrown, in the current page, then the control is transferred in the URL of this attribute.

Example:

```
<%@page errorPage="error.jsp" %>
```

isErrorPage attribute:

This is used to specify the current JSP page as an *errorPage* to other JSP pages.

Example:

```
<%@page isErrorPage="true" %>
```

Default value for this attribute is "false".

language attribute:

It specifies the scripting language that is used when compiling the JSP page. Note that Java is the only language available for JSP currently.

Example:

```
<%@page language="Java" %>
```

Default value for this attribute is "Java".

session attribute:

This is to specify the availability of the session data for a JSP page.

Example:

```
<%@page session="false" %>
```

Default value for this attribute is "true".

isThreadSafe attribute:

If it is *true*, then the current page can service multiple requests at a time, by using multiple threads for each of the request. These threads access the *service()* method of the same Servlet instance simultaneously. If it is *false*, then it prevents simultaneous access to the same Servlet instance i.e., JSP processor queues up requests from clients for a page and it processes one at a time, in the order they were received.

Example:

```
<%@page isThreadSafe="false" %>
```

Default value for this attribute is "true".

buffer attribute:

This is used to set the size of the buffer (for the out object). The document content will be sent to the client only if the buffer is full or if the page is completed.

Examples:

```
<%@page buffer="10kb" %>
<%@page buffer="none" %>
```

Default value fort this attribute is 8 kb.

autoFalsh attribute:

If it is true, the output buffer to the client is flushed (sent out) automatically when it becomes full. If it is false, a runtime exception is raised indicating buffer overflow.

Example:

```
<%@page autoFlash="true" %>
```

Default value for this attribute is "true".

extends attribute:

This attribute can force the generated Servlet (of the JSP file) to extend the class specified in this attribute. This is used in rare case. Note that the implicit objects will not be available to the requested JSP.

Example:

```
<%@page extends="myclasses.DisplayClass" %>
```

info attribute:

The `getServletInfo()` method used in a Servlet returns the String which is specified in this attribute.

```
<%@page info="E-commerce application" %>
```

6.5.2 Include Directive

This directive is used to append static (html) and dynamic (JSP) content with a JSP.

Examples:

```
<%@include file="biodata.html" %>
<%@include file="biodata.jsp" %>
```

6.5.3 Taglib Directive

This directive is used to specify the inclusion of custom tags (XML tags) in a JSP file.

General format is,

```
<%@taglib uri="TagLibraryURI" prefix="tagprefix" %>
```

The attributes `uri` and `prefix` are used to specify the Tag Library Descriptor (TLD) file and a reference name for a particular tag library respectively.

Example:

```
<%@taglib uri="Employee.tld" prefix="emp" %>
```

We will discuss about this *taglib* directive in detail later.

6.6 STANDARD ACTIONS

The Standard Actions are the container tags particularly used for using JavaBeans, including static/dynamic files and forwarding requests.

The following are the available Standard Actions.

```
<jsp:include>
<jsp:forward>
<jsp:param>
<jsp:plugin>
    <jsp:fallback>
<jsp:useBean>
    <jsp:setProperty>
    <jsp:getProperty>
```

6.6.1 <jsp:include> action

This include action is used to include a static (HTML) or dynamic (JSP) file in a JSP page as like include directive.

General format is,

```
<jsp:include page="URL of including file" flush="true" />
```

Note that the `include` directive does not update changes made to the static resources if the parent JSP is called second time. This is not the case in Standard action, every time the changed static contents are also updated.

The page attribute specifies the URL of the static or dynamic resource to be included. The flush attribute must be "true" and it flush (sent out) the buffer in the output stream. If the page output is buffered, then the buffer is flushed prior to the inclusion.

6.6.2 <jsp:forword> action

This standard action is used to forward the request from the current JSP page to another JSP, Servlet or even a static resource at run time.

General format is,

```
<jsp:forward page="URL of the forwarded page" />
```

Example:

```
<jsp:forward page="biodata.jsp" />
```

6.6.3 <jsp:param> action

This is used to send additional parameter name-value pairs (along with the originals from client) to included and forwarded resources.

General format is,

```
<jsp:param name="parameter name" value="parameter value" />
```

Examples:

```
<jsp:include page="biodata.jsp" flush="true">
      <jsp:param name="uname" value="Ibrahim" />
      <jsp:param name="age" value="26" />
</jsp:include>
<jsp:forward page="biodata.jsp" >
      <jsp:param name="uname" value="Ibrahim" />
      <jsp:param name="age" value="26" />
</jsp:forward>
```

When the JSP engine encounters the `jsp:include` / `jsp:forward` action, then the output buffer is flushed and the control is transferred to the included / forwarded page with the original request parameters and the parameters specified in `<jsp:param>` action tags. In the case of `jsp:include`, after the execution of the included file, the control returns back to the parent JSP, but it is not true in the case of `jsp:forward`. In both cases, the parent JSP can not use the parameters specified in the `<jsp:param>` tags, it can only access the original parameters which are sent from the client.

The `jsp:param` action is also used in `jsp:plugin`, which is explained below.

6.6.4 <jsp:plugin> action

This action is used to embed Java component plug-ins like Applets. These `<jsp:plugin>` tags are replaced to `<object>` or `<embed>` HTML tags to display the components in the browser.

(You have to install and run Java plug-in software before executing the JSP which uses `<jsp:plugin>` action.).

General format is,

```
<jsp:plugin
     type  =  "applet|bean"
     code = "Class file name of the plug-in"
     codebase = "URL of the specified class file">
</jsp:plugin>
```

Examples:

```
<jsp:plugin
      type="applet"
      code="Biodata.class"
      width="200"  height="200">
</jsp:plugin>
<jsp:plugin
      type="applet"
      code="Biodata.class"
      width="200"  height="200">
    <jsp:param name="uname"  value="Ibrahim"  />
    <jsp:param name="age" value="26"  />
</jsp:plugin>
```

An `<jsp:fallback>` tag is used to specify the text which is to be displayed in the client browser if the `plugin` is not supported.

```
<jsp:plugin
      type="applet"
      code="Biodata.class"
      width="200"  height="200">
    <jsp:fallback> Your browser does not support this plug-in
    </jsp:fallback>
</jsp:plugin>
```

6.6.5 <jsp:useBean>

This action is used to access a Java bean. (Bean is a program component developed for a particular application.).

```
<jsp:useBean
    id = "instance of the bean"
    class = "bean's class filename"
    scope = "life of the bean">
```

The attribute `class` specifies the class filename of the bean. Its instance is specified in the id attribute. It acts as an object to the bean class. The scope attributes which is used to specify the life of the bean can have any one of the values: `page`, `request`, `session`, and `application`. The default life time of a bean is `page`.

page scope:

Any objects defined within this scope will disappear as soon as the current page finishes generating or the request is forwarded to another resource.

request scope:

Any object defined within this `request` scope is available as long as the HttpRequest object (request) is available. It is similar to page scope, but even though the current page forwards the request to another resource, the scope will still exist.

session scope:

Any objects defined within this `session` scope are available as long as the client session is valid. (A session is initiated when the client first makes a request and ends when the user closes his browser. Also some JSP implementation uses time specifications, for example, session period is one hour. But it is limited to a single client, i.e., single client, multiple pages. The session period starts when a user makes request to a page in a server.)

application scope:

Objects within the application scope are not limited to an individual clients, but to all the clients.

Each bean has properties, methods and events. The bean properties can be accessed by using the *`setXXX()`* and *`getXXX()`* methods. Here, *XXX* represents the corresponding property name. Every bean class should have a public default constructor and get and set methods of each properties.

Example:

```
<jsp:useBean id="bio" class="myclass.Biodata" scope="page" />
```

Here, Biodata is the bean class filename stored at the package `myclasses`.

<jsp:setProperty>

This standard action is used along with the `<jsp:useBean>`, to set the value of the properties of the bean whose class filename is specified in the *class* attribute.

General format is,

```
<jsp:setProperty
      name = "Name of the bean"
      property = "data member of the bean"
      value = "value to the property"
      param = "HTML parameter value to the property" />
```

Here, *name* specifies the instance of the bean, *property* specifies the data member name of the bean to set a value, *value* represents the value for the bean property and, *param* specifies the property name of the request parameter (HTML input element name) to be used to set the value of the bean property. Either *value* or *param* attribute can be used in a `<jsp:setProperty>` tag.

Example:

```
<jsp:useBean id="bio" class="myclass.Biodata" scope="page">
  <jsp:setProperty name="bio" property="name" value="Ibrahim" />
</jsp:useBean>
<jsp:useBean id="bio" class="myclass.Biodata" scope="page">
  <jsp:setProperty name="bio" property="name" param="username"/>
</jsp:useBean>
<jsp:useBean id="bio" class="myclass.Biodata" scope="page">
  <jsp:setProperty name="bio" property="*" />
</jsp:useBean>
```

Making connection between HTML FORM properties and Bean properties:

```
<jsp:setProperty
  name = "beanid"
  peoperty = "beanproperty"
  value = "<% request.getParameter("formproperty") %>" />
```

Here, the value of the "formproperty" is assigned as the value of "beanproperty". If the "beanproperty" and "formproperty" names are same, then the above code can be written as,

```
<jsp:setProperty name="beanid" property="beanproperty" />
```

The value from the HTML form element (whose name is same as "beanproperty") is taken and assigned to the specified property of the bean implicitly.

If the "beanproperty" name and "formproperty" name are different, we have to use the first format or the following format of the `jsp:setProperty`.

```
<jsp:setProperty name = "beanid"
                 property = "beanproperty"
                 param = "formproperty" />
```

Note that when the property is to be set in a bean, then its `setXXX()` method is called. The programmer must write assignment statements within this method.

If a HTML form has form elements named Param1, Param2, and so on. And we want to assign their values into the bean's properties whose names are also Param1, Param2, and so on. Then the following format can be used.

```
<jsp:setProperty name="beanid" property="*" />
```

Then the *setParam1(), setParam2(), ...* methods of the bean will be called automatically to set values to the bean properties *Param1, Paaram2, etc.* i.e., it looks through all the parameters provided by the FORM and all the *set* methods provided by the bean and link them together automatically. If the FORM provides some properties for which there are no *set* methods in the bean, then they will be ignored and no errors will occur. Likewise, if the bean provides set methods for which the FORM does not supply values, these methods will not be called and also no error will occur.

Also we can call the bean's set methods without using `<jsp:setProperty>` as follows.

```
<% beanid.setMethod(Parameters if any) %>
```

<:getProperty>

This Standard action is used along with `<jsp:useBean>`, to get the value of a property of the bean whose class filename is specified in the *class* attribute.

General format is,

```
<jsp:getProperty name="beanid" property="beanproperty" />
```

It calls the corresponding *get* method of the bean property which returns the value of the bean property. The value will be sent to the client automatically.

We can also call the bean's *get* methods using Scriptlets as follows.

```
<% beanid.getMethod("Parameters if any") %>
```

6.7 SESSION TRACKING

A session is time period defined between requests from the single client (single user). When the server sends response data to the client, then the request data that was sent to the server from the client will be destroyed at the server, i.e., the data will not be tracked for the entire user session. To accomplish session tracking, *cookies* and *session* object are used.

Using Cookies:

Cookies are Server-side objects stored at Client. The Cookies can be stored at Clients using *response* object and can be retrieved at Server using *request* object using *addCookies()* and *getCookies()* methods respectively.

Cookies can be manipulated by creating objects of `Cookie class`. The constructor for the *Cookie* class is,

```
Cookie(String cookie-name, String cookie-value)
```

Some of the methods of this class are given below.

`String getName()`

Returns the name of the Cookie associated with the invoking object.

`String getValue()`

Returns the value of the invoking Cookie object.

`void setValue(String value)`

Assigns a new value to the invoking Cookie.

`void setComment(String comment)`

Sets the specified comment with an invoked Cookie object.

`String getComment()`

Returns the comment associated with the invoked Cookie object.

`void setDomain(String DomainName)`

Specifies the domain in which the Cookie should be present.

`void setMaxAge(int seconds)`

Specifies the time period in seconds for a Cookie to live.

6.8 SAMPLE PROGRAMS

This section illustrates the core concepts of JSP with example programs.

Working with Tomcat for running JSPs:

Install the latest version of Tomcat (In our demo, Tomcat version 5.5.11 is used).

Also ensure that the *servlet* tag and *servlet-mapping* tag are not commented in the file *G:/jakarta-tomcat-5.5.11/conf/ web.xml* for using the in-built JspServlet feature.

```
<servlet>
   <servlet-name>jsp</servlet-name>
   <servlet-class>org.apache.jasper.servlet.JspServlet
   </servlet-class>
   <init-param>
         <param-name>fork</param-name>
         <param-value>false</param-value>
   </init-param>
   <init-param>
         <param-name>xpoweredBy</param-name>
         <param-value>false</param-value>
   </init-param>
   <load-on-startup>3</load-on-startup>
</servlet>
<servlet-mapping>
   <servlet-name>jsp</servlet-name>
   <url-pattern>*.jsp</url-pattern>
</servlet-mapping>
```

Create a Sub-directory named *bmijsp* under the directory *G:\jakarta-tomcat-5.5.11\webapps*. In *bmijsp*, create a sub-directory named *WEB-INF* and this *WEB-INF* directory should contain two subdirectories: *classes* and *lib*. The *classes* directory contains all servlet *.class* files and the *lib* directory contains jar files which can be used by *.class* files that are stored in *classes* directory.

The directory structure is as follows.

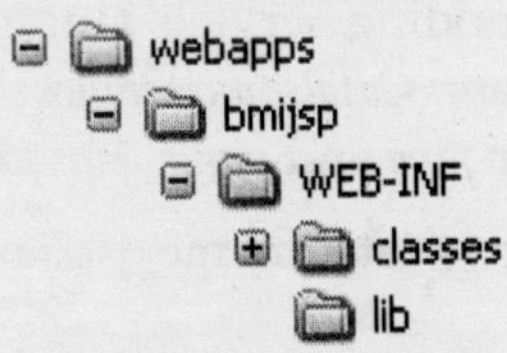

A deployment descriptor file named *web.xml* should be stored in the directory- *G:\jakarta-tomcat-5.5.11\webapps\bmi\WEB-INF*. A typical content of the file is,

```
<?xml version="1.0" encoding="ISO-8859-1"?>
<web-app xmlns="http://java.sun.com/xml/ns/j2ee"
         xmlns:xsi="http://www.w3.org/2001/XMLSchema-instance"
         xsi:schemaLocation="http://java.sun.com/xml/ns/j2ee
         http://java.sun.com/xml/ns/j2ee/web-app_2_4.xsd"
         version="2.4">
```

```
  <description>
   JSP Examples.
  </description>
  <display-name>JSP Examples</display-name>
 </web-app>
```

First JSP Application: Displaying your name

Store the following program as *"name.jsp"* in the directory G:\jakarta-tomcat-5.5.11\webapps\bmijsp.

```
<html>
 <head>
  <title> Name </title>
 </head>
 <body>
  My name is <b> Ibrahim </b>.
 </body>
</html>
```

Start the Tomcat server.

Invoke the browser with the address, http://localhost/bmijsp/name.jsp

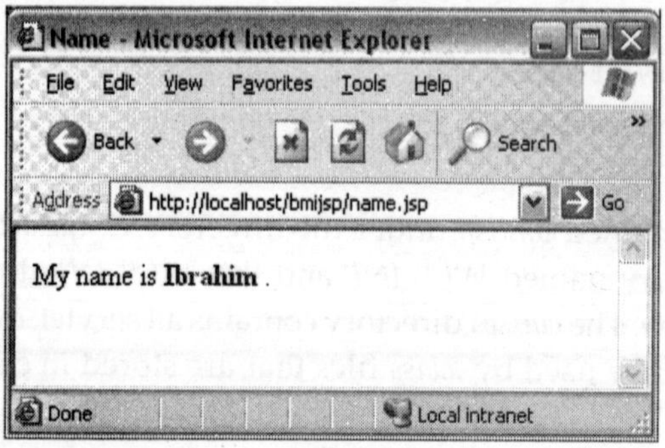

All JSP are converted into corresponding Servlets automatically before execution. To test this, go to the *G:\jakarta-tomcat-5.5.11\work\Catalina\localhost\bmijsp\org\apache\jsp* directory and observe that two files named *name_jsp.java* and *name_jsp.class* are stored.

The content of the automatically generated name_jsp.java file is given below.

```
package org.apache.jsp;
import javax.servlet.*;
import javax.servlet.http.*;
import javax.servlet.jsp.*;
public final class name_jsp extends
   org.apache.jasper.runtime.HttpJspBase
   implements org.apache.jasper.runtime.JspSourceDependent {
private static java.util.List _jspx_dependants;
```

```
public Object getDependants() {
  return _jspx_dependants;
}
public void _jspService(HttpServletRequest request,
                        HttpServletResponse response)
               throws java.io.IOException, ServletException {
  JspFactory _jspxFactory = null;
  PageContext pageContext = null;
  HttpSession session = null;
  ServletContext application = null;
  ServletConfig config = null;
  JspWriter out = null;
  Object page = this;
  JspWriter _jspx_out = null;
  PageContext _jspx_page_context = null;
  try   {
     _jspxFactory = JspFactory.getDefaultFactory();
      response.setContentType("text/html");
      pageContext = _jspxFactory.getPageContext(this, request,
      response, null, true, 8192, true);
      _jspx_page_context = pageContext;
      application = pageContext.getServletContext();
      config = pageContext.getServletConfig();
      session = pageContext.getSession();
      out = pageContext.getOut();
      _jspx_out = out;
      out.write("<html>\r\n");
      out.write(" <head>\r\n");
      out.write(" <title> Name </title>\r\n");
      out.write(" </head>\r\n");
      out.write(" <body>\r\n");
      out.write(" My name is <b> Ibrahim </b>.\r\n");
      out.write(" </body>\r\n");
      out.write("</html>");
    } catch (Throwable t) {
      if (!(t instanceof SkipPageException)){
       out = _jspx_out;
      if (out != null && out.getBufferSize() != 0)
        out.clearBuffer();
      if (_jspx_page_context != null)
           _jspx_page_context.handlePageException(t);
```

```
        }
    } finally {
        if (_jspxFactory != null)
            _jspxFactory.releasePageContext(_jspx_page_context);
    }
  }
}
```

Copy the directory *org* from the directory G:\jakarta-tomcat 5.5.11\work\Catalina\localhost\bmijsp into the directory G:\jakarta-tomcat-5.5.11\webapps\bmijsp\WEB-INF\classes.

Add the following entries in the *G:\jakarta-tomcat-5.5.11\webapps\bmijsp\WEB-INF\web.xml* file.

```
<servlet>
    <servlet-name> na </servlet-name>
    <servlet-class> org.apache.jsp.name_jsp </servlet-class>
</servlet>
<servlet-mapping>
    <servlet-name> na </servlet-name>
    <url-pattern> /myname </url-pattern>
</servlet-mapping>
```

Start the Tomcat server.

Invoke the browser with the address, http://localhost/bmijsp/myname

Note that we are using the servlet class that was automatically generated. We can also use this reference in *action* attribute of the HTML *form* element.

Handling request data

Store the *"yname.html"* file in the directory- G:\jakarta-tomcat-5.5.11\webapps\bmijsp.

Store the *"yname.jsp"* file in the directory- G:\jakarta-tomcat-5.5.11\webapps\bmijsp.

File Name: yname.html

```
<html>
<body>
```

```
<form name="f1" method="GET"
              action="http://localhost/bmijsp/yname.jsp">
  Enter your name <input type="text" name="txtname" size="20">
  <br> <input type="submit" value="SUBMIT">
 </form>
</body>
</html>
```

File Name: yname.jsp

```
<html>
<head>
 <title> Accessing parameter </title>
</head>
<body>
 My name is <b> <%= request.getParameter("txtname") %> </b>.
</body>
</html>
```

Start the Tomcat server. Invoke the browser with the address,

http://localhost/bmijsp/yname.html

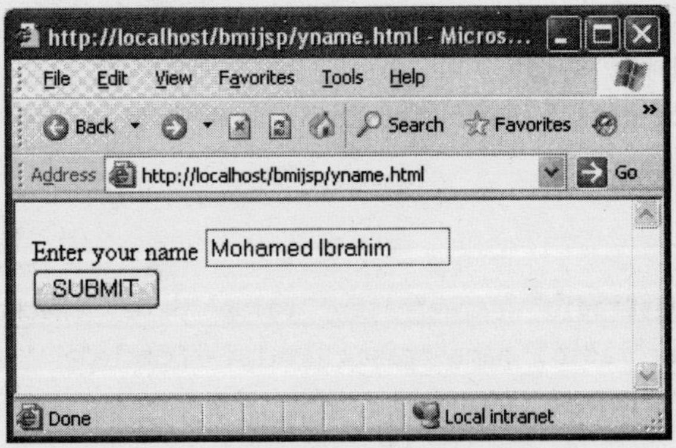

Enter your name in the text box and press the "SUBMIT" button.

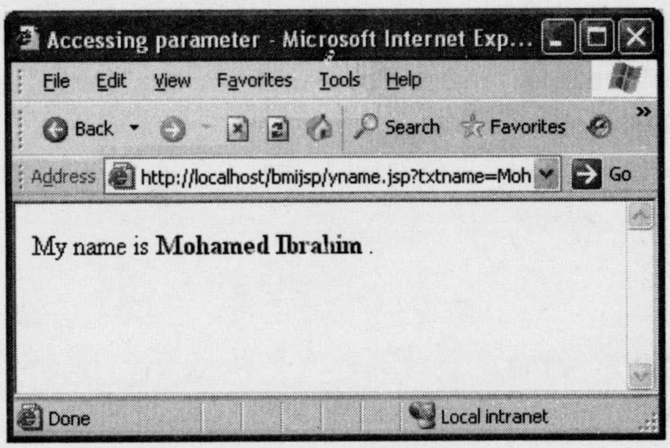

Accessing various types of data from HTML form

Store the *"biodata.html"* file in the directory- G:\jakarta-tomcat-5.5.11\webapps\bmijsp.

Store the *"biodata.jsp"* file in the directory- G:\jakarta-tomcat-5.5.11\webapps\bmijsp.

File Name: biodata.html

```
<html>
 <head>
  <title> Bio-Data </title>
</head>
<body>
  <center>
  <h1> BIO-DATA </h1>
  <form name="f1" action="http://localhost/bmijsp/biodata.jsp"
                                                  method="post">
  <table>
   <tr>
    <td> Employee number: </td>
    <td> <input type="text" name="txteno" size="6"> </td>
   </tr>
   <tr>
    <td> Employee Name: </td>
    <td> <input type="text" name="txtname" size="10"> </td>
  </tr>
  <tr>
    <td> Sex: </td>
    <td> <input type="radio" name="rasex" value="Male" checked> Male
        <input type="radio" name="rasex" value="Female">
                   Female </td>
  </tr>
  <tr>
   <td> Languages Known: </td>
   <td> <input type="checkbox" name="chklan1" value="Tamil" checked>
                 Tamil
       <input type="checkbox" name="chklan2" value="English">
               English </td>
  </tr>
  <tr>
   <td> Specialization: </td>
   <td> <select name="listspecial" size="3">
```

```
        <option value="Web Designing"> Web Designing </option>
        <option value="System Programming">
              System Programming
        </option>
        <option value="Linux Administration">
             Linux Administration
        </option>
        <option value="Windows NT Administration">
              Windows NT Administration
        </option>
        <option value="Object Oriented Programming System">
              OOPS
        </option>
        <option value="Database Administration"> DBA </option>
       </select>
 <td>
</tr>
<tr>
 <td> Nationality: </td>
 <td>
   <select name="chonation" size="1">
   <option value="India"> India </option>
   <option value="America"> America </option>
   <option value="Singapore"> Singapore </option>
   <option value="Malaysia"> Malaisia </option>
   <option value="UAE"> United Arab Embreds </option>
   <option value="Others"> Others </option>
  </select> </td>
 </tr>
 <tr>
  <td> Address: </td>
 <td>
   <textarea name="txtaddress" rows="5" cols="30">
          Type your address here
   </textarea>
  </td>
 </tr>
 </table>
 <input type="hidden" name="sno" value="1">
```

```
    <input type="submit" value="SUBMIT">
    <input type="reset" value="RESET">
   </form>
  </body>
 </html>
```

File Name: biodata.jsp

```
<html>
<head>
 <title> Accessing Form Data </title>
</head>
<body>
<b><u> BIO-DATA </u></b> <br><br>
<%
   java.util.Enumeration e = request.getParameterNames();
   while (e.hasMoreElements())
   {
    String pname = (String) e.nextElement();
    String pvalue = request.getParameter(pname);
    out.println(pname + " = " + pvalue + "<br>");
   }
%>
</body>
</html>
```

Start the Tomcat server. Invoke the browser with the address,

http://localhost/bmijsp/biodata.html

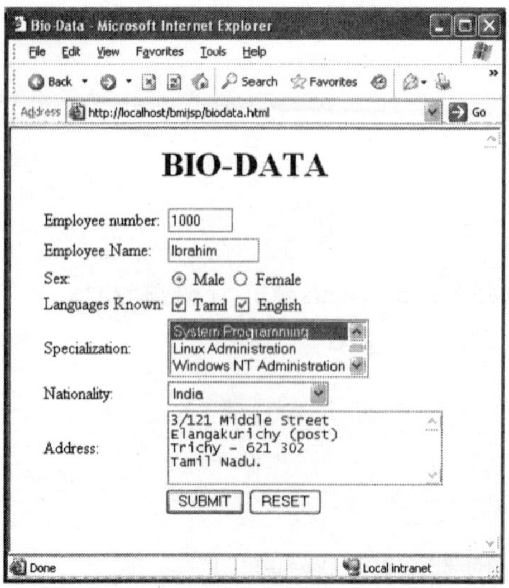

Fill up the form and press the submit button.

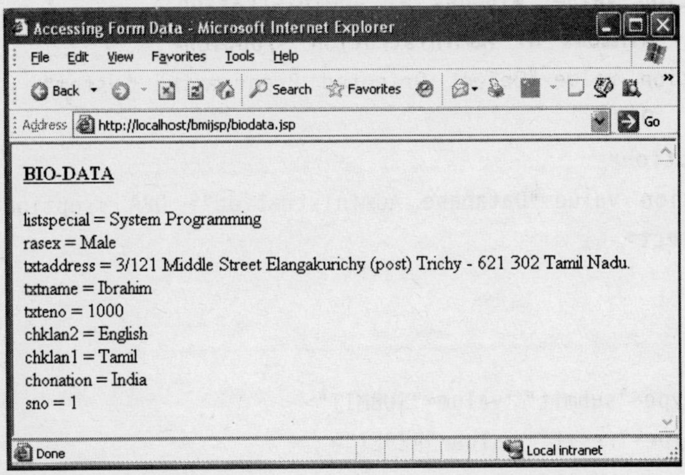

Handling Multi-selection List box

More than one item can be selected in a Multi-selection list box.

Store the *"multilist.html"* file in the directory- G:\jakarta-tomcat-5.5.11\webapps\bmijsp.

Store the *"multilist.jsp"* file in the directory- G:\jakarta-tomcat-5.5.11\webapps\bmijsp.

File Name: multilist.html

```
<html>
 <head>
  <title> List box with Multiple Selection </title>
 </head>
 <body>
  <center>
  <h1> Specialization </h1>
  <form name="form1" action="http://localhost/bmijsp/multilist.jsp"
       method="POST">
  <table>
   <tr>
    <td> Specialization: </td>
    <td> <select name="listspecial" size="3" multiple="true">
        <option value="Web Designing"> Web Designing </option>
        <option value="System Programming">
             System Programming
        </option>
        <option value="Linux Administration">
             Linux Administration
```

```
            </option>
            <option value="Windows NT Administration">
                Windows NT Administration </option>
            <option value="Object Oriented Programming System">
                OOPS
            </option>
            <option value="Database Administration"> DBA </option>
          </select>
      <td>
    </tr>
    </table>
      <input type="submit" value="SUBMIT">
      <input type="reset" value="RESET">
    </form>
  </body>
</html>
```

File Name: multilist.jsp

```
<html>
<head>
  <title> Specialization </title>
</head>
<body>
Your Specialization subjects are, <br><br>
<%
   String values[] = request.getParameterValues("listspecial");
   for (int i=0;i<values.length;i++)
    {
%>
<%= values[i] %>
<br>
<% } %>
</body>
</html>
```

Start the Tomcat server. Invoke the browser with the address,

http://localhost/bmijsp/multilist.html

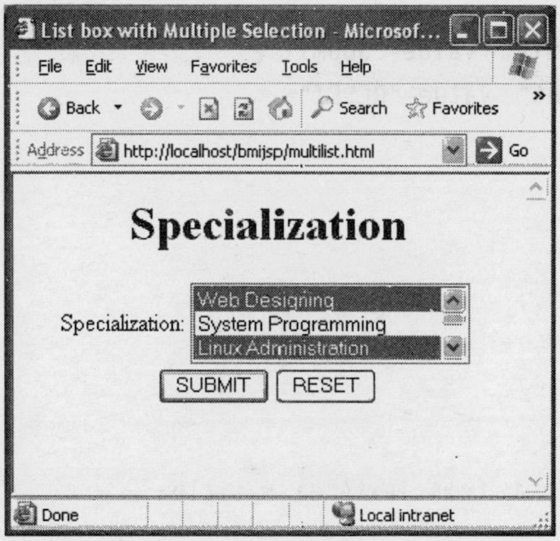

Select your specialization(s) and press the submit button.

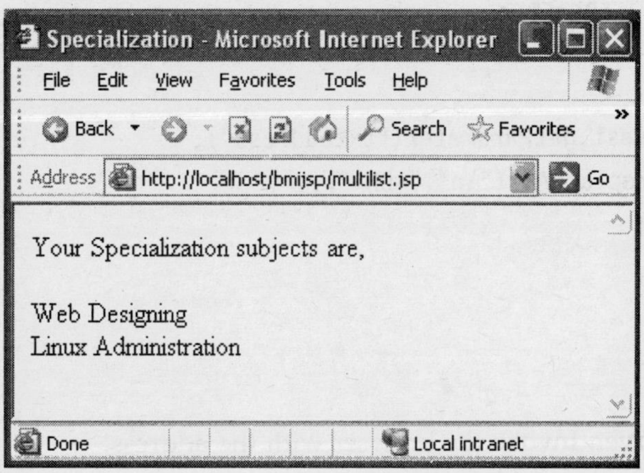

Accessing TextArea data

Store the *"tarea.html"* file in the directory- G:\jakarta-tomcat-5.5.11\webapps\bmijsp.

Store the *"tarea.jsp"* file in the directory- G:\jakarta-tomcat-5.5.11\webapps\bmijsp.

File Name: tarea.html

```
<html>
 <head>
  <title> TextArea </title>
 </head>
<body>
  <center>
  <form name="Form1" action="http://localhost/bmijsp/tarea.jsp">
   Address: <textarea name="txtaddress" rows="5" cols="30">
            Type your address here </textarea>
```

```
      <br>
      <input type="submit" value="SUBMIT">
      <input type="reset" value="RESET">
    </form>
    </center>
  </body>
</html>
```

File Name: tarea.jsp

```
<html>
<head>
 <title> Accessing Data from TextArea </title>
</head>
<body>
 Your Address is, <br><br>
<b>
<%
 String s = request.getParameter("txtaddress");
 String s1 = s.replaceAll("\n","<BR>");
 out.println(s1);
%>
</b>
</body>
</html>
```

Start the Tomcat server. Invoke the browser with the address,

http://localhost/bmijsp/tarea.html

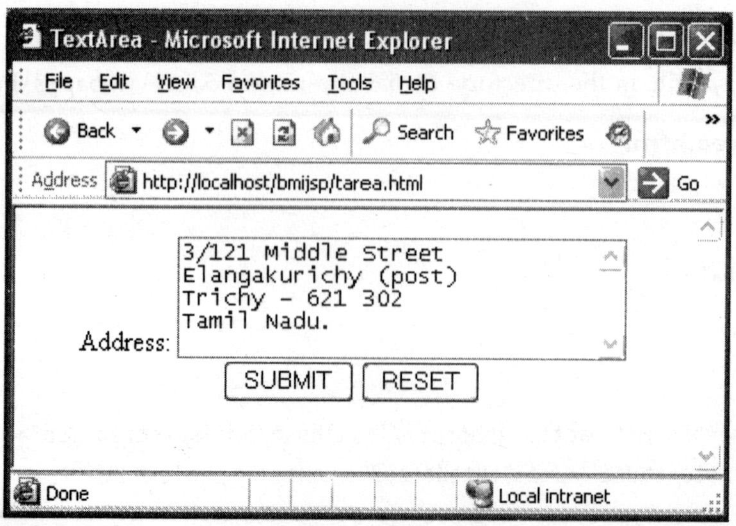

Enter your address and press the submit button.

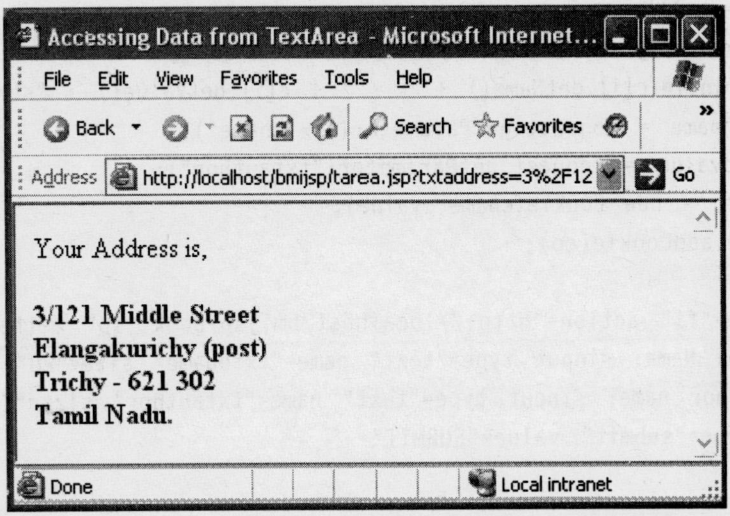

Cookies

Store the *"book.html"* in the directory- G:\jakarta-tomcat-5.5.11\webapps\bmijsp.

Store the *"book.jsp"* in the directory- G:\jakarta-tomcat-5.5.11\webapps\bmijsp.

File Name: book.html

```
<html>
<head>
 <title> Cookies </title>
</head>
<body>
  <form name="f1" action="http://localhost/bmijsp/book.jsp" method="get">
  Enter Book Name: <input type="text" name="txtbname" size="20"> <br>
  Enter Author name: <input type="text" name="txtauthor" size="20"> <br>
  <input type="submit" value="SUBMIT">
 </form>
</body>
</html>
```

File Name: book.jsp

```
<html>
<head>
 <title> Session Tracking </title>
</head>
<body> Cookies Data: <br> <br>
<%@page import="javax.servlet.http.*" %>
```

```
<% Cookie c[] = request.getCookies();
   if (c != null)
    for (int i=0;i<c.length;i++)
     out.println(c[i].getName() + " = " + c[i].getValue() + "<br>");
   String cname = request.getParameter("txtbname");
   String cvalue = request.getParameter("txtauthor");
   Cookie co = new Cookie(cname,cvalue);
   response.addCookie(co);
%>
 <form name="f1" action="http://localhost/bmijsp/book.jsp" method="get">
  Enter Book Name: <input type="text" name="txtbname" size="20"> <br>
  Enter Author name: <input type="text" name="txtauthor" size="20"> <br>
  <input type="submit" value="SUBMIT">
 </form>
</body>
</html>
```

Start the Tomcat server. Invoke the browser with the address, http://localhost/bmijsp/book.html

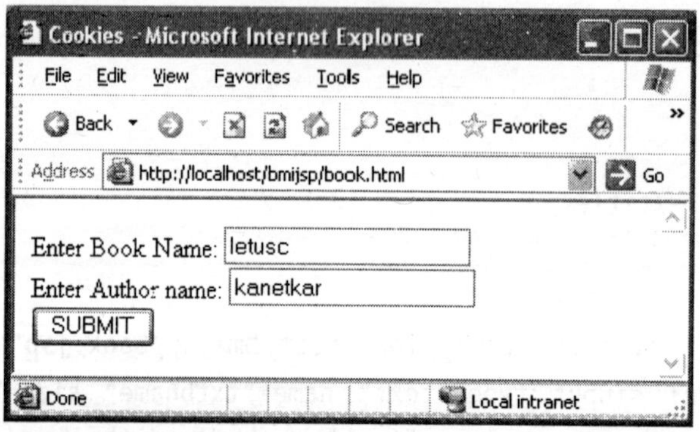

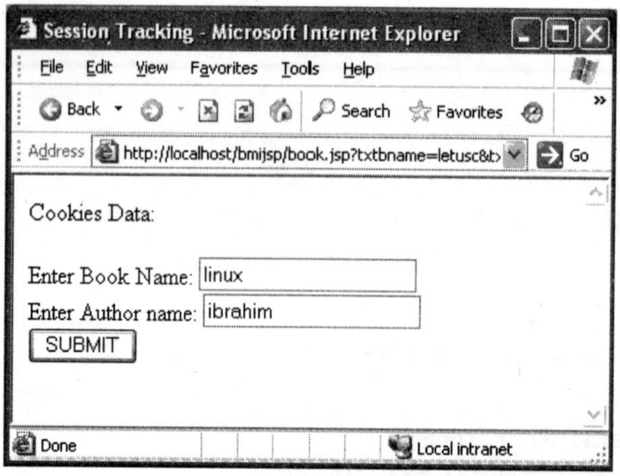

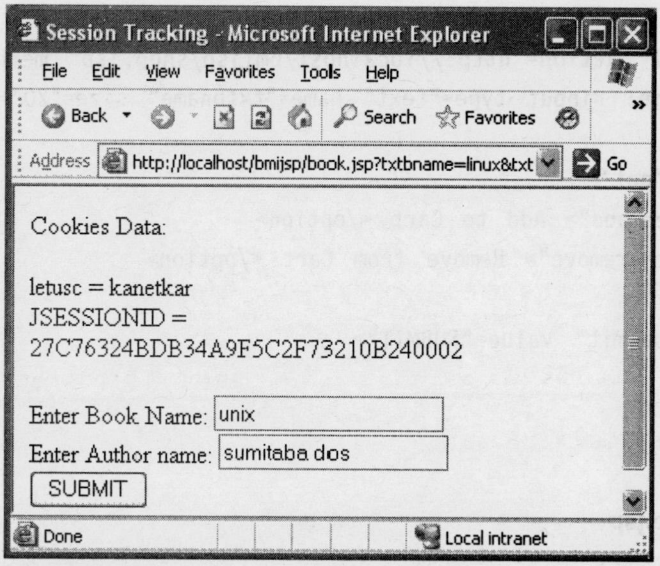

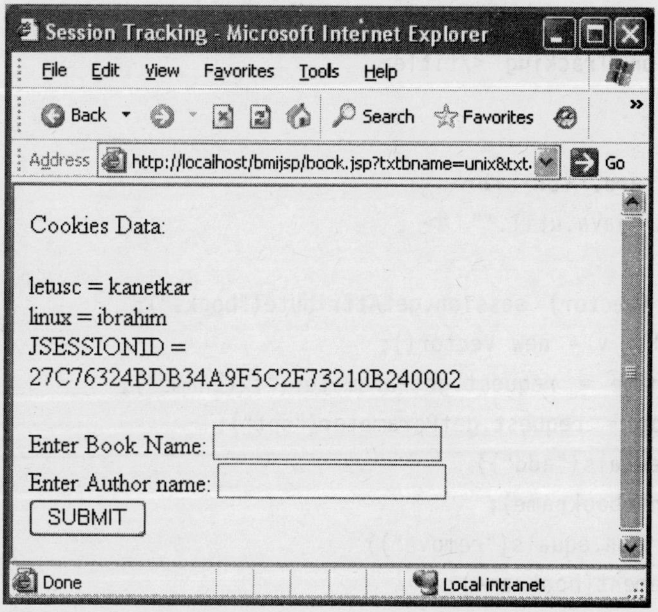

Session Tracking using session object

Store the *"shop.html"* in the directory- G:\jakarta-tomcat-5.5.11\webapps\bmijsp.

Store the *"shop.jsp"* in the directory- G:\jakarta-tomcat-5.5.11\webapps\bmijsp.

File Name: shop.html

```
<html>
<head>
 <title> Session Tracking </title>
</head>
```

```
<body>
<form name="f1" action="http://localhost/bmijsp/shop.jsp" method="get">
Enter Book Name: <input type="text" name="txtbname" size="20">
<br><br>
<select name="opt">
 <option value="add"> Add to Cart </option>
 <option value="remove"> Remove from Cart </option>
</select>
<input type="submit" value="SUBMIT">
</form>
</body>
</html>
```

File Name: store.jsp

```
<html>
<head>
 <title> Session Tracking </title>
</head>
<body>
Selected books are, <br> <br>
<%@page import="java.util.*" %>
<%
  Vector v = (Vector) session.getAttribute("books");
  if (v == null) v = new Vector();
  String bookname = request.getParameter("txtbname");
  String option = request.getParameter("opt");
  if (option.equals("add"))
   v.addElement(bookname);
  else if (option.equals("remove"))
   v.removeElement(bookname);
  Enumeration e = v.elements();
  while (e.hasMoreElements())
  {
   String b = (String) e.nextElement();
   out.println(b + "<br>");
  }
  session.setAttribute("books",v);
%>
<form name="f1" action="http://localhost/bmijsp/shop.jsp" method="get">
```

```
Enter Book Name: <input type="text" name="txtbname" size="20">
<br><br>
<select name="opt">
 <option value="add"> Add to Cart </option>
 <option value="remove"> Remove from Cart </option>
</select>
<input type="submit" value="SUBMIT">
</form>
</body>
</html>
```

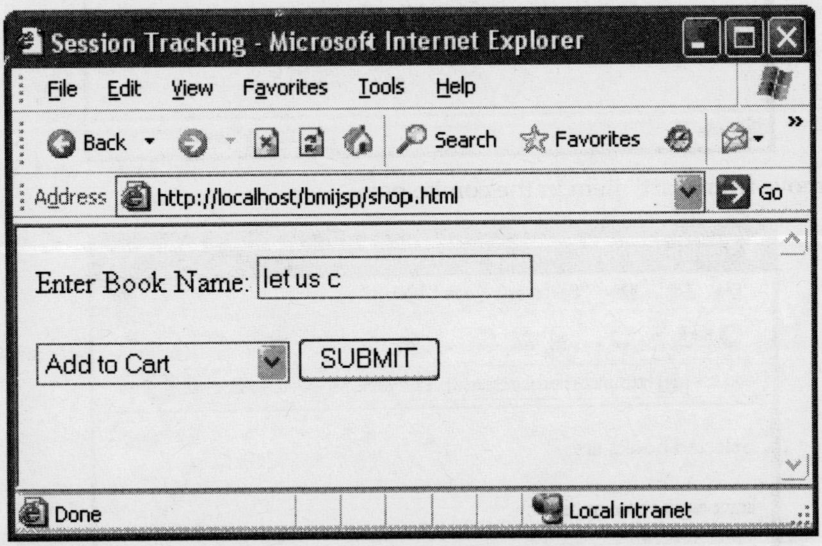

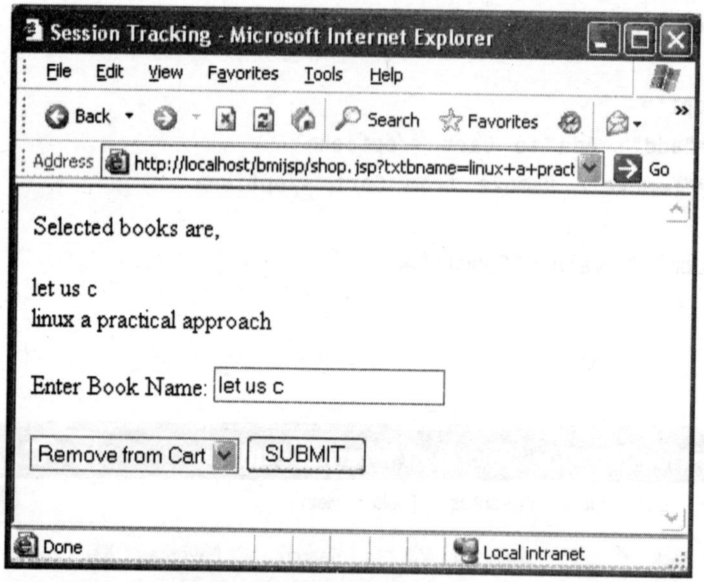

Choose "Remove from Cart" item in the combo box.

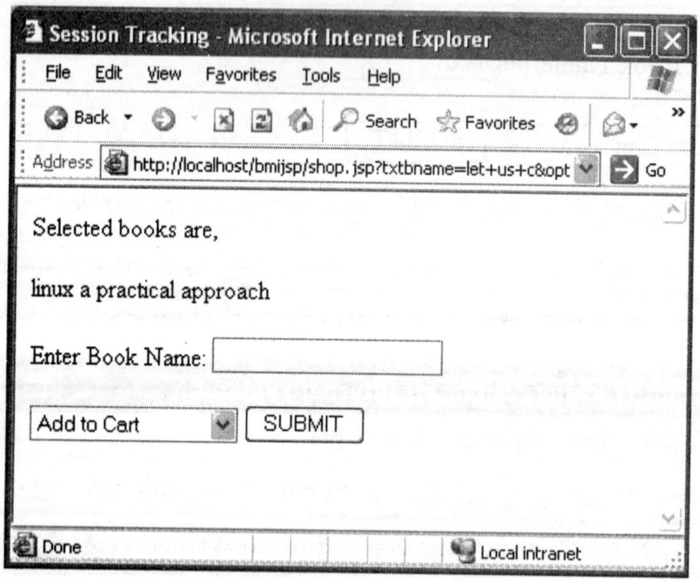

SUMMARY

JSP is one of the core components of Java EE Platform. It enables programmer to embed Java code in HTML document, and supports the features of Java Servlet. In fact, all JSP code will be converted into Java Servlet code by Servlet Container before execution. This chapter explains the core concepts of JSP with adequate example code. Apache Tomcat is used as Servlet Container (Application Server) to test JSP illustrating examples. However, the readers can use and test these examples in any application server which supports Java Servlets and JSP.

7

JSTL

7.0 INTRODUCTION

The JSTL (JSP Standard Tag Library) provides many customized tags to do coding with Java Server Pages (JSP). You can easily accomplish tasks using these JSTL tags, rather than using complex JSP Scriptlet code. This chapter explains the core concepts and features of JSTL in details with illustrating examples.

7.1 INSTALLATION

The latest version of JSTL is 1.2 (at the time of writing), and its binary version can be downloaded from `http://mvnrepository.com/artifact/javax.servlet/jstl`. This version only works on JSP 2.1 supported containers such as Tomcat 6. The latest version of Tomcat (in our demo, Tomcat 6.0.20 is used) can be downloaded from `http://tomcat.apache.org/`.

For Windows users, Download the Tomcat in ZIP format and extract it to a directory (Linux/Mac user can download tomcat compactable to their operating system). Copy the downloaded jstl-1.2.jar file to the lib directory under home directory of Tomcat (/apache-tomcat-6.0.20/lib).

7.2 TAG LIBRARIES

JSTL offers the following categories of tag libraries.

core - Basic scripting functionalities such as Expressions, Conditions, Looping, ...
fmt - Formatting data and Internationalization (I18N)
xml - Processing XML data
sql - Accessing databases

If you want to use these Tag libraries, then you have to import them into your JSP pages. Tag libraries and their corresponding import syntaxes are given below.

```
core  -  <%@ taglib prefix="c" uri="http://java.sun.com/jsp/jstl/core" %>
fmt   -  <%@ taglib prefix="fmt" uri="http://java.sun.com/jsp/jstl/fmt" %>
xml   -  <%@ taglib prefix="x" uri="http://java.sun.com/jsp/jstl/xml" %>
sql   -  <%@ taglib prefix="sql" uri="http://java.sun.com/jsp/jstl/sql" %>
```

You can use any identifier as a Tab library prefix; however it is convention to use "c" for core, "fmt" for fmt, "x" for xml, and "sql" for sql tag libraries.

7.3 EXPRESSION LANGUAGE

The Expression Language (EL) makes easy to access application data without Java Scriplets.

EL Expressions starts with $ and enclosed by braces {}. And the expressions can access the following types of data.

String	Enclosed by single/double quotes
Numbers	Integers/Floating-point numbers
Boolean	True/false values
Collections	List of values

7.3.1 Operators

The following are the operators supported by EL.

Arithmetic operators

+, - (both unary and binary) , *, / and div, % and mod

Logical operators

&& and and, || and or, ! and not

Relational operators

== and eq, != and ne, < and lt, > and gt, <= and le, >= and ge

Ternary operator

exp1 ? exp2: exp3

If exp1 becomes true, then the value of exp2 will be returned, otherwise the value of exp3 will be returned.

empty operator

empty <variable-name>

Checks whether a variable *empty* or *null*.

The empty operation is performed as below.

If the specified variable is *null*, return true,

Otherwise, if the specified variable is the empty string, then return true.

Otherwise, if the specified variable is an empty array, then return true.

Otherwise, if the specified variable is an empty Map, return true

Otherwise, if the specified variable is an empty Collection, return true

We can also use "null" operator to check whether a variable exists or not using the following syntax,

<variable-name> == null

However, the null check will fail to check empty value. So, if you want to check only whether a variable is defined, you can use 'null' check. If you want to check whether a variable is defined or empty, use "empty" operator.

Dot (.) and Index [] operator

In JSTL, we can use dot (.) to access a bean's property directly. (Normally, we will call getter/setter method of that property in JSP scriplet code)

For Example,

<%= obj.getUserName() %> can be written in JSTL as ${obj.userName} where userName is a property defined in the Bean class of obj object.

We can also use [] operator to invoke as below.

${obj["username"]}

Of course, the [] operator is also used to access values in collection (Maps, Lists, Arrays).

Example:

```
<!– File Name: Expressions.jsp –>
<%@ page import="java.util.*" %>
<%@ taglib uri='http://java.sun.com/jsp/jstl/core' prefix='c'%>
<html>
  <body>
    <table border="1" cellspacing="0" cellpadding="5">
          <caption><h2>JSTL Expression Language</h2></caption>
          <tr>
             <td colspan="2" align="center"><b>Arithmetic operators</b></td>
          </tr>
          <tr>
             <td>\${5 + 2}</td>
             <td>${5 + 2}</td>
          </tr>
          <tr>
             <td>\${5 - 2}</td>
             <td>${5 - 2}</td>
          </tr>
          <tr>
             <td>\${5 * 2}</td>
             <td>${5 * 2}</td>
          </tr>
          <tr>
             <td>\${8 / 3}</td>
             <td>${8 / 3}</td>
          </tr>
          <tr>
```

```
            <td>\${8 div 3}</td>
            <td>${8 div 3}</td>
        </tr>
        <tr>
            <td>\${8 % 3}</td>
            <td>${8 % 3}</td>
        </tr>
        <tr>
            <td>\${8 mod 3}</td>
            <td>${8 mod 3}</td>
        </tr>
        <tr>
            <td colspan="2" align="center">
             <b>Relational operators</b>
            </td>
        </tr>
        <tr>
            <td>\${"abc" == "ABC"}</td>
            <td>${"abc" == "ABC"}</td>
        </tr>
        <tr>
            <td>\${"abc" eq "abc"}</td>
          <td>${"abc" eq "abc"}</td>
        </tr>
        <tr>
           <td>\${5 ge 2}</td>
           <td>\${5 ge 2}</td>
        </tr>
        <tr>
           <td colspan="2" align="center">
           <b>Relational and Logical operators</b>
          </td>
    </tr>
    <tr>
    <td>Ternary Condition</td>
    <td>
        <c:set var="msg" value="INFO" />
        <c:set var="display" value="true" />
        ${((msg eq "INFO") and display) ? "Condition became true" :
                                          "Condition became false"}
    </td>
```

```
    </tr>
    <tr>
      <td colspan="2" align="center"><b>Empty operator</b></td>
    </tr>
    <tr>
      <td>empty check</td>
      <td>
          <c:set var="msg1" value="INFO" />
          <c:set var="display1" value="" />
          ${(empty msg1) ? "msg1 is empty" : "msg1 is not empty"}.
          ${(empty display1) ? "display1 is empty" : "display1 is not empty"}.
          ${(empty display2) ? "display2 is empty" : "display2 is not empty"}. <br>
          ${(msg1 == null) ? "msg1 is null" : "msg1 is not null"}.
          ${(display1 == null) ? "display1 is null" : "display1 is not null"}.
          ${(display2 == null) ? "display2 is null" : "display2 is not null"}.
          <!-- Note that the variable 'display2' is not defined -->
      </td>
    </tr>
    <tr>
  <td colspan="2" align="center"><b>Dot (.) and [] operators</b></td>
    </tr>
    <tr>
      <td>using Dot (.) and []</td>
      <td>
        <% Date d = new Date();
           List lst = new ArrayList();
           lst.add("Jan");
           lst.add("Feb");
           lst.add("Mar");
           System.out.println(lst);
           pageContext.setAttribute("d", d);
           pageContext.setAttribute("lst", lst);
        %>
        ${pageScope.d} <br>
        ${pageScope["d"]} <br>
        ${pageScope.lst[0]} <br>
        ${pageScope["lst"][2]}
      </td>
    </tr>
  </table>
 <body>
</html>
```

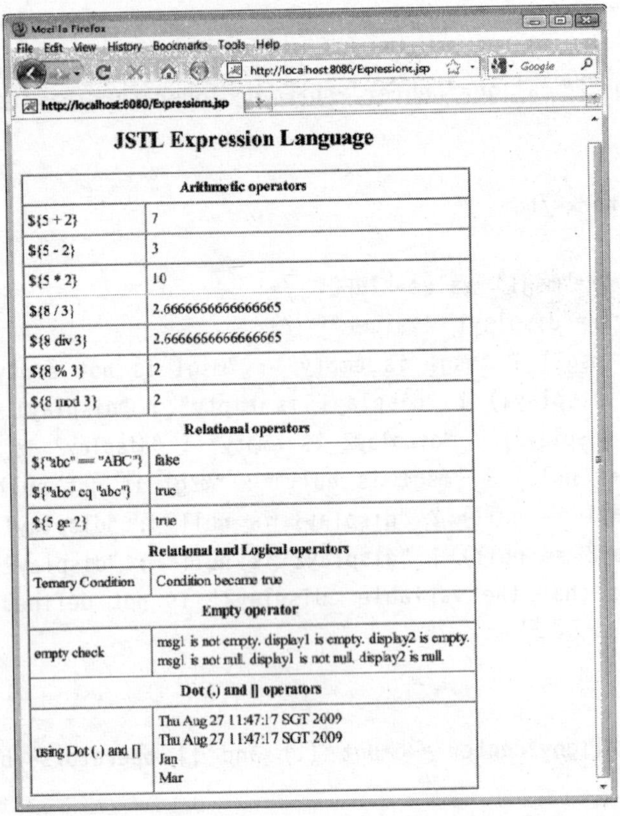

JSTL Expression Language

Arithmetic operators	
${5 + 2}	7
${5 - 2}	3
${5 * 2}	10
${8 / 3}	2.6666666666666665
${8 div 3}	2.6666666666666665
${8 % 3}	2
${8 mod 3}	2
Relational operators	
${"abc" == "ABC"}	false
${"abc" eq "abc"}	true
${5 ge 2}	true
Relational and Logical operators	
Ternary Condition	Condition became true
Empty operator	
empty check	msg1 is not empty. display1 is empty. display2 is empty. msg1 is not null. display1 is not null. display2 is null.
Dot (.) and [] operators	
using Dot (.) and []	Thu Aug 27 11:47:17 SGT 2009 Thu Aug 27 11:47:17 SGT 2009 Jan Mar

7.4 IMPLICIT OBJECTS

The following are the implicit objects available with JSTL.

`PageScope`	: Page scope
`RequestScope`	: Request scope
`SessionScope`	: Session scope
`applicationScope`	: Application scope
`Param`	: Request parameter (single value)
`paramValues`	: Request parameter (multiple values)
`initParam`	: Context initialization parameter
`Cookie`	: Value of a cookie
`pageContext`	: Current page information
`header`	: Header sent by the browser
`headerValues`	: All values of a header

7.4.1 pageScope

Objects are visible only within the JSP page in which they were created and included pages.

Example:

The following example sets an object using JSP's pageContext implicit object, and accessed via JSTL.

Store this content in a file named "PageScopeDemo.jsp" and put it in webapps/ROOT directory of Tomcat installation (Readers can also develop their own web application to test these examples, instead of using default ROOT application). Start the Tomcat by invoking "startup.bat" in "bin" directory of Tomcat installation, for MS Windows (For Linux, invoke "startup.sh").

```
<!–
 File Name: PageScopeDemo.jsp
 This JSP sets an object named "msg" with the page scope,
 which is referred using JSTL expression.
 –>
<html>
 <body>
  <%
    pageContext.setAttribute("msg", "This is a simple test message");
  %>
  <br>
  The Message is [ ${pageScope.msg} ]
 <body>
</html>
```

Invoke browser with the URL "http://localhost:8080/PageScopeDemo.jsp"

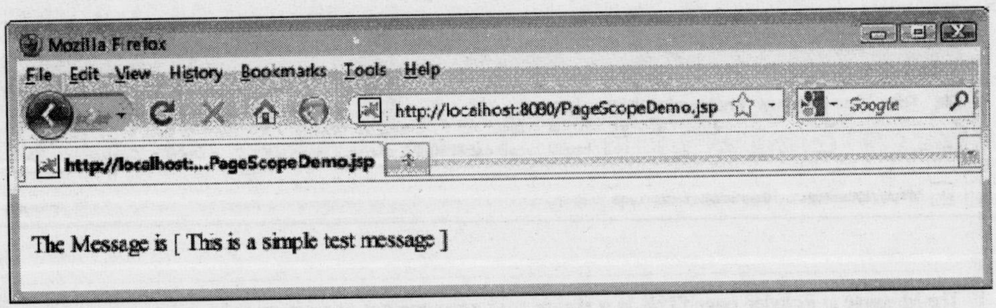

In the following program, we used JSTL to set and access a "page" scoped object.

```
<!– File Name: PageScopeDemo.jsp –>
<%@ taglib uri='http://java.sun.com/jsp/jstl/core' prefix='c'%>
<html>
  <body>
   <c:set var="msg" value="This is a simple test message" />
   <br>
   The Message is [ ${pageScope.msg} ]
  <body>
</html>
```

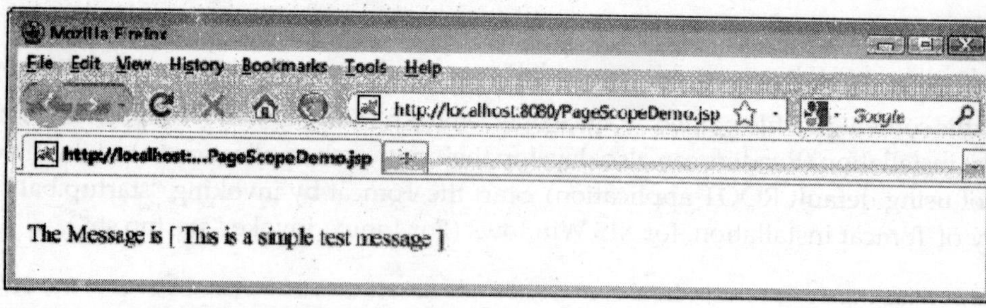

The following example illustrates the "page" scoped object set at main page, will be available to included pages. However, the inclusion should appear after the scoped objects are set.

```
<!-  File Name: PageScopeDemo.jsp ->
<%@ taglib uri='http://java.sun.com/jsp/jstl/core' prefix='c'%>
<html>
  <body>
       <c:set var="msg" value="This is a simple test message set at main page" />
       <br>
       <%@include file="DisplayMessage.jsp" %>
<body>
</html>
<!-  File Name: DisplayMessage.jsp ->
<hr>
The Message at included page [<b>${pageScope.msg}</b>]
<hr>
```

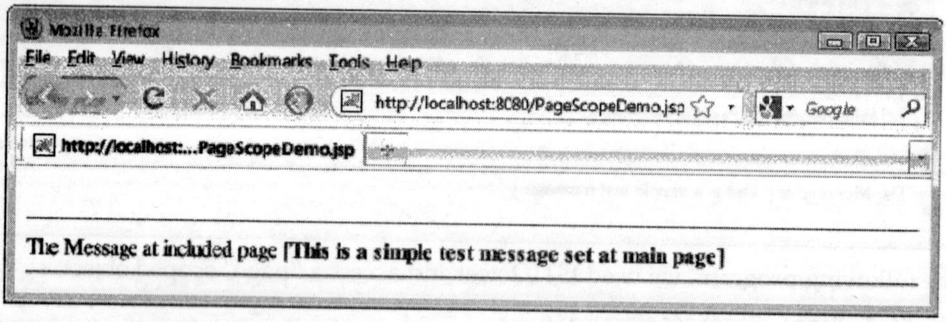

The following example illustrates the "page" scoped object set in an included page is available in main JSP.

```
<!-  File Name: PageScopeDemo.jsp ->
<%@ taglib uri='http://java.sun.com/jsp/jstl/core' prefix='c'%>
<html>
 <body>
      <%@include file="DisplayMessage.jsp" %>
      The Message set at included page [<i>${pageScope.msg}</i>]
 <body>
```

```
</html>
<!- File Name: DisplayMessage.jsp ->
<c:set var="msg" value="This is a simple test message set at DisplayMessage page" />
<hr>
The Message is [<b>${pageScope.msg}</b>]
<hr>
```

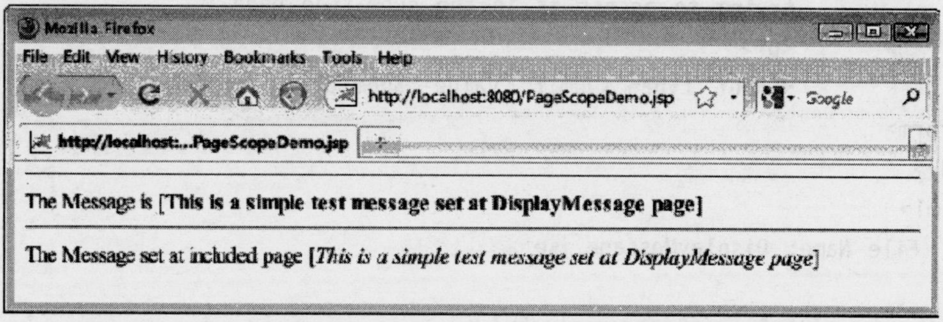

Note that the "page" scoped objects will not be available to forwarded pages.

```
<!- File Name: PageScopeDemo.jsp ->
<%@ taglib uri='http://java.sun.com/jsp/jstl/core' prefix='c'%>
<html>
 <body>
     <c:set var="msg" value="This is a simple test message set at forwarding page" />
     <br>
     <jsp:forward page="DisplayMessage.jsp" />
 <body>
</html>
<!- File Name: DisplayMessage.jsp ->
<hr>
The Message at forwarded page [<b>${pageScope.msg}</b>]
<hr>
```

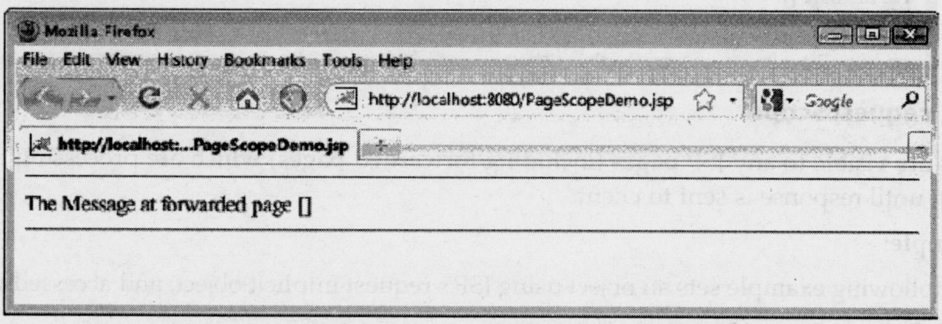

Also the "page" scoped object will not be available in the submitted page (JSP, Servlet ...).

```
<!- File Name: PageScopeDemo.jsp ->
```

```
<%@ taglib uri='http://java.sun.com/jsp/jstl/core' prefix='c'%>
<html>
 <body>
      <form action="DisplayMessage.jsp">
             <c:set var="msg" value="This is a simple test message" />
             A page scoped object is set in this page,
             trying to access it in the submitted page.
             <br>
             <input type="submit" value="Submit"></input>
 </form>
<body>
</html>
<!-  File Name: DisplayMessage.jsp ->
<hr>
The Message [<b>${pageScope.msg}</b>]
<hr>
```

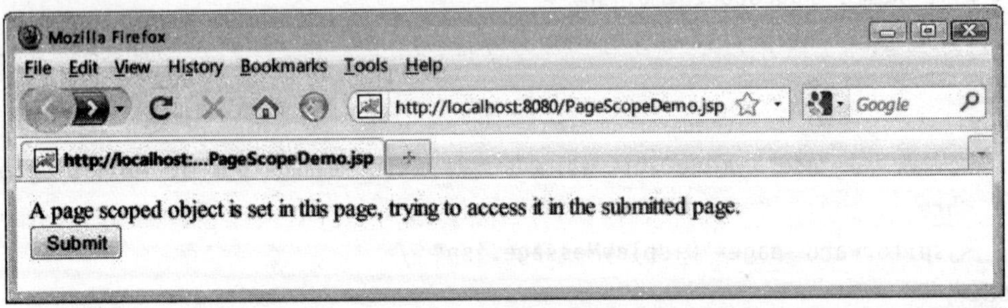

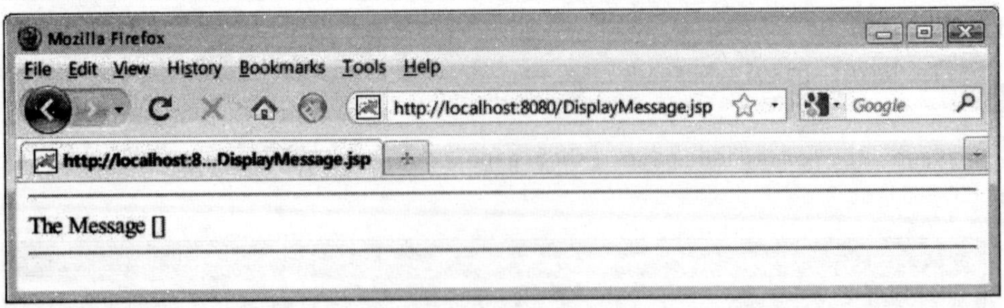

7.4.2 requestScope

Objects are visible to any JSP pages (including forwarded pages) which are processing the same request, until response is sent to client.

Example:

The following example sets an object using JSP's request implicit object, and accessed via JSTL.

```
<!- File Name: RequestScopeDemo.jsp ->
<%@ page import="java.util.Date" %>
<html>
```

```
<body>
      <%
         request.setAttribute("date", new Date());
      %>
      <br>
      The Date is [ ${requestScope.date} ]
 <body>
</html>
```

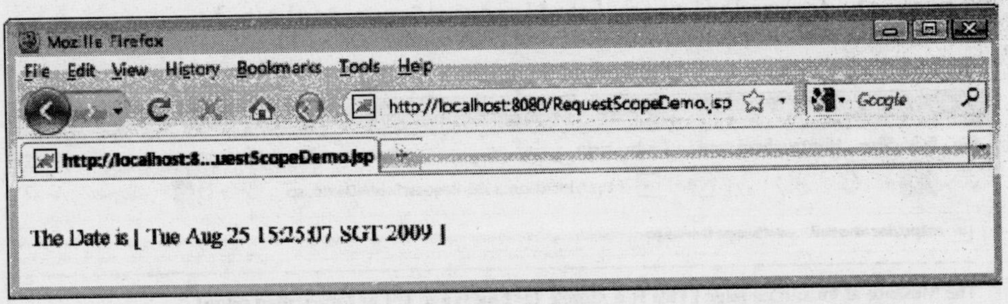

In the following program, we used JSTL to set and access a "request" scoped object.

```
<!- File Name: RequestScopeDemo.jsp ->
<%@ page import="java.util.Date" %>
<%@ taglib uri='http://java.sun.com/jsp/jstl/core' prefix='c'%>
<html>
 <body>
      <c:set var="msg" value="This is a simple test message" scope="request" />
      <br>
      The Message is [ ${requestScope.msg} ]
 <body>
</html>
```

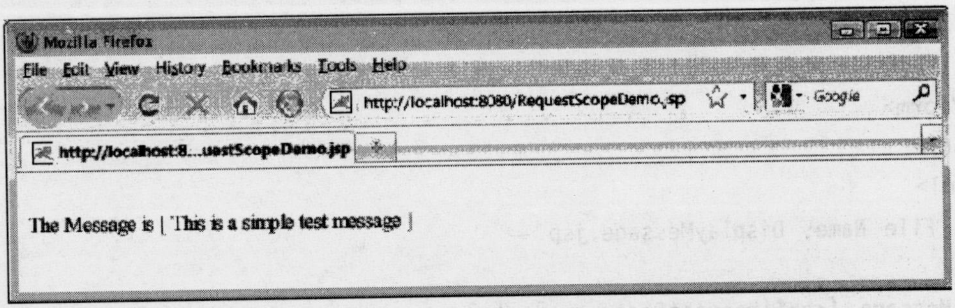

Note that the "request" scoped objects will be available to forwarded pages.

```
<!- File Name: RequestScopeDemo.jsp ->
<%@ taglib uri='http://java.sun.com/jsp/jstl/core' prefix='c'%>
<html>
 <body>
```

```
        <c:set var="msg" value="This is a simple test message set at forwarding page"
                            scope="request"  />
        <br>
        <jsp:forward  page="DisplayMessage.jsp"  />
   <body>
  </html>
  <!-   File Name: DisplayMessage.jsp ->
  <hr>
  The Message at forwarded page [<b>${requestScope.msg}</b>]
  <hr>
```

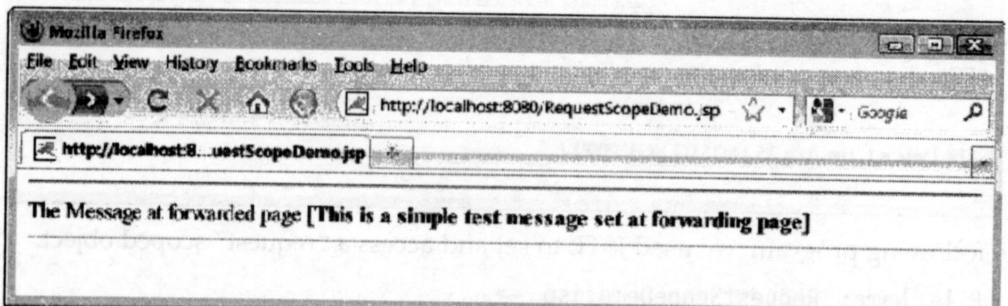

The "request" scoped object will not available in the submitted page (JSP, Servlet ...).

```
<!-   File Name: RequestScopeDemo.jsp ->
<%@ taglib uri='http://java.sun.com/jsp/jstl/core' prefix='c'%>
<html>
 <body>
  <form action="DisplayMessage.jsp">
       <c:set var="msg" value="This is a simple test message" scope="request" />
       A request scoped object is set in this page,
       trying to access it in the submitted page.
       <br>
       <input type="submit" value="Submit"></input>
  </form>
 <body>
</html>
<!-   File Name: DisplayMessage.jsp ->
<hr>
The Message [<b>${requestScope.msg}</b>]
<hr>
```

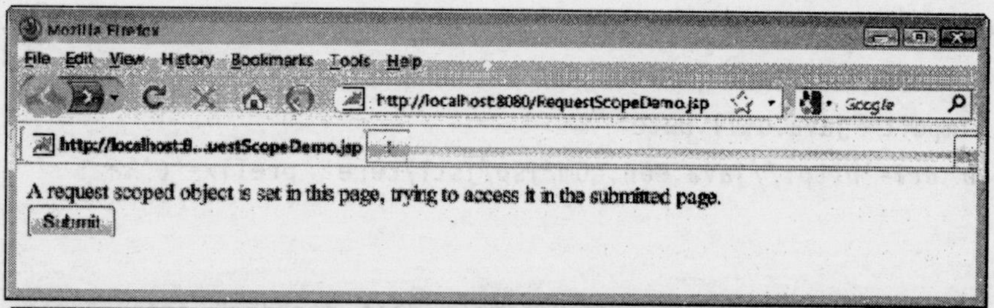

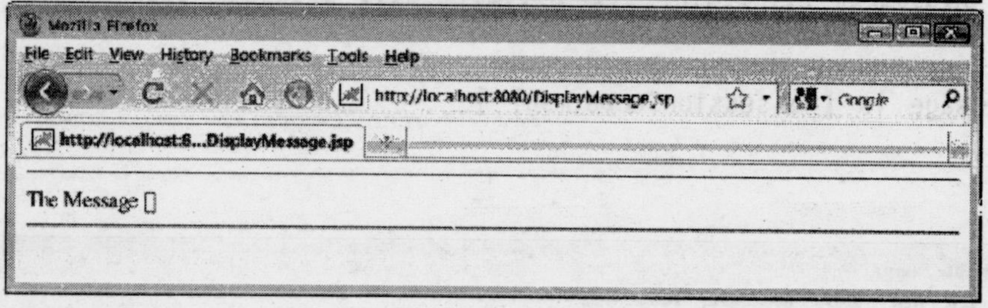

7.4.3 sessionScope

Objects are visible to all the JSP pages which are belonging to the same session in which the objects were set (instantiated).

A session refers to all the connections that a single client (web browser) might make to the web server for accessing (dynamic) web pages. Sessions are also created for each individual user basis, and also time-bound.

Example:

The following example sets an object using JSP's session implicit object, and accessed via JSTL.

```
<!— File Name: SessionScopeDemo.jsp —>
<%@ page import="java.util.Date" %>
<html>
  <body>
        <%
            session.setAttribute("date", new Date());
        %>
        <br>
        The Date is [ ${sessionScope.date} ]
  <body>
</html>
```

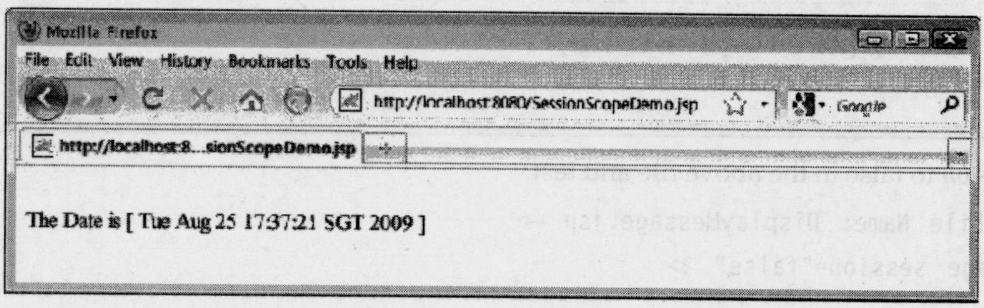

In the following program, we used JSTL to set and access a "session" scoped object.

```
<!-  File Name: SessionScopeDemo.jsp ->
<%@ page import="java.util.Date" %>
<%@ taglib uri='http://java.sun.com/jsp/jstl/core' prefix='c'%>
<html>
 <body>
  <c:set var="msg" value="This is a simple test message" scope="session" />
  <br>
  The Message is [ ${sessionScope.msg} ]
 <body>
</html>
```

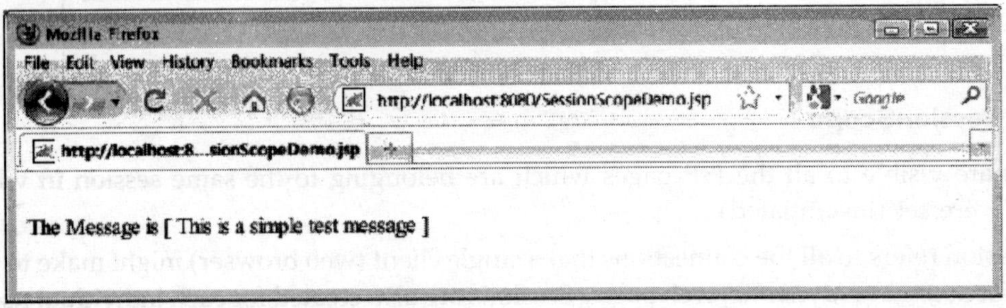

The "session" scoped object will be available to all JSPs (not only forwarded, included, submitted) as long as session is valid and session tracking is enabled. Session can be disabled in a JSP file by setting *session* as *false* in @page directive.

After invoking the above example, open the following "DisplayMessage.jsp" file in the browser. Note that this is just another file in the web application, not directly related with SessionScopeDemo.jsp file.

```
<!-  File Name: DisplayMessage.jsp ->
<hr>
The Message [<b>${sessionScope.msg}</b>]
<hr>
```

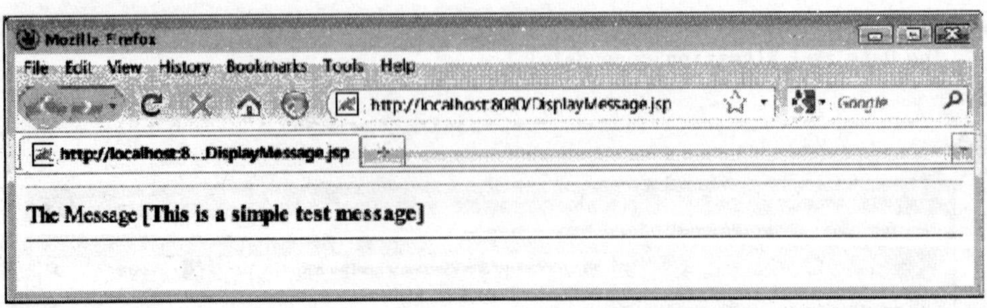

Set *session* to false in the above file and test.

```
<!-  File Name: DisplayMessage.jsp ->
<%@ page session="false" %>
```

```
<hr>
The Message [<b>${sessionScope.msg}</b>]
<hr>
```

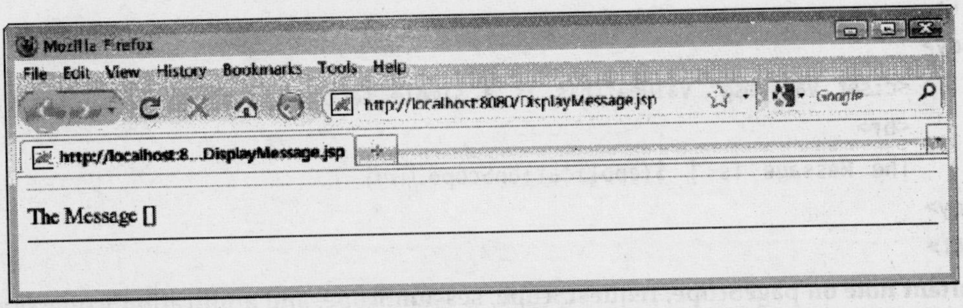

Objects associated with a session will not be available when session time-out is met or session is invalidated. You can specify the timeout of a session in the web.xml (deployment descriptor) file of your web application using session-config tags with in web-app tags, as below.

```
<web-app ...>
   <session-config>
      <session-timeout>60</session-timeout>
   </session-config>
</web-app>
```

A session can be invalidated through the following code.

```
session.invalidate()
```

7.4.4 applicationScope

Objects are visible to all the JSP pages which are belonging to the same web application. An application scoped object will be available even if the session is expired.

Example:

The following example sets an object using JSP's application implicit object, and accessed via JSTL.

```
<!– File Name: ApplicationScopeDemo.jsp –>
<%@ page import="java.util.Date" %>
<html>
 <body>
      <%
       application.setAttribute("date", new Date());
      %>
      <br>
      The Date is [ ${applicationScope.date} ]
 <body>
</html>
```

In the following program, we used JSTL to set and access an "application" scoped object.

```
<!-   File Name: ApplicationScopeDemo.jsp ->
<%@ page import="java.util.Date" %>
<%@ taglib uri='http://java.sun.com/jsp/jstl/core' prefix='c'%>
<html>
 <body>
       <c:set var="msg" value="This is a simple test message" scope="application" />
       <br>
       The Message is [ ${applicationScope.msg} ]
 <body>
</html>
```

Important note on pageScope, requestScope, sessionScope, and applicationScope: If you use an scoped object-name in an expression with out prefixed by any scope like {object-name}, then the scoped object-name will be searched in all the JSP scopes starting from pageScope, if not found, then requestScope, sessionScope and then applicationScope respectively.

7.4.5 param and paramValues

These implicit objects are used to retrieve request parameter value/values (from the client when a HTML form is submitted / from URL with query string).

Example:

```
<!- File Name: Biodata.html ->
<html>
 <head>
  <title>Bio-Data</title>
 </head>
<body>
 <h1>BIO-DATA</h1>
  <form name="form" action="Biodata.jsp" method="post">
   <table>
     <tr>
          <td>Employee number:</td>
          <td><input type="text" name="txtENo" size="6"></td>
     </tr>
     <tr>
          <td>Employee Name:</td>
          <td><input type="text" name="txtName" size="20"></td>
     </tr>
     <tr>
          <td>Sex:</td>
          <td>
            <input type="radio" name="sex" value="Male" checked> Male
```

```
        <input type="radio" name="sex" value="Female"> Female
    </td>
</tr>
<tr>
    <td>Languages Known:</td>
    <td>
        <input type="checkbox" name="chkTamil" value="Tamil" checked> Tamil
        <input type="checkbox" name="chkEnglish" value="English"> English
        <input type="checkbox" name="chkHindi" value="Hindi"> Hindi
    </td>
</tr>
<tr>
    <td>Specialization:</td>
    <td>
        <select name="listSpecialization" size="3" multiple>
            <option value="Web Designing">Web Designing</option>
            <option value="System Programming">System Programming</option>
            <option value="Linux Administration">Linux Administration</option>
            <option value="Windows NT Administration">
                        Windows NT Administration
            </option>
            <option value="Object Oriented Programming System">OOPS </option>
            <option value="Database Administration">DBA</option>
        </select>
     <td>
    </tr>
    <tr>
     <td>Nationality:</td>
     <td>
        <select name="choiceNationality" size="1">
        <option value="India">India</option>
        <option value="America">America</option>
        <option value="Singapore">Singapore</option>
        <option value="Malaysia">Malaisia</option>
        <option value="UAE">United Arab Embreds</option>
        <option value="Others">Others</option>
      </select>
    </td>
  </tr>
  <tr>
    <td>Address:</td>
```

```
            <td>
                <textarea name="txtAddress" rows="5" cols="30">
                    Type your address here
                </textarea>
            </td>
          </tr>
        </table>
        <input type="hidden" name="sno" value="1">
        <input type="submit" value="SUBMIT">
        <input type="reset" value="RESET">
      </form>
    </body>
  </html>
<!— Biodata.jsp —>
<%@ taglib uri='http://java.sun.com/jsp/jstl/core' prefix='c' %>
<%@ taglib prefix="fn" uri="http://java.sun.com/jsp/jstl/functions" %>
<html>
  <head>
    <title>Bio-Data</title>
  </head>
  <body>
      <h1>BIO-DATA</h1>
      <table>
          <tr>
              <td>Sno:</td>
              <td> ${param.sno} </td>
          </tr>
          <tr>
              <td>Employee number:</td>
              <td> ${param.txtENo} </td>
          </tr>
          <tr>
              <td>Employee Name:</td>
              <td> ${param.txtName} </td>
          </tr>
          <tr>
              <td>Sex:</td>
              <td> ${param.sex} </td>
          </tr>
          <tr>
              <td>Languages Known:</td>
```

```
            <td> ${param.chkTamil} ${param.chkEnglish} ${param.chkHindi}</td>
        </tr>
        <tr>
            <td valign="top">Specialization:</td>
            <td>
             <c:forEach items ="${paramValues.listSpecialization}" var =
             "specialization">
                ${specialization} <br>
             </c:forEach>
           <td>
        </tr>
        <tr>
           <td>Nationality:</td>
           <td> ${param.choiceNationality} </td>
        </tr>
        <tr>
           <td valign="top">Address:</td>
           <td>
              <% pageContext.setAttribute("newLineChar", "\n"); %>
              ${fn:replace(param.txtAddress, newLineChar, "<br>")} </td>
        </tr>
      </table>
   </body>
</html>
```

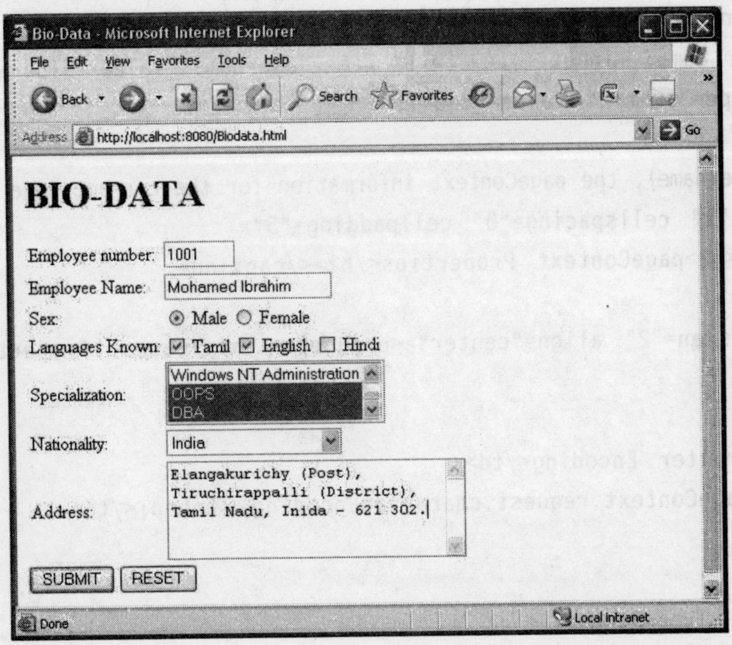

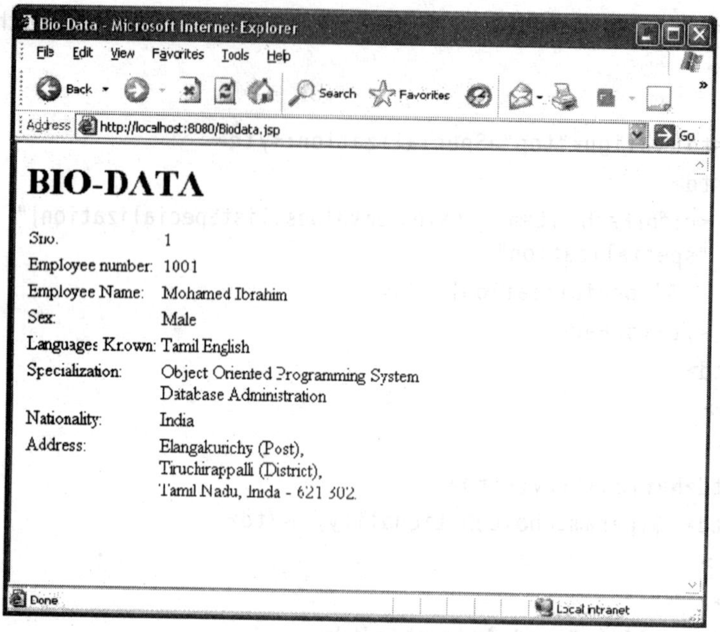

7.4.6 pageContext

This implicit object provides context information of the current JSP page.

```
<!– File Name: PageContextDemo.jsp –>
<%@ taglib uri='http://java.sun.com/jsp/jstl/core' prefix='c'%>
<%@ taglib uri='http://java.sun.com/jsp/jstl/fmt' prefix='fmt'%>
<html>
 <body>
  <form action="PageContextDemo.jsp">
    Enter your name: <input type="text" name="username" value="${param.username}">
    <input type="submit" value="Submit">
  </form>
Dear ${param.username}, the pageContext information for the current page are as below.
<table border="1" cellspacing="0" cellpadding="5">
    <caption><h2>pageContext Properties</h2></caption>
    <tr>
      <td colspan="2" align="center"><b>pageContext.request Properties</b></td>
    </tr>
    <tr>
      <td>Character Encoding</td>
      <td>${pageContext.request.characterEncoding}  </td>
    </tr>
    <tr>
      <td>MIME Type</td>
```

```
    <td>${pageContext.request.contentType}  </td>
  </tr>
  <tr>
    <td>Locale</td>
    <td>${pageContext.request.locale}  </td>
  </tr>
  <tr>
    <td>Protocol</td>
    <td>${pageContext.request.protocol}  </td>
  </tr>
  <tr>
    <td>Client IP Address</td>
    <td>${pageContext.request.remoteAddr}  </td>
  </tr>
  <tr>
    <td>Client Host Name</td>
   <!-- The host name of the client, or the IP address if the host name is
   undefined ->
    <td>${pageContext.request.remoteHost}  </td>
  </tr>
  <tr>
    <td>Current Request Scheme</td>
    <td>${pageContext.request.scheme}  </td>
  </tr>
  <tr>
    <td>Server Name</td>
    <td>${pageContext.request.serverName}  </td>
 </tr>
 <tr>
    <td>Request received port number</td>
    <td>${pageContext.request.serverPort}  </td>
 </tr>
 <tr>
    <td>Request on secure channel</td>
    <td>${pageContext.request.secure}  </td>
 </tr>
 <tr>
    <td>The type of authentication used by the page</td>
    <td>${pageContext.request.authType}  </td>
 </tr>
```

```
<tr>
   <td>Query String (Request parameters while method is GET)</td>
   <td>${pageContext.request.queryString}  </td>
</tr>
<tr>
   <td>Web application context</td>
   <td>${pageContext.request.contextPath}  </td>
</tr>
<tr>
   <td>The HTTP Method to access the page</td>
   <td>${pageContext.request.method}  </td>
</tr>
<tr>
   <td>Page's cookies</td>
   <td>
     <c:forEach var="item" items="${pageContext.request.cookies}">
       ${item.name} - ${item.value}
     </c:forEach>
    </td>
  </tr>
  <tr>
   <td>URL used to access the page</td>
   <td>${pageContext.request.requestURL}  </td>
</tr>
<tr>
   <td colspan="2" align="center"><b>pageContext.response Properties</b></td>
</tr>
<tr>
   <td>Buffer size used for the response</td>
   <td>${pageContext.response.bufferSize}  </td>
</tr>
<tr>
   <td>Character Encoding used for the response</td>
   <td>${pageContext.response.characterEncoding}  </td>
</tr>
<tr>
   <td>Locale assigned for the response</td>
   <td>${pageContext.response.locale}  </td>
</tr>
<tr>
```

```
    <td colspan="2" align="center"><b>pageContext.session Properties</b></td>
  </tr>
  <tr>
    <td>Session created Time</td>
    <td>
       <jsp:useBean id="creationTime" class="java.util.Date" />
         <c:set target="${creationTime}"
               value="${pageContext.session.creationTime}" property="time" />
       ${creationTime}
   </tr>
   <tr>
     <td>Session Id</td>
     <td>${pageContext.session.id}  </td>
   </tr>
   <tr>
     <td>Is Session new</td>
     <td>${pageContext.session.new}  </td>
   </tr>
   <tr>
     <td>The last time the session was accessed</td>
   <td>
     <jsp:useBean id="lastAccessedTime" class="java.util.Date" />
        <c:set target="${lastAccessedTime}"
             value="${pageContext.session.lastAccessedTime}" property="time" />
        ${lastAccessedTime}
     </td>
   </tr>
   <tr>
     <td colspan="2" align="center"><b>pageContext.servletContext Properties</b></td>
   </tr>
   <tr>
     <td>Servlet API used</td>
     <td>${pageContext.servletContext.majorVersion}.
           ${pageContext.servletContext.minorVersion}  </td> .....
   </tr>
   <tr>
     <td>Servlet container information</td>
     <td>${pageContext.servletContext.serverInfo}</td>    ............
   </tr>
</table>
```

```
<body>
</html>
```

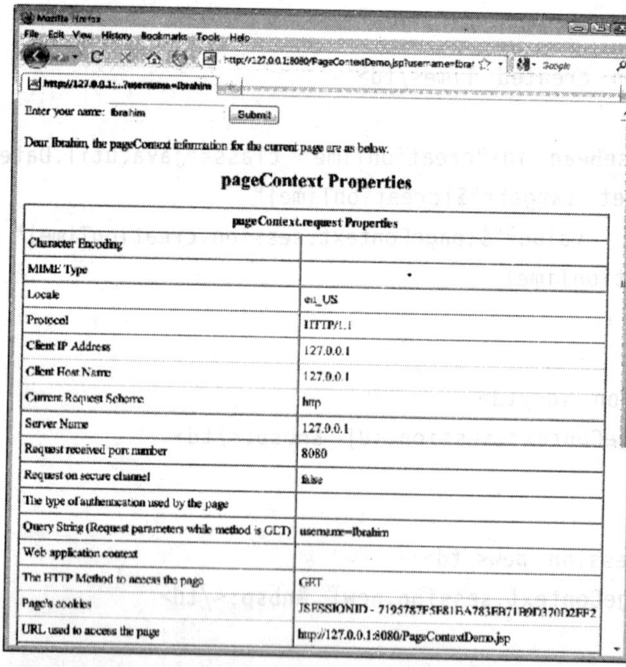

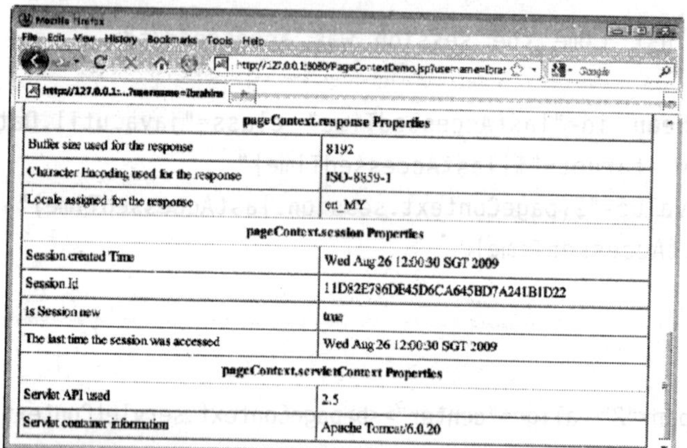

7.4.7 header and headerValues

A header is a unit of information, which are used by the web servers and web clients (usually, browsers) in order to communicate.

The header object returns a single value of the specified header property, where as the headerValues returns a collection of values for the specified header property.

```
<!— File Name: HeaderDemo.jsp —>
<%@ taglib uri='http://java.sun.com/jsp/jstl/core' prefix='c'%>
<%@ taglib uri="http://java.sun.com/jsp/jstl/functions" prefix="fn" %>
<html>
```

```
<body>
     <c:set var="browser" value="${header['user-agent']}" />
     You are using
     <c:choose>
       <c:when test="${fn:contains(browser,'MSIE')}">
              Internet Explorer
       </c:when>
       <c:when test="${fn:contains(browser,'Firefox')}">
              Firefox
       </c:when>
       <c:otherwise>
              ${browser}
       </c:otherwise>
     </c:choose>
 <body>
</html>
```

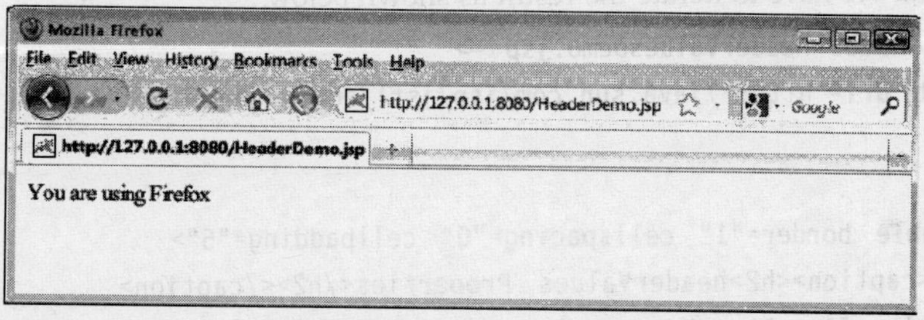

The following program lists all the header informations.

```
<!- File Name: HeaderDemo.jsp ->
<%@ taglib uri='http://java.sun.com/jsp/jstl/core' prefix='c'%>
<html>
 <body>
     <table border="1" cellspacing="0" cellpadding="5">
       <caption><h2>header Properties</h2></caption>
       <!- Iterating Map ->
       <c:forEach items='${header}' var='item'>
        <tr>
            <td>${item.key}</td>
            <td>${item.value}</td>
        </tr>
       </c:forEach>
     </table>
 <body>
</html>
```

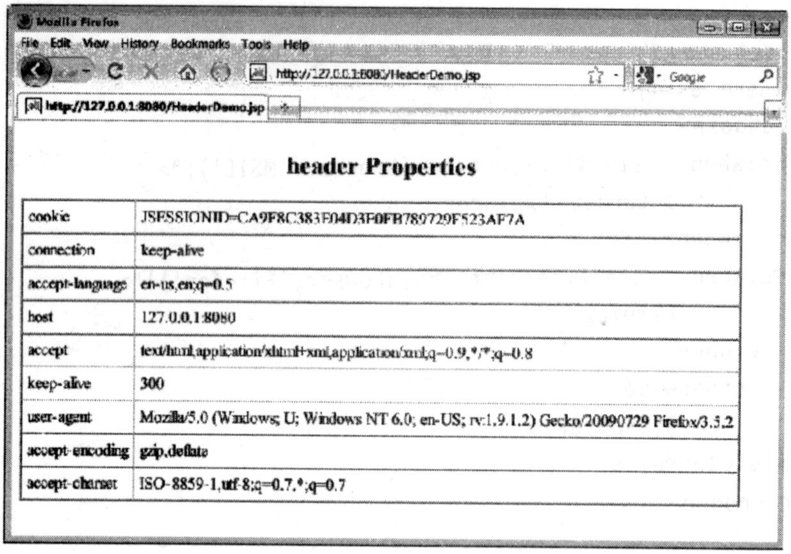

We can achieve the above task by using "headerValues" object, but it returns a collection of values as result. We have to iterate the result as shown below.

```
<!-  File Name: HeaderValuesDemo.jsp ->
<%@ taglib uri='http://java.sun.com/jsp/jstl/core' prefix='c'%>
<html>
 <body>
      <table border="1" cellspacing="0" cellpadding="5">
        <caption><h2>headerValues Properties</h2></caption>
        <!-- Iterating Map ->
        <c:forEach items='${headerValues}' var='item'>
         <tr>
             <td>${item.key}</td>
             <td>
              <c:forEach items='${item.value}' var='itemvalue'>
                     ${itemvalue}
              </c:forEach>
             </td>
         </tr>
        </c:forEach>
       </table>
 <body>
</html>
```

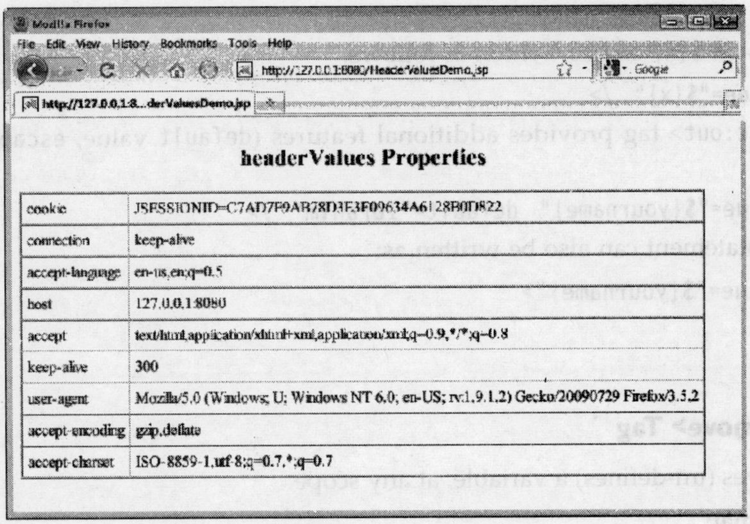

7.5 ACCESSING CUSTOM VARIABLES

The `<c:set>` tag defines a variable, `<c:out>` tag is used to output the value of a variable, and `<c:remove>` tag deletes the already defined variable.

7.5.1 <c:set> Tag

This tag sets (defines) a value to a variable.

General format:

```
<c:set var="variable-name" value="expression"
                            scope="scope"  />
```

The attribute `var` is mandatory and upon which the result of the specified expression will be stored. The `scope` attribute specifies in which scope (`page`, `request`, `session`, and `application`) the variable should be assigned, default to "page" (pageScope).

Example:

```
<c:set var="yourname" value="Mohamed Ibrahim" scope="session" />
```

7.5.2 <c:out> Tag

This tag outputs the result of the specified expression.

General format:

```
<c:out value="expression" default="default text"
                           escapeXml="true|false" />
```

The attribute `value` is mandatory and the result of the specified expression will be outputted. If the result of the expression is nothing (no value, may be due to the expression variable is not defined), then the default text will be outputted. If the result contains HTML specific special characters (`<`, `>`, `"`, `'`, `&`), then the characters will be converted into HTML entity references (`<` , `>` , `"` , `'` , `&`) if escapeXml is set to true. The default value to escapeXml is true.

Example:

The expression ${x} can be written as follows.

```
<c:out value="${x}" />
```

However, <c:out> tag provides additional features (`default` value, `escapeXml`) over direct expression.

```
<c:out value="${yourname}" default="Ibrahim" />
```

The above statement can also be written as:

```
<c:out value="${yourname}">
  Ibrahim
</c:out>
```

7.5.3 <c:remove> Tag

This tag removes (un-defines) a variable, at any scope.

General format:

```
<c:remove var="variable-name" scope="scope" />
```

The variable specified in var (mandatory attribute) at the specified scope will be removed and if the same variable-name present in many scopes, then removing of a variable in one scope will not remove the same variable-names in other scopes.

If the scope attribute is not specified, then that variable-name in all the scope (if found) will be removed.

Example:

```
<c:remove var="x" scope="session" />
```

The above code will remove the variable named "x" associated with "`session`" will be removed.

```
<!- File Name: Variables.jsp ->
<%@ taglib uri='http://java.sun.com/jsp/jstl/core' prefix='c'%>
<html>
 <body>
       <h2>Setting, Outputting, and Removing variables</h2>
       <c:set var="yourname" value="Mohamed Ibrahim" /> <!- Defaults to 'page'
        scope - >
       <c:set var="yourname" value="Mohamed" scope="request" />
       <c:set var="yourname" value="Ibrahim" scope="application" />
       <c:set var="x" value="5" />
       <c:set var="y" value="" />
       <b><u>Outputting without default value</u></b> <br>
       Without specifying Scope: <c:out value="${yourname}" />
     <!- Searches the variable from page, request, session, and then application
       scopes ->
       <br>
       page Scope: <c:out value="${pageScope.yourname}" /> <br>
       request Scope: <c:out value="${requestScope.yourname}" /> <br>
```

```
session Scope: <c:out value="${sessionScope.yourname}" /> <br>
application Scope: <c:out value="${applicationScope.yourname}" /> <br>
x * 10 value: <c:out value="${x * 10 }" /> <br>
y value: <c:out value="${y}" /> <br>
z value: <c:out value="${z}" /> <br> <br>
<b><u>Outputting with default value</u></b> <br>
Without specifying Scope: <c:out value="${yourname}" default="Not specified"
/> <br>
page Scope: <c:out value="${pageScope.yourname}" default="Not specified" />
<br>
request Scope: <c:out value="${requestScope.yourname}" default="Not specified" />
<br>
session Scope: <c:out value="${sessionScope.yourname}" default="Not specified"
/> <br>
application Scope:
<c:out value="${applicationScope.yourname}" default="Not specified" /> <br>
x value: <c:out value="${x}"> Not specified </c:out> <br>
y value: <c:out value="${y}" default="Not specified" /> <br>
z value: <c:out value="${z}" default="Not specified" /> <br> <br>
<c:set var="yourname" value="<b>Mohamed Ibrahim</b>" />
<b><u>Outputting with escapeXml to true (default)</u></b> <br>
Without specifying Scope: <c:out value="${yourname}" default="<u>Not specified
</u>" />
<br>
session Scope:
<c:out value="${sessionScope.yourname}" default="<u>Not specified</u>" />
<br><br>
<b><u>Outputting with escapeXml to false</u></b> <br>
Without specifying Scope:
<c:out value="${yourname}" default="<u>Not specified</u>" escapeXml="false"
/> <br>
session Scope:
  <c:out value="${sessionScope.yourname}"
        default="<u>Not specified</u>" escapeXml="false" />
<br> <br>
<b><u>Removing page scopped variable</u></b> <br>
<c:remove var="yourname" scope="page" />
Without specifying Scope: <c:out value="${yourname}" default="Not specified"
/> <br>
page Scope: <c:out value="${pageScope.yourname}" default="Not specified" />
<br>
request Scope: <c:out value="${requestScope.yourname}" default="Not speci-
fied" /> <br>
```

```
        session Scope: <c:out value="${sessionScope.yourname}" default="Not speci-
        fied" /> <br>
        application Scope: <c:out value="${applicationScope.yourname}"
                                          default="Not specified" /> <br> <br>
        <b><u>Removing a variable without specifying scope</u></b> <br>
        <c:remove var="yourname" /> <!— Removes the variable 'yourname'
                                               in all the scopes (if found) —>
        Without specifying Scope: <c:out value="${yourname}" default="Not speci-
        fied" /> <br>
        page Scope: <c:out value="${pageScope.yourname}" default="Not specified" />
        <br>
        request Scope: <c:out value="${requestScope.yourname}" default="Not speci-
        fied" /> <br>
        session Scope: <c:out value="${sessionScope.yourname}" default="Not speci-
        fied" /> <br>
        application Scope: <c:out value="${applicationScope.yourname}"
                                          default="Not specified" /> <br>

   <body>
  </html>
```

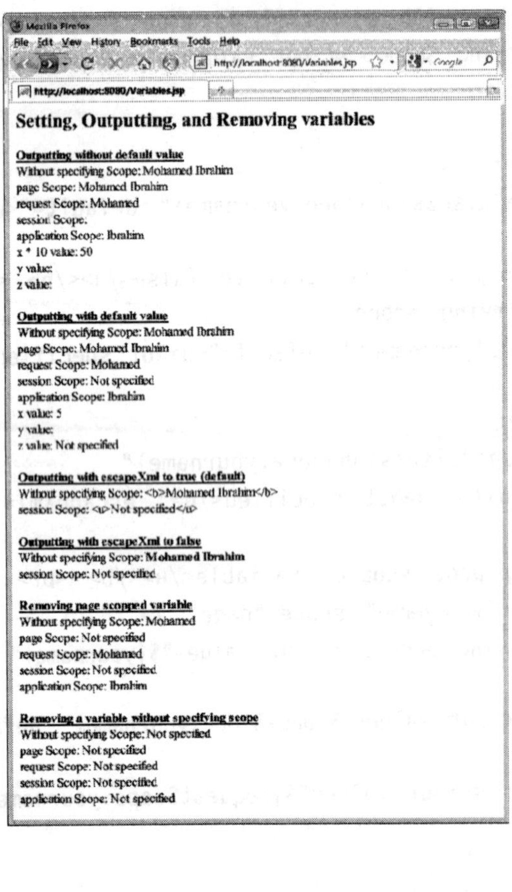

7.6 CONDITIONAL CONSTRUCTS AND LOOPING TAGS

JSTL provides conditional check and multi-branch statements and looping statement.

7.6.1 <c:if>

It is a conditional check statement; if the specified test condition becomes true, then the specified set of code (HTML code, scriplets, JSTL code ...) written between <c:if> and </c:if> will be executed.

General format:

```
<c:if test="condition">
  code
</c:if>
```

Two additional attributes namely "var" and "scope" can be used with <c:if> tag along with mandatory attribute "test". If used, the boolean result of the test condition will be stored on the specified variable in the specified scope. Then, you can refer this variable elsewhere in the program.

Note that JSTL currently does not provide direct if-else statement. You can use <c:choice> statement for testing if-else condition.

Example:

```
<!– File Name: if.jsp –>
<%@ taglib uri='http://java.sun.com/jsp/jstl/core' prefix='c'%>
<html>
<body>
      <h3>Conditional Constructs: if</h3>
      <p>Display day of the corresponding day-code present in the variable 'daycode'
      </p>
      <c:set var="daycode" value="3" />
      Daycode is ${daycode}
      <br>
      <c:if test="${daycode lt 0 or daycode gt 6}">
         <u>Invalid daycode. Should be within the reange [0-6]</u> </c:if>
      <c:if test="${daycode == 0}"> <b>Sunday</b> </c:if>
      <c:if test="${daycode == 1}"> <i>Monday</i> </c:if>
      <c:if test="${daycode == 2}"> <i>Tuesday</i> </c:if>
      <c:if test="${daycode == 3}"> <i>Wednessday</i> </c:if>
      <c:if test="${daycode == 4}"> <i>Thursday</i> </c:if>
      <c:if test="${daycode == 5}"> <i>Friday</i> </c:if>
      <c:if test="${daycode == 6}"> <i>Saturday</i> </c:if>
      <br>
      <c:if test="${(daycode ge 1) and (daycode le 5)}"> <b><i>Working day</i></b>
      </c:if>
```

```
    <c:if test="${(daycode eq 1) or (daycode eq 6)}"> <b><i>Holiday day</i></b>
    </c:if>
  <body>
</html>
```

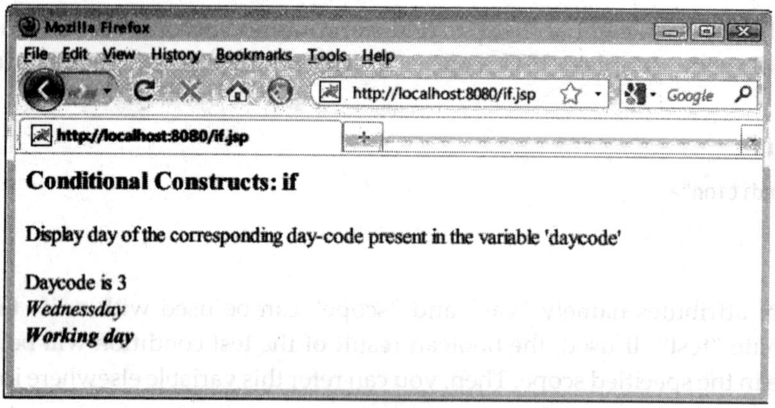

7.6.2 <c:choose> and <c:when>

It is a multi-branch conditional statement.

General format:

```
<c:choose>
  <c:when test="condition">
   code
  </c:when>
  <c:when test="condition">
   code
  </c:when>
  ...
  ...
  <c:otherwise>
   code
  </c:otherwise>
</c:choose>
```

Each `<c:when>` tag specifies one condition, thus this `<c:choose>` may have multiple conditions. The `<c:when>` conditions are evaluated from top to bottom, when a condition becomes true, then its corresponding code will be executed and `<c:choose>` will end without executing remaining `<c:when>` conditions and `<c:otherwise>` part. If none of the `<c:when>` conditions becomes true, then `<c:otherwise>` part will be executed.

Example:

```
<!– File Name: choose.jsp –>
<%@ taglib uri='http://java.sun.com/jsp/jstl/core' prefix='c'%>
```

```
<html>
   <body>
        <h3>Conditional Constructs: choose</h3>
        <p>Display day of the corresponding day-code present in the variable
           'daycode'</p>
        <c:set var="daycode" value="10" />
        Daycode is ${daycode}
        <br>
        <c:choose>
        <c:when test="${daycode == 0}">
              <b>Sunday</b>
        </c:when>
        <c:when test="${daycode == 1}">
              <i>Monday</i>
        </c:when>
        <c:when test="${daycode == 2}">
              <i>Tuesday</i>
        </c:when>
        <c:when test="${daycode == 3}">
              <i>Wednessday</i>
        </c:when>
        <c:when test="${daycode == 4}">
              <i>Thursday</i>
        </c:when>
        <c:when test="${daycode == 5}">
              <i>Friday</i>
        </c:when>
        <c:when test="${daycode == 6}">
              <i>Saturday</i>
        </c:when>
        <c:otherwise>
           <u>Invalid daycode. Should be within the reange [0-6]</u>
        </c:otherwise>
     </c:choose>
     <br>
     <c:choose>
        <c:when test="${(daycode ge 1) and (daycode le 5)}">
                 <b><i>Working day</i></b>
        </c:when>
        <c:when test="${(daycode eq 1) or (daycode eq 6)}">
```

```
                <b><i>Holiday day</i></b>
        </c:when>
       </c:choose>
   <body>
</html>
```

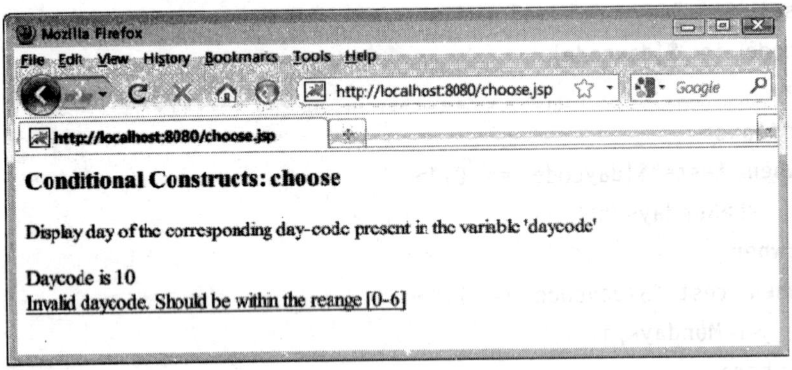

7.6.3 <c:forEach>

It is a powerful looping tag in JSTL. It is generally used to iterate collection of values.

General format:

```
<c:forEach items="collection" var="variable"
           begin="start-index" end="end-index"
           step="step-increment"
           varStatus="current_iteration_status">
    code
</c:forEach>
```

The attribute `items` specifies a collection of data to iterate, which includes Java Collection data (List, Set, Iterator), Arrays, Enumeration, and Map.

The attribute `var` specifies the variable-name, which contains the current fetched value of the iteration, and its scope is *page*.

The attribute `begin` specifies the starting index of the loop; the body of the loop (code) will be executed from this (n^{th}) iteration. The index starts from 0 and it is the default value also. If you specify a value for this attribute which is greater than the collection's last index, then the body of the loop will not executed at all. However, no error/exception will occur.

The attribute end specifies the ending index of the loop; the body of the loop will be executed up to this (n^{th}) iteration. The index starts from 0 and it is the default value is the index of the last item in the specified collection. If you specify a value for this attribute which is greater than the collection's last index, then the collection's last index will be taken as ending index for iteration, and this attribute value will be simply ignored.

The attribute `step` instructs the iteration to execute the body of the loop every `step`th item. It defaults to 1, i.e., the body of the loop will be executed for every item in the specified collection. For example, if attribute is set to 3, then the body of the loop will be executed for every third element (0, 3, 6, 9, 12 …).

The attribute `varStatus` assigns the current status of the iteration to the specified variable. It is a page scoped variable and it provides the following properties to access the status information.

`index`	Returns the index of the current fetched item from the specified collection. (Index starts from 0)
`count`	Returns the current round of iteration (Count starts from 1)
`first`	Returns true if it is the first round in the iteration, else returns false.
`last`	Returns true if it is the last round in the iteration, else returns false.

For example, if you specified varStatus="status" in the loop, then status.count gives the current round of the iteration.

Example:

```
<!- File Name: forEach.jsp ->
<%@ page import="java.util.*" %>
<%@ taglib uri='http://java.sun.com/jsp/jstl/core' prefix='c' %>
<html>
  <body>
        <h2>c:forEach Tag</h2>
        <%
                List<String> lstCountries = new ArrayList<String>();
                lstCountries.add("India");
                lstCountries.add("Pakistan");
                lstCountries.add("Bangladesh");
                lstCountries.add("Sri Lanka");
                lstCountries.add("China");
                lstCountries.add("Afghanistan");
                lstCountries.add("Australia");
                lstCountries.add("America");
                lstCountries.add("Malaysia");
                lstCountries.add("Singapore");
                lstCountries.add("Japan");
                lstCountries.add("Thailand");
                pageContext.setAttribute("countries", lstCountries);
        %>
        <hr>
        <h2>List all countries</h2>
        <ol>
                <c:forEach items="${pageScope.countries}" var="country">
                   <li>${country}</li>
                </c:forEach>
        </ol>
        <hr>
```

```
    <h2>List countries [4-8]</h2>
    <!-- In JSTL, index starts from zero ->
    <ul>
        <c:forEach items="${pageScope.countries}" var="country" be-
         gin="3 end="7">
         <li>${country}</li>
        </c:forEach>
    </ul>
    <hr>
    <h2>List countries (odd numbers; 1, 3, 5, 7, ...)</h2>
    <ul>
        <c:forEach items="${pageScope.countries}" var="country" step="2">
        <li>${country}</li>
        </ul> </c:forEach>
   <hr>
   <h2>List countries (even numbers; 2, 4, 6, 8, ...)</h2>
   <ul>
        <c:forEach items="${pageScope.countries}" var="country" begin="1"
        step="2">
           <li>${country}</li>
        </c:forEach>
   </ul>
   <hr>
   <h2>List countries (1, 5, 9, 13, ...)</h2>
   <ul>
        <c:forEach items="${pageScope.countries}" var="country" step="4">
           <li>${country}</li>
        </c:forEach>
   </ul>
   <hr>
   <h2>List countries (1, 5, 9, 13, ...) with their Indexes at Collection</h2>
   <table border="1" cellspacing="0" cellpadding="5">
        <tr>
            <th>Index at Collection</th>
            <th>Country</th>
        </tr>
        <c:forEach items="${pageScope.countries}"
                 var="country" step="4" varStatus="status">
           <tr>
               <td>${status.index}</td>
               <td>${country}</td>
           </tr>
```

```
            </c:forEach>
        </table>
        <hr>
        <h2>List countries with their Iteration Counts in Loop</h2>
        <table border="1" cellspacing="0" cellpadding="5">
                <tr>
                    <th>Iteration Count</th>
                    <th>Country</th>
                </tr>
                <!- This loop will be executed 3 times ->
                <c:forEach items="${pageScope.countries}"
                            var="country" step="2" varStatus="status">
                <tr <c:if test="${status.count % 2 eq 1}"> bgcolor="#FF0000" </
                c:if> >
                    <td>${status.count}</td>
                    <td>${country}</td>
                </tr>
            </c:forEach>
        </table>
        <hr>
        <c:forEach items="${pageScope.countries}" var="country" varStatus="status">
          <c:if test="${status.first}"> <h2>List of countries</h2> </c:if>
          <c:out value="${country}" default="" /> <br>
          <c:if test="${status.last}"> <br> <u>Total ${status.count} countries
          </u> </c:if>
        </c:forEach>
    <body>
</html>
```

Invoke the browser with the URL: http://localhost:8080/forEach.jsp

Then, you will get the output as below.

```
c:forEach Tag
```

```
List all countries
1. India
2. Pakistan
3. Bangladesh
4. Sri Lanka
5. China
6. Afghanistan
7. Australia
8. America
9. Malaysia
10. Singapore
```

```
11. Japan
12. Thailand
```

```
List countries [4-8]
Sri Lanka
China
Afghanistan
Australia
America
```

```
List countries (odd numbers; 1, 3, 5, 7, ...)
India
Bangladesh
China
Australia
Malaysia
Japan
```

```
List countries (even numbers; 2, 4, 6, 8, ...)
Pakistan
Sri Lanka
Afghanistan
America
Singapore
Thailand
```

```
List countries (1, 5, 9, 13, ...)
India
China
Malaysia
```

```
List countries (1, 5, 9, 13, ...) with their Indexes at Collection
Index at Collection Country
0 India
4 China
8 Malaysia
```

```
List countries with their Iteration Counts in Loop
Iteration Count Country
1 India
```

```
2 Bangladesh
3 China
4 Australia
5 Malaysia
6 Japan
```

```
List of countries
India
Pakistan
Bangladesh
Sri Lanka
China
Afghanistan
Australia
America
Malaysia
Singapore
Japan
Thailand
Total 12 countries
```

Suppose you want to execute a loop for "n" times, then you can use this <c:forEach> with begin and end attributes as shown in the following example.

```
<!— File Name: forEach.jsp —>
<%@ taglib uri='http://java.sun.com/jsp/jstl/core' prefix='c' %>
<html>
  <body>
      <h2>c:forEach Executing the loop for "n" times</h2>
      <hr>
      Execuing a loop for 10 times: 1-10
      <c:forEach begin="1" end="10" var="i">
          <li>${i}</li>
      </c:forEach>
      <hr>
      Displaying numbers from 1 to 10, sterp 3
      <c:forEach begin="1" end="10" var="i" step="3">
          <li>${i}</li>
      </c:forEach>
   <body>
 </html>
```

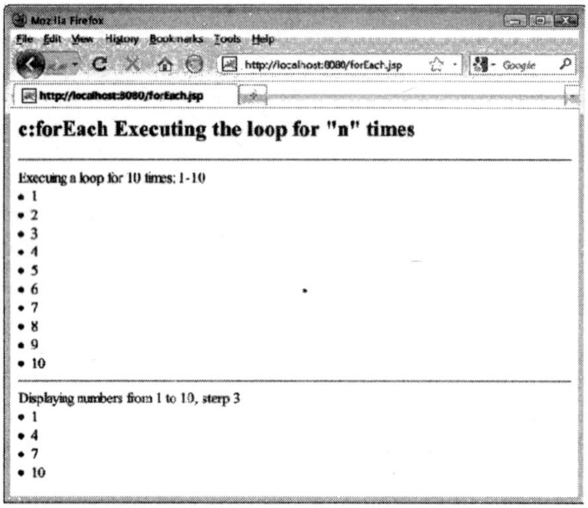

7.6.4 <c:forTokens>

It parses tokens (strings) from a specified source string which contains tokens separated by one or many delimiter(s), and iterates the loop for each parsed token.

Instead of specifying a collection upon which to iterate, you can also specify a series of tokens (normally strings) separated by delimiters such as comma, semi-colon, dot, etc.

General format:

```
<c:forTokens  items="string"  delims="delimiters"  var="variable"
               begin="start-index"  end="end-index"
              step="step-increment"
               varStatus="current_iteration_status">
    code
</c:forTokens >
```

The `items` attribute accepts an input string which is separated by one or more delimiters specified in `delims` attribute.

The functions of the attributes `var`, `begin`, `end`, `step`, `varStatus` are same as in `<c:forEach>`.

Example:

Let us take the same example used to illustrate `<c:forEach>` tag, and we change to Commas Separated Values to specify items instead of `ArrayList`.

```
<!–  File Name: forTokens.jsp –>
<%@ taglib uri='http://java.sun.com/jsp/jstl/core' prefix='c' %>
<html>
  <body>
      <h2>c:forTokens Tag</h2>
      <%
```

```
String csvCountries =
        "India, Pakistan, Bangladesh, Sri Lanka,
          China, Afghanistan, Australia, America, Malaysia, Singapore, Japan,
        Thailand";
          pageContext.setAttribute("countries", csvCountries);
%>
<hr>
<h2>List all countries</h2>
<ol>
   <c:forTokens items="${pageScope.countries}" delims="," var="country">
      <li>${country}</li>
   </c:forTokens>
</ol>
<hr>
<h2>List countries [4-8]</h2>
<!- In JSTL, index starts from zero ->
<ul>
   <c:forTokens items="${pageScope.countries}"
                   delims="," var="country" begin="3" end="7">
      <li>${country}</li>
   </c:forTokens>
</ul>
<hr>
<h2>List countries (odd numbers; 1, 3, 5, 7, ...)</h2>
<ul>
  <c:forTokens items="${pageScope.countries}" delims="," var="country"
step="2">
      <li>${country}</li>
   </c:forTokens>
</ul>
<hr>
<h2>List countries (even numbers; 2, 4, 6, 8, ...)</h2>
<ul>
   <c:forTokens items="${pageScope.countries}"
                   delims="," var="country" begin="1" step="2">
     <li>${country}</li>
   </c:forTokens>
</ul>
<hr>
```

```
<h2>List countries (1, 5, 9, 13, ...)</h2>
<ul>
  <c:forTokens items="${pageScope.countries}" delims="," var="country"
 step="4">
      <li>${country}</li>
  </c:forTokens>
</ul>
<hr>
<h2>List countries (1, 5, 9, 13, ...) with their Indexes at Collection</h2>
<table border="1" cellspacing="0" cellpadding="5">
  <tr>
      <th>Index at Collection</th>
      <th>Country</th>
  </tr>
  <c:forTokens items="${pageScope.countries}"
                 delims="," var="country" step="4" varStatus="status">
  <tr>
     <td>${status.index}</td>
     <td>${country}</td>
   </tr>
  </c:forTokens>
 </table>
 <hr>
 <h2>List countries with their Iteration Counts in Loop</h2>
 <table border="1" cellspacing="0" cellpadding="5">
  <tr>
     <th>Iteration Count</th>
     <th>Country</th>
  </tr>
  <!– This loop will be executed 3 times –>
  <c:forTokens items="${pageScope.countries}"
                 delims="," var="country" step="2" varStatus="status">
     <tr <c:if test="${status.count % 2 eq 1}"> bgcolor="#FF0000" </c:if> >
        <td>${status.count}</td>
        <td>${country}</td>
  </tr>
 </c:forTokens>
</table>
<hr>
```

```
        <c:forTokens items="${pageScope.countries}"
              delims="," var="country" varStatus="status">
         <c:if test="${status.first}"> <h2>List of countries</h2> </c:if>
         <c:out value="${country}" default="" /> <br>
         <c:if test="${status.last}"> <br> <u>Total ${status.count} countries</u>
        </c:if>
        </c:forTokens>
  <body>
</html>
```

Invoke the browser with the URL: http://localhost:8080/forTokens.jsp

You will get the same result as shown in `<c:forEach>` example.

You can also use Comma Separated Values string as the source to `items` attribute of `<c:forEach>` tag as shown in the following example, but we can not use other than comma to separate tokens. If you want to use other character (including comma) as delimiter to parse tokens, then you have to choose `<c:forTokens>` tag.

```
<!- File Name: forEach.jsp ->
<%@ taglib uri='http://java.sun.com/jsp/jstl/core' prefix='c' %>
<html>
 <body>
      <h2>c:forEach Tag with CSV</h2>
      <%
        String csvCountries =
        "India,Pakistan,Bangladesh,Sri Lanka,
        China, Afghanistan, Australia, America, Malaysia, Singapore, Japan,
        Thailand";
      pageContext.setAttribute("countries", csvCountries);
      %>
      <hr>
      <h2>List all countries</h2>
      <ol>
        <c:forEach items="${pageScope.countries}" var="country">
          <li>${country}</li>
        </c:forEach>
      </ol>
  <body>
 </html>
```

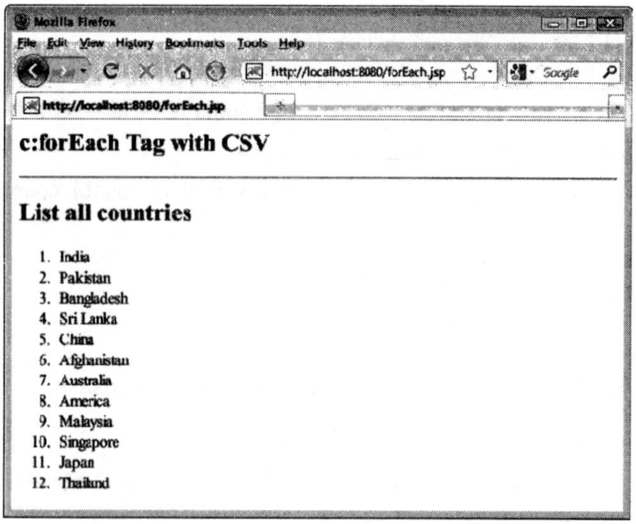

If you want to parse the input string using multiple delimiters, then simply specify them in delims attribute.

```
<!- File Name: forTokens.jsp ->
<%@ taglib uri='http://java.sun.com/jsp/jstl/core' prefix='c' %>
<html>
 <body>
      <h2>c:forTokens Tag, multiple delimiters</h2>
      <%
        String csvCountries = "India, Pakistan, Bangladesh, Sri Lanka|China#
        Af ghanistan#
             Australia|,A m e r i    ca,Malaysia, ,|Singapore||,Japan##Thailand";
        pageContext.setAttribute("countries", csvCountries);
      %>
      <hr>
      <h2>List all countries</h2>
      <ol>
         <c:forTokens items="${pageScope.countries}" delims=",|#" var="country">
            <li><pre>${country}</pre></li>
         </c:forTokens>
      </ol>
 <body>
</html>
```

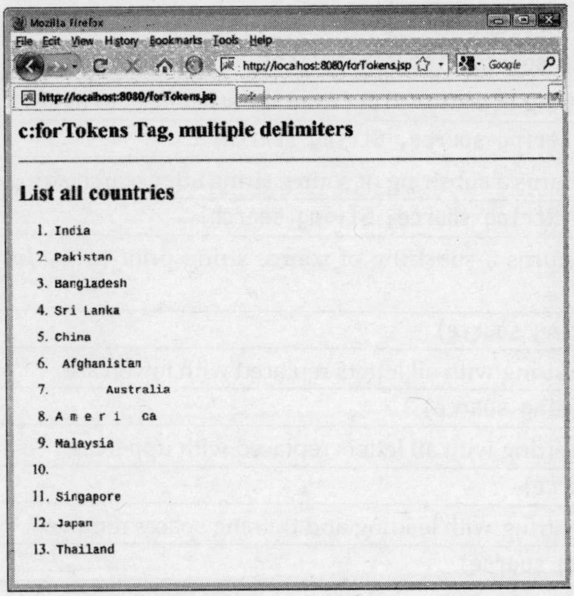

7.7 JSTL BUILT-IN FUNCTIONS

JSTL provides the many standard built-in functions, which can be used in your JSP by importing the following Tag library.

```
<%@ taglib prefix="fn" uri="http://java.sun.com/jsp/jstl/functions" %>
```

The functions available at the above Tag library are briefed below.

`boolean contains(String source, String search)`	
	Returns true if source string contains the search string, where search is case-sensitive. Otherwise returns false.
`boolean containsIgnoreCase (String source, String search)`	
	Returns true if source string contains the search string, where search is not case-sensitive. Otherwise returns false.
`boolean startsWith(String source, String prefix)`	
	Returns true if source string starts with prefix string. Otherwise returns false.
`boolean endssWith(String source, String suffix)`	
	Returns true if source string ends with suffix string. Otherwise returns false.
`int indexOf(String source, String search)`	
	Returns the index of first occurrence of search string in source string. Index starts from 0.
`int length(Object)`	
	Returns total number of items, if parameter is an Collection; Returns total number of characters if parameter is a String.
`String replace(String source, String search, String replace)`	

	Returns string after replacement of all search string in source string with replace string.
`String substring(String source, int startOffset, int endOffset)`	
	Returns a substring of source string from the startOffset to (endOffset – 1).
`String substringAfter(String source, String search)`	
	Extracts and returns a substring of source string after search string is appeared.
`String substringBefore(String source, String search)`	
	Extracts and returns a substring of source string prior to the location of found search string.
`String toLowerCase(String source)`	
	Returns source string with all letters replaced with lowercase.
`String toUpperCase( String source)`	
	Returns source string with all letters replaced with uppercase.
`String trim(String source)`	
	Returns source string with leading and training spaces removed.
`String escapeXml(String source)`	
	Escapes XML specific characters. Displays < for <, > for >, " for ", &apos for ', & for &
`String join(String source[], String delimiter)`	
	Converts and returns the delimiter separated string of source string array.
`String[] split(String source, String delimiters)`	
	Converts and returns string array for the specified string values in source separated by one or many delimiter(s).

Example:

```
<!-  File Name: FunctionsDemo.jsp ->
<%@ taglib uri='http://java.sun.com/jsp/jstl/core' prefix='c'%>
<%@ taglib prefix="fn" uri="http://java.sun.com/jsp/jstl/functions" %>
<html>
<body>
 <table border="1" cellspacing="0" cellpadding="5">
  <caption><h2>JSTL Built-in Functions</h2></caption>
  <c:set var="name" value="Mohamed Ibrahim" />
  <tr>
      <td> boolean contains(String, String) </td>
      <td> ${fn:contains(name, 'ibrahim')} </td>
  </tr>
  <tr>
      <td> boolean containsIgnoreCase(String, String) </td>
      <td> ${fn:containsIgnoreCase(name, 'ibrahim')} </td>
  </tr>
  <tr>
      <td> boolean startsWith(String, String) </td>
```

```
        <td> ${fn:startsWith(name, 'rahim')} </td>
    </tr>
    <tr>
        <td> boolean endsWith(String, String) </td>
        <td> ${fn:endsWith(name, 'rahim')} </td>
    </tr>
    <tr>
        <td> int indexOf(String, String) </td>
        <td> ${fn:indexOf(name, 'a')} </td>
    </tr>
    <tr>
        <td> int length(Object) </td>
        <td> ${fn:length(name)} </td>
    </tr>
    <tr>
        <td> String replace(String, String, String) </td>
        <td> ${fn:replace(name, 'a', 'A')} </td>
    </tr>
    <tr>
        <td> String substring(String, int, int) </td>
        <td> ${fn:substring(name, 2, 5)} </td>
    </tr>
    <tr>
        <td> String substringAfter(String, String) </td>
        <td>
          ${fn:substringAfter(name, "Mohamed ")}, ${fn:substringAfter(name, "a")},
          [${fn:substringAfter(name, "XYZ")}]
        </td>
    </tr>
    <tr>
        <td> String substringBefore(String, String) </td>
        <td>
          ${fn:substringBefore(name, "rahim")}, ${fn:substringBefore(name, "a")},
          [${fn:substringBefore(name, "XYZ")}]
        </td>
    </tr>
    <tr>
        <td> String toLowerCase(String) </td>
        <td> ${fn:toLowerCase(name)} </td>
    </tr>
    <tr>
        <td> String toUpperCase(String) </td>
```

```
        <td> ${fn:toUpperCase(name)} </td>
    </tr>
    <tr>
        <td> String trim(String) </td>
        <td> ${fn:replace(fn:trim("  Mohamed      Ibrahim    "), ' ', ' ')} </td>
    </tr>
    <tr>
        <td> String escapeXml(String) </td>
        <td> <b>Ibrahim</b> <br> ${fn:escapeXml("<b>Ibrahim</b>")} </td>
    </tr>
    <%
        String countriesArray[] = {"India", "Pakistan", "Bangladesh", "Sri Lanka",
        "China",
        "Afghanistan", "Australia", "America", "Malaysia", "Singapore", "Japan",
        "Thailand"};
        String csvCountries = "India,Pakistan,Bangladesh,
          Sri Lanka, China, Afghanistan, Australia, America, Malaysia|
          Singapore|Japan|Thailand";
        pageContext.setAttribute("countriesArray", countriesArray);
        pageContext.setAttribute("csvCountries", csvCountries);
    %>
    <tr>
        <td> String join(String[], String) </td>
        <td> ${fn:join(countriesArray, "#")} </td>
    </tr>
    <tr>
        <td> String[] split(String, String) </td>
        <td> <c:set var="cArray" value="${fn:split(csvCountries, ',|')}" />
              <ul>
              <c:forEach items="${pageScope.cArray}" var="country">
                      <li>${country}</li>
              </c:forEach>
              </ul>
        </td>
    </tr>
  </table>
<body>
</html>
```

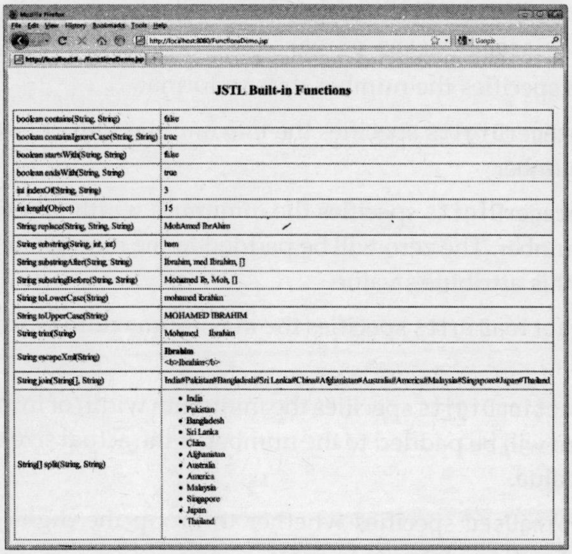

JSTL Built-in Functions

boolean contains(String, String)	false
boolean containsIgnoreCase(String, String)	true
boolean startsWith(String, String)	false
boolean endsWith(String, String)	true
int indexOf(String, String)	3
int length(Object)	15
String replace(String, String, String)	MohAmed IbrAhim
String substring(String, int, int)	ham
String substringAfter(String, String)	Ibrahim, med Ibrahim, []
String substringBefore(String, String)	Mohamed Ib, Moh, []
String toLowerCase(String)	mohamed ibrahim
String toUpperCase(String)	MOHAMED IBRAHIM
String trim(String)	Mohamed Ibrahim
String escapeXml(String)	**Ibrahim** <b>Ibrahim</b>
String join(String[], String)	India#Pakistan#Bangladesh#Sri Lanka#China#Afghanistan#Australia#America#Malaysia#Singapore#Japan#Thailand
String[] split(String, String)	• India • Pakistan • Bangladesh • Sri Lanka • China • Afghanistan • Australia • America • Malaysia • Singapore • Japan • Thailand

7.8 DATA FORMATTING WITH JSTL

Using JSTL, we can format the data in order to display in the required format. JSTL tags are available to intensively format numbers and date values. We can also use a message bundle with JSTL, to separate messages from your JSP files. Locale specific data formatting and message display are also possible with JSTL.

7.8.1 Formatting Tag

Include the following tag library in your JSPs to use the formatting features.

```
<%@ taglib uri="http://java.sun.com/jsp/jstl/fmt" prefix="fmt" %>
```

7.8.2 <fmt:formatNumber>

This tag formats numbers based on set attributes and outputs the result / stores the result to a scoped variable.

General format:

```
<fmt:formatNumber value="number_value"
        maxIntegerDigits     ="maximum_digits_before_dot"
        minIntegerDigits  ="minimum_digits_before_dot"
        maxFractionDigits ="maximum_digits_after_dot"
        minFractionDigits="minimum_digits_after_dot"
        type="value_type#number|currency|percent"
        currencyCode="currency_code"
        currencySymbol="currency_symbol"
        groupingUsed="boolean_to_group_digits"
        pattern="pattern_to_format_number"
```

```
var="variable_to_store_result"
scope="scope_of_var" />
```

The attribute `value` specifies the number data to format.

The attribute `maxIntegerDigits` specifies the maximum width of integer number / integer part of the floating point number.

The attribute `minIntegerDigits` specifies the minimum width of integer number / integer part of the floating point number. The zero will be padded to the number, if the actual size of the value is less in width than this attribute's value.

The attribute `maxFractionDigits` specifies the maximum width of fractional part of the floating point number.

The attribute `minFractionDigits` specifies the minimum width of infractional part of the floating point number. The zero will be padded to the number, if the actual size of the value is less in width than this attribute's value.

The attribute `groupingUsed` specifies whether to group the digits (separator between every three digits) while outputting, defaults to true.

The attribute `type` specifies for what type the value should formatted. The attribute may have one of the following three values:

`number`	Number (default)
`currency`	Currency (Locale specific, the value will be formatted according to the browser's preferred locale. That is, if you invoke the page in US set locale machine, then the value formatted to US currency, $value.)
`percent`	Percentage (the value will be multiplied by 100)

The attribute `pattern` decides how the number should be displayed. For example, the setting `pattern="###.##E0"` displays the corresponding number in scientific format.

The attribute `currencyCode` specifies the country code, for which the currency value should be formatted instead of formatting based on current locale. The default currency indicator such as (INR, EUR ...) will be prefixed to the currency value. We can also display some other symbol by using currencySymbol attribute.

Note: For list of `currencyCode` values, search "ISO 4217 Currency Code List" in Internet. The following are some of the currency codes.

Currency	Country Code
India	INR
Pakistan	PKR
Bangladesh	BDT
Sri Lanka	LKR
China	CNY
Afghanistan	AFN

Australia	AUD
America	USD
Malaysia	MYR
Singapore	SGD
Japan	JPY
Thailand	THB

The attribute var stores the result of this tag, instead of outputting, and its scope can be specified using scope attribute (defaults to page).

```
<!-  File Name: FormatNumber.jsp ->
<%@ taglib uri='http://java.sun.com/jsp/jstl/core' prefix='c'%>
<%@ taglib prefix="fmt" uri="http://java.sun.com/jsp/jstl/fmt" %>
<html>
 <body>
  <table border="1" cellspacing="0" cellpadding="5">
  <caption><h2><c:out value="<fmt:formatNumber>" /></h2></caption>
  <c:set var="num1" value="1234567.867523" />
  <tr>
    <td> <c:out value='<fmt:formatNumber value="${num1}" />' /> </td>
    <td> <fmt:formatNumber value="${num1}" /> <br>
        (Observe Rounding at decimal part)
    </td>
  </tr>
  <tr>
    <td> <c:out value='<fmt:formatNumber value="${num1}" maxIntegerDigits="5"
    />' /> </td>
    <td> <fmt:formatNumber value="${num1}" maxIntegerDigits="5" /> </td>
  </tr>
  <tr>
    <td> <c:out value='<fmt:formatNumber value="${num1}" minIntegerDigits="10"
               groupingUsed="false" />' /> </td>
    <td> <fmt:formatNumber value="${num1}" minIntegerDigits="10" groupingUsed=
    "false" /> </td>
  </tr>
  <tr>
    <td> <c:out value='<fmt:formatNumber value="${num1}" maxFractionDigits="5"
    />' /> </td>
    <td> <fmt:formatNumber value="${num1}" maxFractionDigits="5" /> </td>
  </tr>
  <tr>
    <td> <c:out value='<fmt:formatNumber value="${num1}" minFractionDigits="8"
    />' /> </td>
```

```
      <td> <fmt:formatNumber value="${num1}" minFractionDigits="8" /> </td>
    </tr>
    <tr>
      <td> <c:out value='<fmt:formatNumber value="${num1}" groupingUsed="false"
      />' /> </td>
      <td> <fmt:formatNumber value="${num1}" groupingUsed="false" /> </td>
    </tr>
    <tr>
      <td> <c:out value='<fmt:formatNumber value="${num1}" type="number"
      minIntegerDigits="10"
                 maxFractionDigits="5" groupingUsed="false" />' /> </td>
     <td> <fmt:formatNumber value="${num1}" type="number" minIntegerDigits="10"
                           maxFractionDigits="5" groupingUsed="false" /> </td>
     </tr>
     <tr>
       <td> <c:out value='<fmt:formatNumber value="72" type="percent" />' /> </td>
       <td> <fmt:formatNumber value="72" type="percent" /> </td>
     </tr>
     <tr>
       <td> <c:out value='<fmt:formatNumber value=".728952" type="percent" />'/> </td>
       <td> <fmt:formatNumber value=".728952" type="percent" /> </td>
     </tr>
     <tr>
       <td>
       <c:out value='<fmt:formatNumber value=".728952" type="percent"
       minFractionDigits="2" />' />
      </td>
      <td> <fmt:formatNumber value=".728952" type="percent" minFractionDigits="2"
      /> </td>
     </tr>
     <tr>
       <td> <c:out value='<fmt:formatNumber value="1728952" type="currency" />'
       /> </td>
       <td> <fmt:formatNumber value="1728952" type="currency" /> </td>
     </tr>
      <tr>
       <td>
        <c:out value='<fmt:formatNumber value="1728952" type="currency" currency
        Code="INR" />' />
        </td>
        <td> <fmt:formatNumber value="1728952" type="currency" currencyCode="INR"
        /> </td>
```

```
    </tr>
   <tr>
  <td>
    <c:out value='<fmt:formatNumber value="1728952" type="currency" currency
    Code="EUR" />' />
  </td>
    <td> <fmt:formatNumber value="1728952" type="currency" currencyCode="EUR"
    /> </td>
    </tr>
  <tr>
  <td>
    <c:out value='<fmt:formatNumber value="1728952" type="currency" currency
    Symbol="Rs." />' />
  </td>
  <td> <fmt:formatNumber value="1728952" type="currency" currencySymbol="Rs."
  /> </td>
</tr>
<tr>
 <td>
  <c:out value='<fmt:formatNumber value="1728952" type="currency"
                  currencySymbol="&euro;" />' /> </td>
  <td> <fmt:formatNumber value="1728952" type="currency" currencySymbol="&euro;"
  /> </td>
 </tr>
 <fmt:setLocale value="en_GB" />
 <tr>
   <td> <c:out value='<fmt:formatNumber value="1728952.1234" type="currency"
   />' /> </td>
   <td> <fmt:formatNumber value="1728952.1234" type="currency" /> </td>
 </tr>
 <fmt:setLocale value="fr_FR" />
 <fmt:formatNumber value="1728952.1234" var="franceLocale" scope="page" />
 <tr>
   <td>
   <c:out value='<fmt:formatNumber value="1728952.1234" var="franceLocale"
   scope="page" />' />
   </td>
   <td> ${franceLocale} </td>
  </tr>
  </table>
 <body>
</html>
```

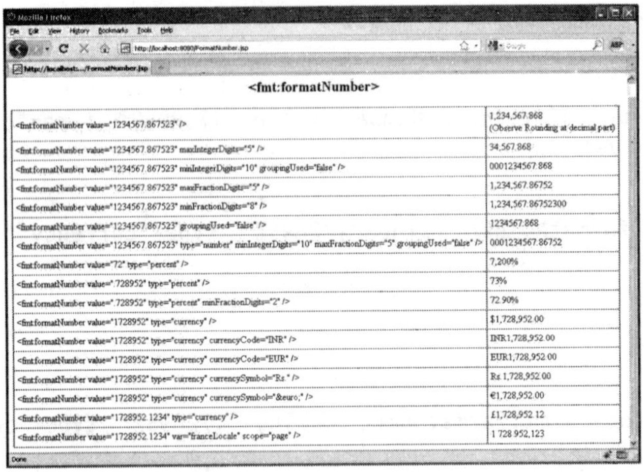

<fmt:formatNumber>

<fmt:formatNumber value="1234567.867523" />	1,234,567.868 (Observe Rounding at decimal part)
<fmt:formatNumber value="1234567.867523" maxIntegerDigits="5" />	34,567.868
<fmt:formatNumber value="1234567.867523" minIntegerDigits="10" groupingUsed="false" />	0001234567.868
<fmt:formatNumber value="1234567.867523" maxFractionDigits="5" />	1,234,567.86752
<fmt:formatNumber value="1234567.867523" minFractionDigits="8" />	1,234,567.86752300
<fmt:formatNumber value="1234567.867523" groupingUsed="false" />	1234567.868
<fmt:formatNumber value="1234567.867523" type="number" minIntegerDigits="10" maxFractionDigits="5" groupingUsed="false" />	0001234567.86752
<fmt:formatNumber value="72" type="percent" />	7,200%
<fmt:formatNumber value=".728952" type="percent" />	73%
<fmt:formatNumber value=".728952" type="percent" minFractionDigits="2" />	72.90%
<fmt:formatNumber value="1728952" type="currency" />	$1,728,952.00
<fmt:formatNumber value="1728952" type="currency" currencyCode="INR" />	INR1,728,952.00
<fmt:formatNumber value="1728952" type="currency" currencyCode="EUR" />	EUR1,728,952.00
<fmt:formatNumber value="1728952" type="currency" currencySymbol="Rs." />	Rs.1,728,952.00
<fmt:formatNumber value="1728952" type="currency" currencySymbol="€" />	€1,728,952.00
<fmt:formatNumber value="1728952.1234" type="currency" />	£1,728,952.12
<fmt:formatNumber value="1728952.1234" var="franceLocale" scope="page" />	1 728 952,123

Locale Specific Formatting: A Locale is generally a specific region on living earth based on some key factors such as geography and culture including currency format, number representation, and date format. It is generally referred by using two lower case letters representing language code, and then an underscore, then two upper case letters representing country code (languagecode_COUNTRYCODE), where underscore and country code are optional.

The server page gets locale information from the client (Web Browser) request header. However, we can change this default locale using `<fmt:setLocale>` tag. A simple syntax of this `<fmt:setLocale>` tag is given below.

```
<fmt:setLocale value="locale_name" />
```

The following example displays the default locale (found from client) and list of all available locales.

```
<!- File Name: LocaleList.jsp ->
<%@ page import="java.util.Locale" %>
<%@ taglib uri='http://java.sun.com/jsp/jstl/core' prefix='c'%>
<%@ taglib prefix="fmt" uri="http://java.sun.com/jsp/jstl/fmt" %>
<html>
<body>
    Default Locale (from Web Browser's header):
        <c:out value="${pageContext.request.locale.language}" />_
        <c:out value="${pageContext.request.locale.country}" />
  <br><br>
  <%
    Locale listLocales[] = Locale.getAvailableLocales();
    pageContext.setAttribute("listLocales", listLocales);
  %>
  <table border="1" cellspacing="0" cellpadding="5">
  <tr>
```

```
<th>Locale</th>
<th>Description</th>
</tr>
<c:forEach  items="${listLocales}"  var="locale">
    <tr>
<td>${locale}</td>
<td>${locale.displayName}</td>
</tr>
    </c:forEach>
</table>
    <body>
</html>
```

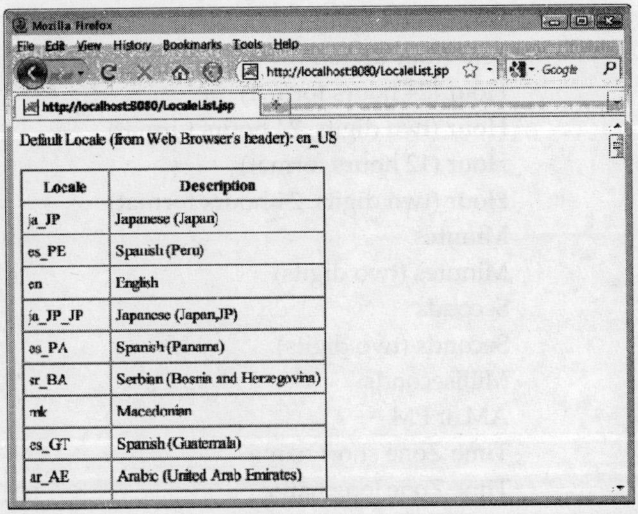

7.8.3 <fmt:formatDate>

This tag is used to format date/time values.

General format:

```
<fmt:formatDate value="date/time_value"
                type="date|time|both"
                dateStyle="date_style_string"
                timeStyle="time_style_string"
                timeZone="time_zone"
                pattern="pattern_to_format_date_time"
                var="variable_to_store_result"
                scope="scope_of_var"  />
```

The attribute `value` specifies the actual date/time value to format.

The attribute type defines whether to display date, or time, or both (date | time | both).

The attribute dateStyle specifies in what style the date value should displayed.

(Acceptable values: default, short, medium, long, full).

The attribute timeStyle specifies in what style the time value should displayed.

(Acceptable values: default, short, medium, long, full).

The attribute pattern specifies a format string, in which the date/time value will be formatted. The format string can be constructed in the combination of the following format characters.

Format Character	Format Effect
D	Day of month
dd	Day of month (two digits)
M	Month
MM	Month (two digits)
MMM	Short Month Name (Eg., Sep)
MMMM	Long Month Name (Eg., September)
yy	Year (two digits)
yyyy	Year (four digits)
H	Hour (24 hours format)
HH	Hour (two digits, 24 hours format)
H	Hour (12 hours format)
hh	Hour (two digits, 24 hours format)
M	Minutes
mm	Minutes (two digits)
S	Seconds
ss	Seconds (two digits)
S	Milliseconds
A	AM or PM
zz	Time Zone short name
zzzz	Time Zone long name

The attribute var stores the result of this tag, instead of outputting, and its scope can be specified using scope attribute (defaults to page).

The attribute timeZone specifies a time zone to use while formatting date/time value, instead of default time zone recognized by JSP. The time zone includes IST, AST, EST, CST, MST, PST, KSA, and HST.

Example:

```
<!– File Name: FormatDate.jsp –>
<%@ page import="java.util.Date" %>
<%@ taglib uri='http://java.sun.com/jsp/jstl/core' prefix='c'%>
<%@ taglib prefix="fmt" uri="http://java.sun.com/jsp/jstl/fmt" %>
<html>
 <body>
 <table border="1" cellspacing="0" cellpadding="5">
  <caption><h2><c:out value="<fmt:formatDate>" /></h2></caption>
```

```
<%
 Date d = new Date();
 pageContext.setAttribute("date", d);
%>
<tr>
 <td> <c:out value='<fmt:formatDate value="${date}" />' /> </td>
 <td> <fmt:formatDate value="${date}" /> </td>
</tr>
<tr>
  <td> <c:out value='<fmt:formatDate value="${date}" type="date" />' /> </td>
  <td> <fmt:formatDate value="${date}" type="date" /> </td>
</tr>
  <td> <c:out value='<fmt:formatDate value="${date}" type="time" />' /> </td>
  <td> <fmt:formatDate value="${date}" type="time" /> </td>
</tr>
<tr>
  <td> <c:out value='<fmt:formatDate value="${date}" type="both" />' /> </td>
  <td> <fmt:formatDate value="${date}" type="both" /> </td>
</tr>
<tr>
  <td> <c:out value='<fmt:formatDate value="${date}" dateStyle="full" />' /> </td>
  <td> <fmt:formatDate value="${date}" dateStyle="full" /> </td>
</tr>
<tr>
 <td>
   <c:out value='<fmt:formatDate value="${date}" type="both" dateStyle="short"
          timeStyle="full" />' />
 </td>
 <td>
  <fmt:formatDate value="${date}" type="both" dateStyle="short" timeStyle="full"/>
 </td>
</tr>
<tr>
   <td> <c:out value='<fmt:formatDate value="${date}" type="both" dateStyle="short"
          timeStyle="short" />' />
</td>
<td>
  <fmt:formatDate value="${date}" type="both" dateStyle="short" timeStyle="short" />
</td>
</tr>
  <tr>
```

```
    <td>
     <c:out value='<fmt:formatDate value="${date}" type="both"
            pattern="dd/MM/yyyy HH:mm:ss" />' />
    </td>
   <td> <fmt:formatDate value="${date}" type="both" pattern="dd/MM/yyyy HH:mm:ss" />
  </td>
  </tr>
  <tr>
    <td>
     <c:out value='<fmt:formatDate value="${date}" type="both" pattern="d/M/yy
     H:m:s" />' />
  </td>
  <td> <fmt:formatDate value="${date}" type="both" pattern="d/M/yy H:m:s" /> </td>
  </tr>
  <tr>
   <td> <c:out value='<fmt:formatDate value="${date}"
          type="both" pattern="dd/MM/yyyy HH:mm:ss" timeZone="EST" />' /> </td>
   <td> <fmt:formatDate value="${date}"
             type="both" pattern="dd/MM/yyyy HH:mm:ss" timeZone="EST" /> </td>
  </tr>
  <tr>
   <td> <c:out value='<fmt:formatDate value="${date}"
         type="both" pattern="dd/MM/yyyy HH:mm:ss" timeZone="PST" />' /> </td>
   <td> <fmt:formatDate value="${date}"
             type="both" pattern="dd/MM/yyyy HH:mm:ss" timeZone="PST" /> </td>
  </tr>
  <tr>
   <td> <c:out value='<fmt:formatDate value="${date}"
         type="both" pattern="dd/MM/yyyy HH:mm:ss" timeZone="KSA" />' /> </td>
   <td> <fmt:formatDate value="${date}"
            type="both" pattern="dd/MM/yyyy HH:mm:ss" timeZone="KSA" /> </td>
  </tr>
   <fmt:formatDate value="${date}"
            type="both" pattern="dd/MM/yyyy HH:mm:ss" timeZone="IST"
            var="datetime" />
  <tr>
    <td> <c:out value='<fmt:formatDate value="${date}"
            type="both" pattern="dd/MM/yyyy HH:mm:ss" timeZone="IST" />' /> </td>
    <td> ${datetime} </td>
  </tr>
 </table>
```

```
  <body>
</html>
```

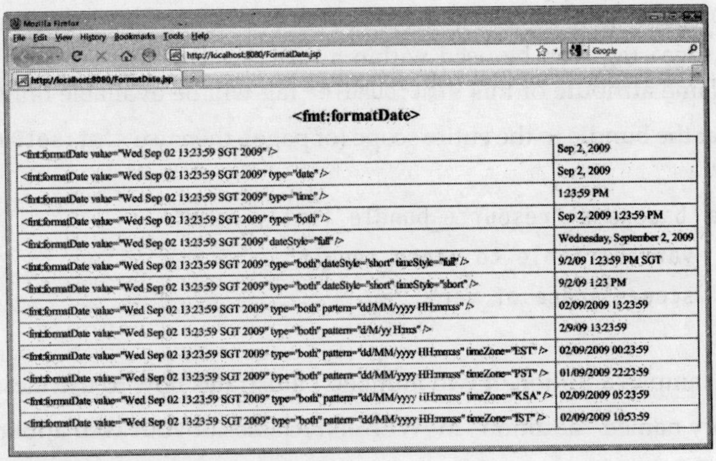

7.8.4 Message Bundle and Internalization

Message texts (captions, messages ...) used in a web page can be separated out into a message bundle as key-value pairs and can be referred in JSPs.

7.8.4.1 <fmt:message>

This tag outputs the value of the specified key from the message bundle.

General format:

```
<fmt:message key="key"
             bundle="resource_bundle_path"
             var="variable_to_store_result"
             scope="scope_of_var" />
```

The attribute key specifies the property-name to get its value from the resource bundle (properties file).

The attribute bundle refers the resource bundle to use.

The attribute var stores the result of this tag, instead of outputting, and its scope can be specified using scope attribute (defaults to page).

7.8.4.2 <fmt:param>

The messages in the resource bundle can have placeholders, which will be filled up at run-time. Multiple <fmt:param> tag can be used within <fmt:message> to pass (parameter) values for the placeholders (positional parameters) in the corresponding message in the resource bundle.

General format

```
<fmt:param value="parameter_value" />
```

7.8.4.3 <fmt:bundle> and <fmt:setBundle>

Both these tags load a resource bundle with your JSP pages.

General format:

```
<fmt:bundle baseName="resource_bundle_family_name"
            prefix="prefix_to_each_key" />
```

Many `<fmt:message>` tags can be used within a `<fmt:bundle>` tag. And the resource bundle specified in baseName attribute of this `<fmt:bundle>` tag will be available only to its child tags.

If you want to set the bundle to the entire scope (of page), then use `<fmt:setBundle>` tag, whose syntax is as below.

```
<fmt:setBundle basename="resource_bundle_family_name"
               var="variable_to_store_result"
               scope="scope_of_var" />
```

Example:

The following example (addition of two numbers) illustrates how to use message bundle.

Create a directory named "addition" in /WEB-INF/classes of your web application.

Store the following properties file (messages.properties) in this newly created "addition" directory.

```
page.title=Addition of Two Numbers
first.number=Enter the first number
second.number=Enter the second number
result=Result: {0} + {1} = {2}
```

Store the following file (addition.jsp) in the web-root (in our example, it is /webapps/ROOT).

```
<!– File Name: addition.jsp –>
<%@ taglib uri='http://java.sun.com/jsp/jstl/fmt' prefix='fmt' %>
<fmt:setLocale value='en'/>
<!– 'message' is the properties filename which is stored in 'addition' directory –>
<fmt:setBundle basename='addition.messages'/>
<html>
 <head>
  <title>
       <fmt:message key='page.title'/>
  </title>
</head>
<body>
 <form name="form" action="addition.jsp">
  <fmt:message key='first.number'/>:
      <input type="text" name="num1" value="${param.num1}"> <br>
  <fmt:message key='second.number'/>:
      <input type="text" name="num2" value="${param.num2}"> <br>
  <input type="submit" value="ADD">
```

```
        <br>
          <b>
            <fmt:message key='result'>
              <fmt:param value="${param.num1}" />
              <fmt:param value="${param.num2}" />
              <fmt:param value="${param.num1 + param.num2}" />
            </fmt:message>
          </b>
    </form>
  </body>
</html>
```

Invoke the addition.jsp in the browser.

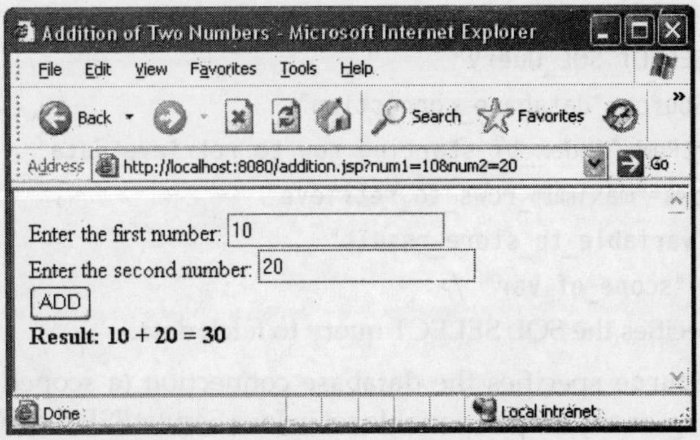

7.9 DATABASE ACCESS WITH JSTL

JSTL provides tags to manipulate with Relational Database Management Systems. These tags simplify database access code; usually these operations are performed through JSP Scriplets.

7.9.1 Tag Library: sql

The JSP should include the following tag library in order to use this sql tags.

```
<%@ taglib uri="http://java.sun.com/jsp/jstl/sql" prefix="sql" %>
```

7.9.2 <sql:setDataSource>

It defines a database connection.

General format:

```
<sql:setDataSource dataSource="existing_data_source"
                   driver="JDBC_driver_class_name"
                   url="JDBC_connection_URL"
```

```
                    user="user_name_of_database"
                    password="password_of_user"
                    var="variable_to_refer_database"
                    scope="scope_of_var" />
```

The attributes `driver, url, user, password` are JDBC parameters to create a database connection.

The attribute var stores the opened database connection in a variable-name and its scope can be specified in the scope attribute. This variable (or a scoped variable which is created in Java Servlet/JSP code that refers database connection) can be specified as dataSource in this tag, instead of specifying JDBC related parameters to open a new connection.

7.9.3 <sql:query>

This tag is used to obtain the result of an SELECT SQL query.

General format:

```
<sql:query  sql="SELECT_SQL_Query"
            dataSource="database_connection"
            startRow="index_of_starting_row_to_retrieve_data"
            maxRows="maximum_rows_to_retrieve"
            var="variable_to_store_result"
            scope="scope_of_var" />
```

The attribute `sql` specifies the SQL SELECT query to fetch data.

The attribute `dataSource` specifies the database connection (a scoped variable defined in `<sql:setDataSource>` tag, or any scoped variable set in Java Servlet/JSP code which refers database connection).

The attribute `startRow` defines the starting row (index start from 0), from which data records should be retrieved from the result of the specified query, defaults to 0. Row means a record in the database table.

The attribute maxRows specifies the maximum number of rows to retrieve from the result of the specified query. The result of the <sql:query> tag will vary based on both startRow and maxRows attributes.

The result (of the tag) will be stored in the variable specified in `var` and its scope is defined in scope attribute, defaults to page. The following are the some properties which can be used with this variable to access the resultant data.

`RowCount`	Returns the numbers of rows in the result.
`ColumnNames`	It is an array, contains list of column names of the resultant rows.
`Rows`	It is the collection of retrieved rows. The columns in each iterated row can be accessed by specifying column-names.
`RowsByIndex`	It is the collection of retrieved rows. The columns in each iterated row can be accessed by specifying column-numbers. The column-numbers start from 0 (in the order of columns-selection in the SELECT statement).

7.9.4 <sql:update>

This tag is used to execute all SQL statements other than SELECT. That is we can execute Data Definition and Data Manipulation (other than Data Selection) operation statements such as CREATE, INSERT, UPDATE, and DELETE.

General format:

```
<sql:update sql="SQL_Statement"
      dataSource="database_connection"
      var="variable_to_affected_row_count"
      scope="scope_of_var" />
```

The attribute sql specifies the SQL statement (other than SELECT) to execute.

The attribute dataSource specifies the database connection (a scoped variable defined in <sql:setDataSource> tag, or any scoped variable set in Java Servlet/JSP code which refers database connection).

The total number of records affected (update, deleted …) while executing the specified query will be stored in the variable specified in var attribute, and its scope is specified in scope attribute, defaults to page.

7.9.5 <sql:param>

This tag is used to assign values for positional parameters (placeholders, question marks) in SQL statements.

General format:

```
<sql:param value="value_for_placeholder" />
```

Multiple <sql:param> can be used with <sql:query> or <sql:update> tags, to assign values for each placeholder vales. The values should be assigned in the order of <sql:param>.

Example:

```
<sql:query sql="select * from student where mark1 >= ? and mark2 >= ?"
                                          dataSource="ds">
   <sql:param value="40" />
      <sql:param value="50" />
</sql:query>
```

Here, we used two placeholders to specify two marks.

7.9.6 <sql:dateParam>

This tag is used to assign date value for a placeholder.

General format:

```
<sql:dateParam value="date_value"
          type="value_type#date#time#timestamp" />
```

The attribute `value` specifies a date value which should be assigned to a placeholder, and the value's date type whether date only (date), time only (time), or both (timestamp) is specified type attribute, defaults to timestamp.

7.9.7 <sql:transaction>

A transaction is a unit of database operations that should be completed all or none. For example, let us consider a typical banking transaction: Transfer amount X from Customer A to Customer B. This operation can be performed in two steps: Debit amount X from Customer A and Credit amount X to Customer B. Case 1: If these two steps are successfully performed, then operation will be successful. Case 2: If none of these steps are performed, then it means no operation performed. Now come to severe case, Case 3: the step 'Debit amount X from Customer A' became successful, but while executing the step 'Credit amount X to Customer B', exception/error occurred so that this step became failed. It is not a successful transaction; we have to bring into old status (rollback) in order to keep correct accounts. In this case, we can use `<sql:transaction>` tag, which rollback the database operations when fatal error occurred which results in failure of database operation.

General format:

```
<sql:transaction dataSource="database_connection"
            isolation="isolation_level_of_transaction" />
```

The attribute `dataSource` specifies the database connection (a scoped variable defined in `<sql:setDataSource>` tag, or any scoped variable set in Java Servlet/JSP code which refers database connection).

Many `<sql:query>`, `<sql:update>` tags can be used within a `<sql:transaction>` tag, and all its child elements (`<sql:query>`, `<sql:update>`) do not specify dataSource attributes as they will use the same database connection used by `<sql:transaction>` tag.

Database Isolation Levels:

The Isolation defines how the database changes made in one operation are available to other concurrent operations, based on status of the operations.

The potential undesirable read (data from database) arises in concurrent (at the same time) transactions are as follows.

Note that many SQL statements can be used in a transaction; the effect of each statement will not be committed to database as soon as it is executed, at the end of the transaction, all the operations (effects) within the transaction will be committed (due to successfully done the operations) or rolled back (due to error).

The following are the three different possibilities that may occur in a database transaction.

(i) **Dirty Read:** A transaction reads the rows, which are used by and have not been committed by another transaction. For example,

There are two concurrent transactions A and B both accessing a database table.

- Txn A reads table rows and modifies some data (but not committed yet).
- Txn B reads table rows (it gets the modified uncommitted version of data done by Txn A).
- Txn A rolls back the changes on the table.
- Txn B now has data inconsistency with the table (do not read again). The read of Txn B is known as "Dirty Read".

(*ii*) **Non-repeatable Read:** The same SELECT query returns different results (in existing data) when executed another time within the same transaction. For example,

There are two concurrent transactions A and B both accessing a database table.

- Txn A reads the table rows.
- Txn B updates the table rows.
- Txn A once again reads the table rows; it gets rows updated by Txn B.

  Txn A finds data that are different now. The read of Txn A is known as "Non-repeatable Read".

(*iii*) **Phantom Read:** The same SELECT query returns different number of rows when executed another time with in the same transaction.

For example,

There are two concurrent transactions A and B both accessing a database table.

- Txn A reads the table rows. It returns say "n" rows.
- Txn B inserts/deletes "m" rows into the table.
- Txn A once again reads the table rows; it gets (n+m) or (n-m) rows (actual rows added/subtracted with the rows affected by Txn B).

  Txn A finds row count that is different now.
- Txn B rolls back the insertion/deletion of rows with the table. So that the database table will contain "n" rows.

  However, at this stage (without re-read) Txn A is looking at (n+m) or (n-m) rows at the table.

  If Txn B inserted "m" rows at second step, then after its rollback Txn A now is wrongly looking for rows that do not exist in the database table.

  If Txn B deleted "m" rows at second step, then after its rollback Txn A now is wrongly not looking for "m" rows which are present in the database table.

The read of Txn A is known as "Phantom Read".

Isolation Levels: Now we will look into database isolation levels. The following are the database transaction isolation levels with their effect on undesirable reads; however it is not guaranteed that all available RDBMS software products support all the four isolation levels.

Isolation Level	Dirty Read	Non-repeatable Read	Phantom Read
READ UNCOMMITTED	Permitted	Permitted	Permitted
READ COMMITTED	Not_Permitted	Permitted	Permitted
REPEATABLE READ	Not_Permitted	Not_Permitted	Permitted
SERIALIZABLE	Not_Permitted	Not_Permitted	Not_Permitted

The `isolation` attribute in the `sql:transaction` tag accepts any one of the values: `read_uncommitted`, `read_committed`, `repeatable_read`, and `serializable`.

Example: Inserting and Retrieving Records with Database Table

The following web application inserts *Employee* record with the given values, and lists all the *Employee* records: Illustrates `sql` tags.

Store the following two files "Employee.jsp" and "InsertEmployee.jsp" in web-root of your web application (in our case, /webapps/ROOT).

The "Employee.jsp" is just a user-interface for getting Employee data from the user. It submits the form to "InsertEmployee.jsp" file. In the "InsertEmployee.jsp" file, we used `sql` tag library for database operations. In this example, Oracle is chosen as database, so that necessary JDBC Oracle Driver (which can be downloaded from Internet, file name looks like 'ojdbc14x.jar') should be place in the lib directory (in our case, \webapps\ROOT\WEB-INF\lib). Specify correct JDBC URL and database user-name with password in the `<sql:setDataSource>` tag.

Use the following SQL statement to create a table EMPLOYEE in the underlying database, which is used in our example code.

```
CREATE TABLE EMPLOYEE (
        EMP_NUM        NUMBER(10) NOT NULL,
        EMP_NAME       VARCHAR2(32) NULL,
        BASIC_PAY      NUMBER(10,2) NULL,
        ALLOWANCES     NUMBER(10,2) NULL,
        DEDUCTIONS     NUMBER(10,2) NULL,
        NETPAY         NUMBER(10,2) NULL
)
```

```
<!– Employee.jsp –>
<html>
<head>
  <title>Inserting Employee Data into Database</title>
</head>
<body>
<h2>Enter the Employee Datails</h2>
<form name="form" action="InsertEmployee.jsp" method="post">
<table>
  <tr>
     <td>Employee Number</td>
    <td><input type="text" name="txtEmpNum" size="15"></td>
  </tr>
  <tr>
    <td>Employee Name</td>
    <td><input type="text" name="txtEmpName" size="15"></td>
  </tr>
  <tr>
     <td>Basic Pay</td>
     <td><input type="text" name="txtBasicpay" size="15"></td>
  </tr>
  <tr>
     <td>Allowances</td>
     <td><input type="text" name="txtAllowances" size="15"></td>
```

```
  </tr>
  <tr>
    <td>Deductions</td>
    <td><input type="text" name="txtDeductions" size="15"></td>
  </tr>
  </table>
  <input type="submit" value="SUBMIT">
  <input type="reset" value="RESET">
</form>
</body>
</html>
<!- InsertEmployee.jsp ->
<%@ taglib uri="http://java.sun.com/jsp/jstl/core" prefix="c" %>
<%@ taglib uri="http://java.sun.com/jsp/jstl/fmt" prefix="fmt" %>
<%@ taglib uri="http://java.sun.com/jsp/jstl/sql" prefix="sql"%>
<sql:setDataSource driver="oracle.jdbc.driver.OracleDriver"
                   url="jdbc:oracle:thin:@192.168.1.2:1521:RBTDEV"
                  user="wstar" password="wstar" var="ds" />
<html>
<head>
  <title>Insert and Select Data from Database</title>
</head>
<body>
<sql:update sql="INSERT INTO EMPLOYEE (EMP_NUM, EMP_NAME, BASIC_PAY, ALLOWANCES,
   DEDUCTIONS, NETPAY) VALUES (?, ?, ?, ?, ?, ?)" dataSource="${ds}" var="rowcount">
  <sql:param value="${param.txtEmpNum}" />
  <sql:param value="${param.txtEmpName}" />
  <fmt:formatNumber value="${param.txtBasicpay}" maxFractionDigits="2" var="basicpay"
                                                           groupingUsed="false" />
  <fmt:formatNumber value="${param.txtAllowances}" maxFractionDigits="2"
                   var="allowances" groupingUsed="false" />
  <fmt:formatNumber value="${param.txtDeductions}" maxFractionDigits="2"
                   var="deductions" groupingUsed="false" />
  <fmt:formatNumber value="${basicpay + allowances - deductions}"
                   maxFractionDigits="2" var="netpay" groupingUsed="false" />
  <sql:param value="${basicpay}" />
  <sql:param value="${allowances}" />
  <sql:param value="${deductions}" />
  <sql:param value="${netpay}" />
```

```
</sql:update>
<c:if test="${rowcount > 0}">
   <b>Employee Record inserted successfully.</b>
  <br>
</c:if>
<br>
<sql:query sql="SELECT * FROM EMPLOYEE" dataSource="${ds}" var="employeeRecords" />
<table cellpadding="5" cellspacing="0" border="1">
   <caption>Employee Records</caption>
  <tr>
    <th nowrap>Emp. Number</th>
    <th nowrap>Emp. Name</th>
     <th nowrap>Basic Pay</th>
     <th nowrap>Allowances</th>
    <th nowrap>Deductions</th>
    <th nowrap>Netpay</th>
    </tr>
<c:forEach items="${employeeRecords.rows}" var="row">
     <tr>
 <td><c:out value="${row.EMP_NUM}" /></td>
 <td><c:out value="${row.EMP_NAME}" /></td>
 <td align="right">
            <fmt:formatNumber value="${row.BASIC_PAY}" minFractionDigits="2" />
        </td>
  <td align="right">
            <fmt:formatNumber value="${row.ALLOWANCES}" minFractionDigits="2" />
        </td>
  <td align="right">
            <fmt:formatNumber value="${row.DEDUCTIONS}" minFractionDigits="2" />
        </td>
         <td align="right">
            <fmt:formatNumber value="${row.NETPAY}" minFractionDigits="2" />
        </td>
     </tr>
    </c:forEach>
</table>
</body>
</html>
```

Invoke the "Employee.jsp" in a browser (assumed that Database Server is on, Tomcat is started).

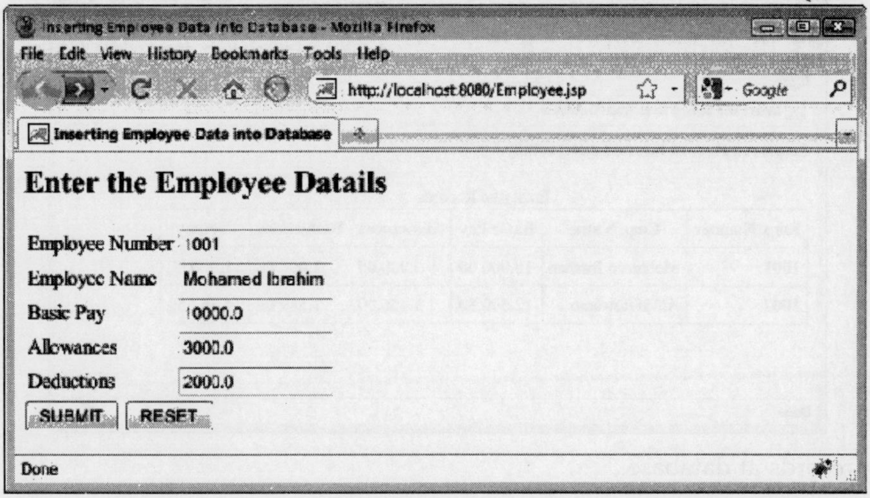

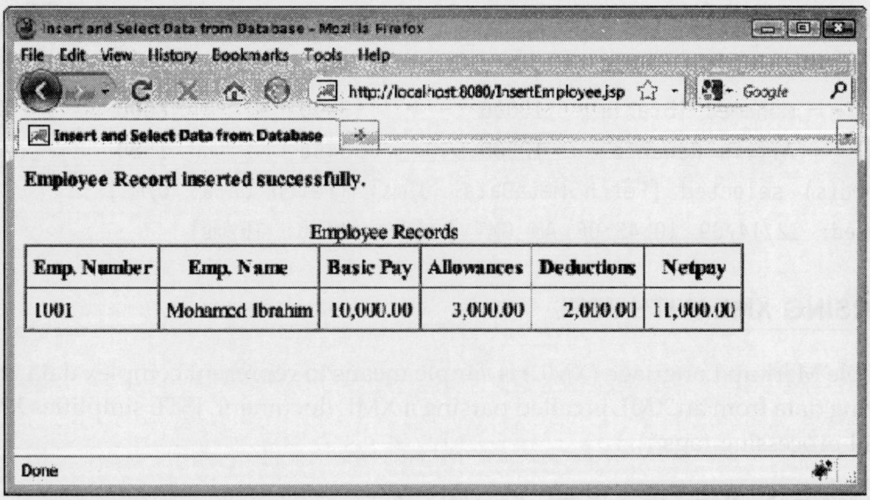

Inserting another record.

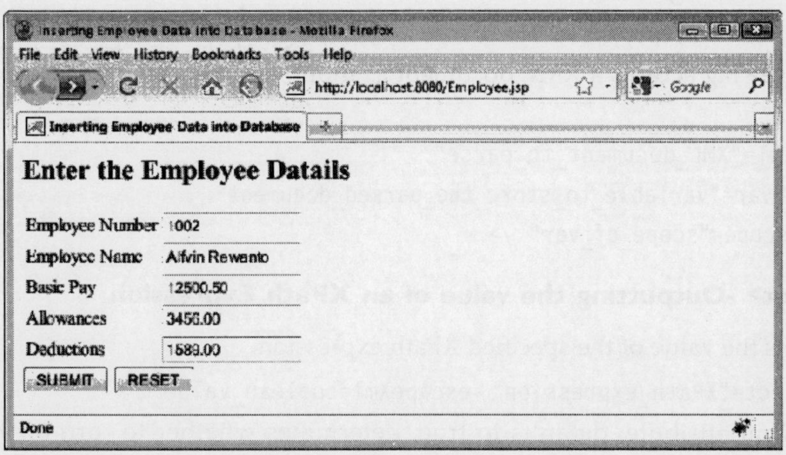

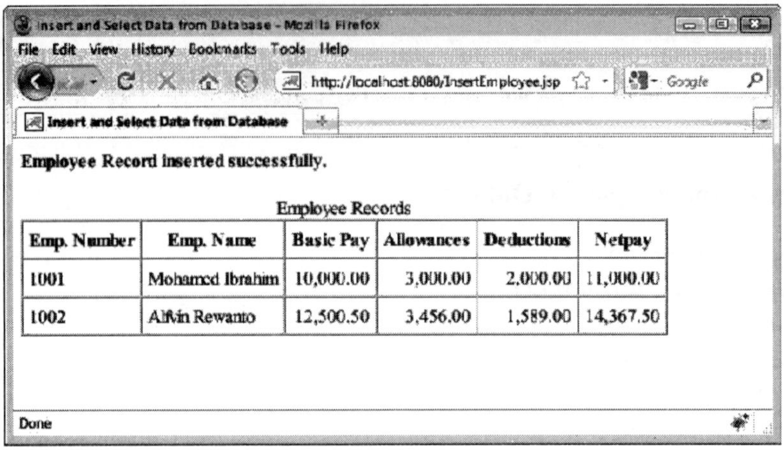

Selecting records at database.

```
SELECT * FROM EMPLOYEE
 EMP_NUM    EMP_NAME          BASIC_PAY    ALLOWANCES   DEDUCTIONS  NETPAY
 - - - - -  - - - - - - - -   - - - - - -  - - - - -    - - - - -   - - - -
 1001       Mohamed Ibrahim   10000        3000         2000        11000
 1002       Alfvin Rewanto    12500.5      3456         1589        14367.5
 2 record(s) selected [Fetch MetaData: 0/ms] [Fetch Data: 0/ms]
 [Executed: 12/14/09 10:45:06 AM GMT ] [Execution: 16/ms]
```

7.10 PARSING XML WITH JSTL

The eXtensible Markup Language (XML) is simple means to represent complex data. Interpreting and Acquiring data from an XML is called parsing a XML document. JSTL simplifies XML Parsing through xml processing tags.

7.10.1 <x:parse> -Parsing a XML document

Include the JSTL xml tag library in the JSP files to use xml related tags.

```
<%@ taglib uri="http://java.sun.com/jsp/jstl/xml" prefix="x" %>
```

This `<x:parse>` tag accepts a XML document as input, and exposes the parsed version of the document.

```
<x:parse xml="XML_document_to_parse"
          var="variable_to_store_the_parsed_document"
         scope="scope_of_var" />
```

7.10.2 <x:out> -Outputting the value of an XPath Expression

This tag outputs the value of the specified XPath expression.

```
<x:out select="XPath_expression" escapeXml=boolean_value />
```

The escapeXml attribute, defaults to true, determines whether to turn-off HTML Special characters or not. If the result contains HTML specific special characters (<, >, ", ', &), then the characters will be converted into HTML entity references (`<` , `>` , `"` , `'` , `&`) if escapeXml is set to true.

XPath:

// (double back slash) refers to any descendents of an element in XML document.

@ (at symbol) refers attributes of an element in XML document.

7.10.3 <x:set> -Storing the value of an XPath expression into a variable

This is similar to <x:out> tag in functionality, but it stores the result into a specified variable instead of outputting.

```
<x:set  select="XPath_expression"
         var="variable_to_store_the_result"
        scope="scope_of_var" />
```

7.10.4 <x:if> -Conditional Construct

If the specified XPath_expression becomes true, then the body will be executed.

```
<x:if  select="XPath_expression">
    body_statements
</x:if>
```

7.10.5 <x:choose> -Multi-branch Conditional Construct

This is a multi-branch conditional construct, an alternate to the use of multiple <x:if> tags.

```
<x:choose>
    <x:when  select="XPath_expression">  statements  <x:when>
    <x:when  select="XPath_expression">  statements  <x:when>
    <x:when  select="XPath_expression">  statements  <x:when>
    ...
    ...
    ...
    <x:otherwise>  statements  </x:otherwise>
</x:choose>
```

Based on the condition (XPath_expression) specified in the <x:when> tag, the corresponding statements block will be executed. If no XPath_expression returns true, then the <x:otherwise> block will be executed.

7.10.6 <x:forEach> -Looping Construct

This tag is used to iterate values.

```
<x:forEach  select="XPath_expression"
                       var="variable_to_expose_current_node">
  loop_body
</x:forEach>
```

The result of the XPath_expression is going to be iterated; for each node in the result, the loop body will be executed.

Example:

The following example, which uses almost all the above explained concept of parsing XML document by JSTL.

Store the following two files (Employee.xml, AccessEmployee.jsp) in the web-root of your web application (in our case, /webapps/ROOT).

```
<?xml version="1.0" encoding="UTF-8"?>
<company>
        <employee>
                <empnumber>1001</empnumber>
                <empname sex="M">Mohamed Ibrahim</empname>
                <salary>10000.0</salary>
                <doj>
                     <day>01</day>
                     <month>06</month>
                     <year>2001</year>
                </doj>
        </employee>
        <employee>
                <empnumber>1002</empnumber>
                <empname sex="M">John Peter</empname>
                <salary>12000.0</salary>
                <doj>
                      <day>15</day>
                      <month>06</month>
                      <year>2001</year>
                </doj>
        </employee>
        <employee>
               <empnumber>1003</empnumber>
               <empname sex="F">Sopna</empname>
               <salary>6000.0</salary>
               <doj>
                     <day>01</day>
                     <month>10</month>
                     <year>2007</year>
               </doj>
        </employee>
```

```
    <employee>
        <empnumber>1004</empnumber>
        <empname sex="M">Suresh</empname>
        <salary>4000.0</salary>
        <doj>
            <day>22</day>
            <month>01</month>
            <year>2009</year>
        </doj>
    </employee>
    <employee>
        <empnumber>1005</empnumber>
        <empname sex="F">Geetha</empname>
        <salary>16000.0</salary>
        <doj>
            <day>01</day>
            <month>02</month>
            <year>1995</year>
        </doj>
    </employee>
</company>
<!- AccessEmployee.jsp ->
<%@ taglib uri="http://java.sun.com/jsp/jstl/core" prefix="c" %>
<%@ taglib uri="http://java.sun.com/jsp/jstl/xml" prefix="x" %>
<c:import var="EmployeeXML" url="Employee.xml" />
<x:parse xml="${EmployeeXML}" var="employeeDoc" />
<html>
<head>
 <title>Parsing XML with JSTL </title>
</head>
<body>
   <table cellpadding="5" cellspacing="0">
   <caption><big><u>Parsing XML with JSTL</u></big></caption>
    <tr>
      <td nowrap valign="top">
         <c:out value='<x:out select="$employeeDoc" />' />
      </td>
      <td>
        <x:out select="$employeeDoc" />
```

```
      </td>
    </tr>
    <tr>
       <td nowrap valign="top">
          <c:out value='<x:out select="$employeeDoc/company/employee/salary" />' />
      </td>
      <td>
         <x:out select="$employeeDoc/company/employee/salary" />
      </td>
    </tr>
   <tr>
       <td nowrap valign="top">
          <c:out value='<x:out select="$employeeDoc//salary" />' />
      </td>
      <td>
        <x:out select="$employeeDoc//salary" />
      </td>
    </tr>
   <tr>
       <td nowrap valign="top">
         <c:out value='<x:set> Tag' />
      </td>
      <td>
         <x:set select="$employeeDoc//salary" var="empSalary" />
        <x:out select="$empSalary" />
      </td>
    </tr>
    <tr>
       <td nowrap valign="top">
          <c:out value='<x:out select="$employeeDoc//empname/@sex" />' />
      </td>
      <td>
         <x:out select="$employeeDoc//empname/@sex" />
      </td>
    </tr>
    <tr>
       <td nowrap valign="top">
         <c:out value='<x:out
                 select="$employeeDoc/company/employee/empname[@sex = \'F\']" />' />
```

```
    </td>
    <td>
       <x:out select="$employeeDoc/company/employee/empname[@sex = 'F']" />
    </td>
  </tr>
 <tr>
    <td nowrap valign="top">
       <c:out value='Selecting Particular Record using Index. Index starts with 1' />
    </td>
    <td>
       <x:out select="$employeeDoc/company/employee[3]/empname" />
    </td>
  </tr>
  <tr>
    <td nowrap valign="top">
       <c:out value='<x:if>, <x:choose>, <x:forEach> Tags' />
    </td>
    <td>
       <x:forEach var="node" select="$employeeDoc//employee" >
<table cellpadding="2" cellspacing="0">
 <tr>
   <td>Emp. Number</td>
   <td><x:out select="$node/empnumber" /></td>
 </tr>
 <tr>
   <td>Emp. Name</td>
   <td><x:out select="$node/empname" /></td>
 </tr>
 <tr>
   <td>Sex</td>
   <td>
    <x:if select="$node/empname/@sex = 'M'" >
     Male
    </x:if>
    <x:if select="$node/empname/@sex = 'F'" >
     Female
    </x:if>
   </td>
 </tr>
```

```
<tr>
  <td>Salary</td>
  <td><x:out select="$node/salary" /></td>
</tr>
    <tr>
  <td>DOJ</td>
  <td><x:out select="$node/doj/day" />
      -<x:out select="$node/doj/month" />
      -<x:out select="$node/doj/year" /></td>
</tr>
<tr>
  <td>Grade</td>
    <td>
         <x:choose>
           <x:when select="$node/doj/year <= 2000"> Grade A </x:when>
           <x:when select="$node/doj/year <= 2005"> Grade B </x:when>
           <x:when select="$node/doj/year <= 2008"> Grade C </x:when>
           <x:otherwise> Junior Employee </x:otherwise>
         </x:choose>
    </td>
    </tr>
     <tr><td height="10"></td></tr>
    </table>
   </x:forEach>
  </td>
</tr>
</table>
</body>
</html>
```

Start the Tomcat Server and open the AccessEmployee.jsp file in a browser.

Parsing XML with JSTL		
<x:out select="$employeeDoc" />	1001 Mohamed Ibrahim 10000.0 01 06 2001 1002 John Peter 12000.0 15 06 2001 1003 Sopna 6000.0 01 10 2007 1004 Suresh 4000.0 22 01 2009 1005 Geetha 16000.0 01 02 1995	
<x:out select="$employeeDoc/company/employee/salary" />	10000.0	
<x:out select="$employeeDoc//salary" />	10000.0	
<x:set> Tag	10000.0	
<x:out select="$employeeDoc//empname/@sex" />	M	
<x:out select="$employeeDoc/company/employee/empname[@sex = 'F']" />	Sopna	
Selecting Particular Record using Index. Index starts with 1	Sopna	
<x:if>, <x:choose>, <x:forEach> Tags	Emp. Number	1001
	Emp. Name	Mohamed Ibrahim
	Sex	Male
	Salary	10000.0
	DOJ	01-06-2001
	Grade	Grade B
	Emp. Number	1002
	Emp. Name	John Peter
	Sex	Male
	Salary	12000.0
	DOJ	15-06-2001
	Grade	Grade B
	Emp. Number	1003
	Emp. Name	Sopna
	Sex	Female
	Salary	6000.0
	DOJ	01-10-2007
	Grade	Grade C
	Emp. Number	1004
	Emp. Name	Suresh
	Sex	Male
	Salary	4000.0
	DOJ	22-01-2009
	Grade	Junior Employee
	Emp. Number	1005
	Emp. Name	Geetha
	Sex	Female
	Salary	16000.0
	DOJ	01-02-1995
	Grade	Grade A

SUMMARY

JSTL provides sophisticated custom tags, which simplifies JSP code. JSTL is available in a separate jar file, and can be downloaded for free of cost. JSTL basically offers tags for scripting functionalities, formatting data, processing XML documents and performing database operations. JSTL implicit objects are used to interpret data, particularly for accessing scoped objects, accessing request parameters, accessing cookies, and accessing context information. The conditional constructs and looping tags eliminates the complexities of using Java code in JSP for condition-based operations.

This chapter started explaining the uses of formatting tags especially to format numbers and date. Internalization (i18n) concepts are outlined and locale specific settings are outlined. An example is given to illustrate how to use message bundles. We can use Unicode characters with locale setting for messages with locale specific languages such as Spanish, Arabic, and Hindi.

JSTL provides adequate tags to do database manipulation such as creation of tables, insertion, deletion, updation of records. It provides support for positional parameter substitution. JSTL also supports database transactions mechanisms for accessing critical data on transactions.

XML provides a flexible means for representing structured data. Since the XML format is just simple text, it is well suited for exchanging data particularly between loosely coupled systems and it is possible that all applications can understand and parse XML contents. The XPath is used to navigate through elements and attributes in an XML document. This chapter explains briefly the JSTL support for parsing and manipulating XML data.

8

Service Oriented Architecture and Web Services

8.0 INTRODUCTION

To integrate the required applications in the enterprises, Enterprise Application Integration (EAI), several technologies are applied; among them, the popular one is Service Oriented Architecture (SOA). In other words, SOA is used for developing loosely coupled distributed applications. Loosely coupled applications are a group of applications (to form EAI) which can operate independent of each other. Earlier SOA was achieved by using many architectures including DCOM (Distributed Component Object Model), ORB (Object Request Broker), and RMI (Remote Method Invocation). However, these architectures work on their own defined protocols and the applications using different architectures can not be able to communicate each other. Currently SOA works based on Web Services, which uses common Internet protocols. This chapter briefly explains the architecture of SOA with Web Services with an example using WTP (Web Tool Platform) available with Eclipse IDE.

8.1 SERVICE ORIENTED ARCHITECTURE (SOA) AND WEB SERVICES

A service is a self-contained software component (subroutine) that performs a specific task. A Service Oriented Architecture is essentially a collection of services; these services communicate with each other and each service does not depend on the context of any other services.

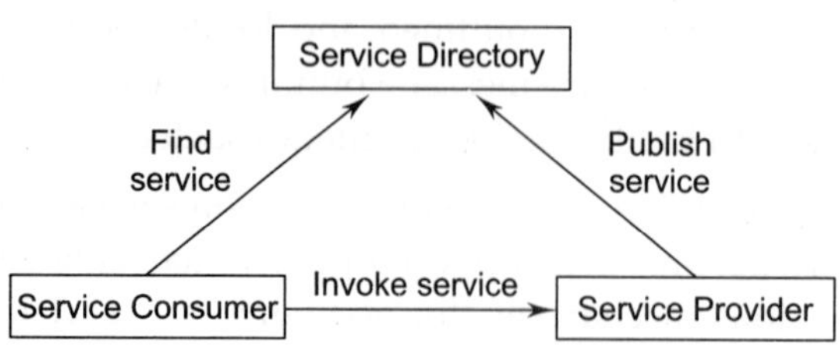

Sevice Oriented Architecture

Earlier CORBA object request brokers were preferred choice, which works based on SOA. Currently, Web services are widely used due to its simplicity and works on Internet protocols.

A Web Service is an application functionality service that can be accessed by any application via standard Internet Protocols such as HTTP.

In a simple term, any procedures (methods in Java) in a web application can be accessed by any other application, which is developed on any programming tool and running on any platform, via web. Web Services are using XML as data exchange format, and the XML format is supported by all modern programming languages. Here, the word "service" refers the endpoint of a connection of web applications (programming functionality).

8.2 COMPONENTS OF WEB SERVICES

The following are few important components that are related to Web Services.

XML (eXtensible Mark-up Language) [Tag the data]: In Web Service, request and response data will be exchanged between applications in this XML format.

WSDL (Web Services description Language) [Describe the service]: It is used to describe a web service, and it used XML format to describe.

SOAP (Simple Object Access Protocol) [Transfer the data]: It is XML based protocol, which is used to define requests / responses for a Web Service (mandatory, optional, minimum / maximum occurrences of elements for defining data in requests / responses). HTTP (Hyper-Text Transport Protocol) is used to deliver web service requests and responses.

UDDI (Universal Description, Discovery and Integration) [listing of available services]: It is a server, which acts as web service directory; web services can be registered and discovered on this server.

8.3 WEB SERVICE EXAMPLE: ARITHMETIC OPERATIONS ON NUMBERS

We are going to develop web service for Arithmetic Operations using Eclipse WTP Bottom-Up Approach. Four Java methods `add()`, `subtract()`, `multiply()`, and `divide()` that are to be serviced as web-methods and will be called by any application over the web via web-service.

Top-Down vs Bottom-Up Web Service

Web services can be created in two methods: Top-Down Approach and Bottom-Up Approach. In Top-Down approach, create the WSDL file and then generate Java skeletons (preferably using tools). In Bottom-Up approach, create the Java Beans / EJBs and then generate WSDL (possibly using tools / IDE). The Bottom-Up approach is fast and easy since the WSDL file is generated automatically during the build.

Thus, Top-Down development starts from requirements and ends with implementation, however Bottom-Up is a reverse engineering process that starts from available components.

Web Tool Platform (WTP)

Web Tool Platform (WTP) is an Eclipse platform extension, which is in-built into all latest Eclipse IDEs. It provides wizards and automatic code generation for developing Web and Java EE applications. Latest WTP can be downloaded from http://www.eclipse.org/webtools/.

In our example, Eclipse JEE Galileo SR1 (can be downloaded from http://www.eclipse.org/) is used with in-built WTA.

Configuring Application Server

Since Web Service example is a web application, a web / application server is needed to deploy the application. I chose Apache Tomcat as the application server. Download the latest version of Tomcat form its official site: http://tomcat.apache.org/. I am using Tomcat version 6.0.24 in our demo. Unzip the downloaded Tomcat zip file, if downloaded in .zip format, and extract into any folder, say C:/Development/apache-tomcat-6.0.24. The readers are also encouraged to use any Servlet container (Application server) of their choice.

Setting up Server Runtime in Eclipse

Invoke Eclipse IDE.

Choose Window → Preferences → Server → Runtime Environment

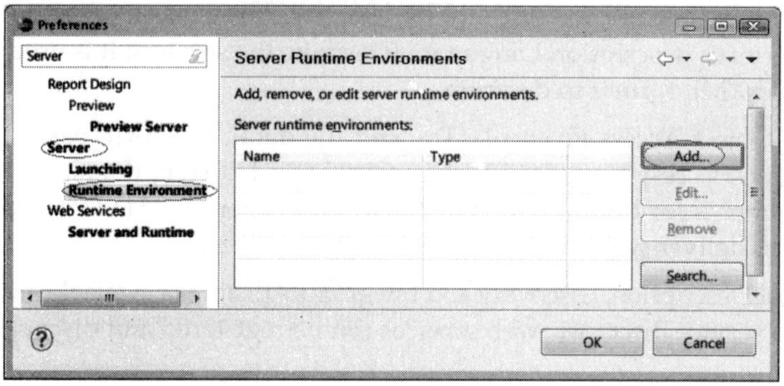

Click on "Add..." button. Choose "Apache Tomcat v6.0". Click "Next".

Select the Home directory of Tomcat for 'Tomcat installation directory' text box. Click "Finish".

Then, click on "OK" on the main window.

Setting up Axis2 Runtime

Apache Axis2 is an open-source, which serves as Web Services / SOAP / WSDL engine. The latest version of Axis2 can be downloaded from http://ws.apache.org/axis2. I am using Axis2 version 1.4.1 and extracted the downloaded Axis2 .zip file into C:\Development\axis2-1.4.1 directory.

In Eclipse IDE, choose Java EE Perspective (Window → Open Perspective → Other .. → Java EE). Then, choose Window → Preferences → Web Services → Axis2 Preferences → Choose Axis2 Home directory for 'Axis2 runtime location' text box. Note that the message 'Azis2 runtime loaded successfully' is displayed on the window.

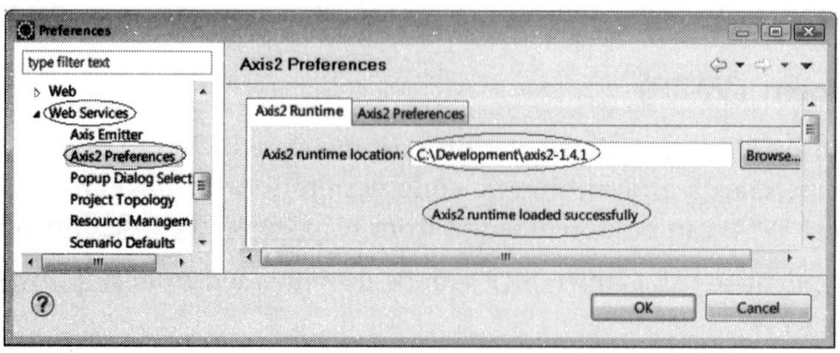

Choose "Server and Runtime" under "Web Services", and then choose "Tomcat v6.0 Server" as Server and "Apache Axis2" as Web service runtime.

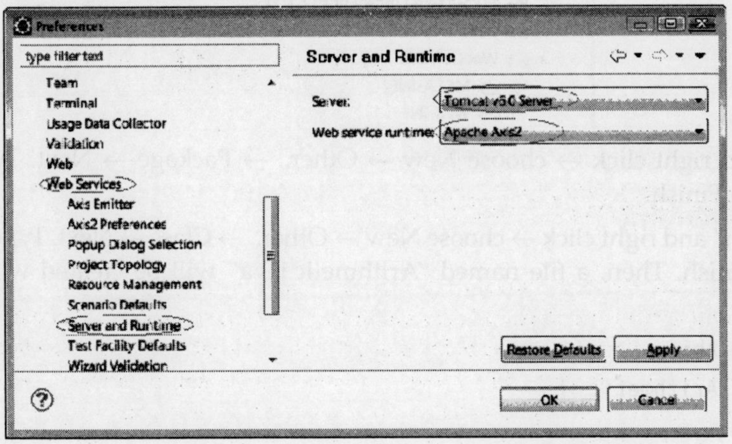

Click on "OK".

Create a Dynamic Web Project

In Eclipse IDE, choose File → New → Other… → Web → Dynamic Web Project.

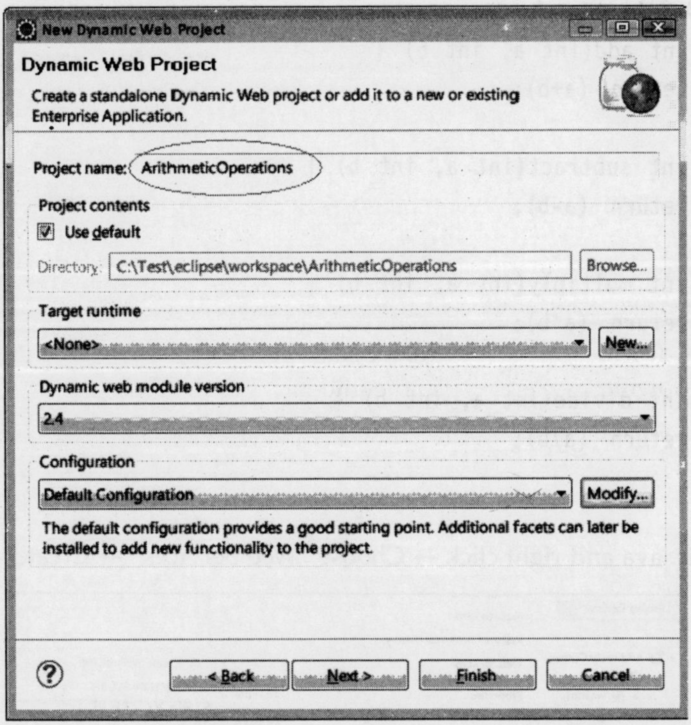

Specify Project name: *ArithmeticOperations*. Accept all other defaults and click on "Finish".

The created project at Package Explorer view is as below.

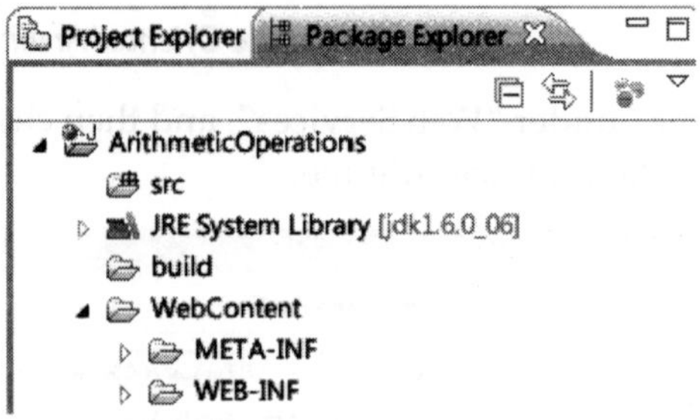

Select 'src' and right click → choose New → Other.. → Package → Next. Type "wsarith" as package-name → Finish.

Select "wsarith" and right click → choose New → Other.. → Class → Next. Type "Arithmetic" as class-name → Finish. Then, a file named "Arithmetic.java" will be created with the following content.

```
package wsarith;
public class Arithmetic {
}
```

Put your logic in this file. In our demo, we are manipulating simple data type, however you can use complex data types such as objects also.

Now, the Arithmetic.java file contains code as below.

```
package wsarith;
public class Arithmetic {
        public int add(int a, int b) {
                return (a+b);
        }
        public int subtract(int a, int b) {
                return (a-b);
        }
        public int multiply(int a, int b) {
                return (a*b);
        }
        public int divide(int a, int b) {
                return (a/b);
        }
}
```

Select Arithmetic.java and right click → Choose "Web Services" → Create Web Service.

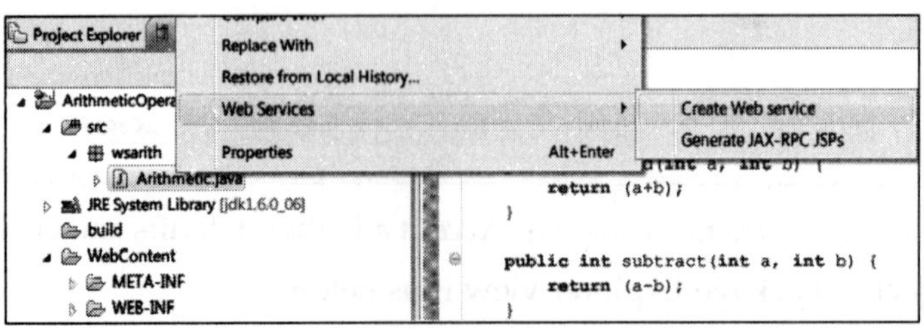

A window with title "Web Service" will be opened. Make sure that web service type is "Bottom Up" and Scroll bar at 'Start service' stage. And also ensure that Web service runtime is "Apache Axis2", if not set, click the hyperlink to change the runtime.

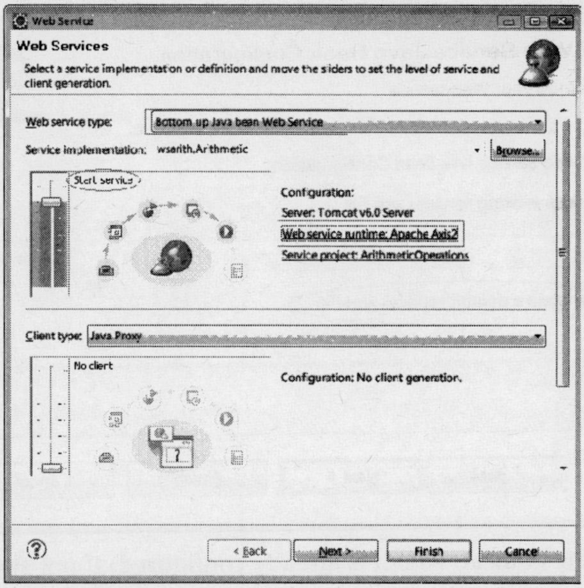

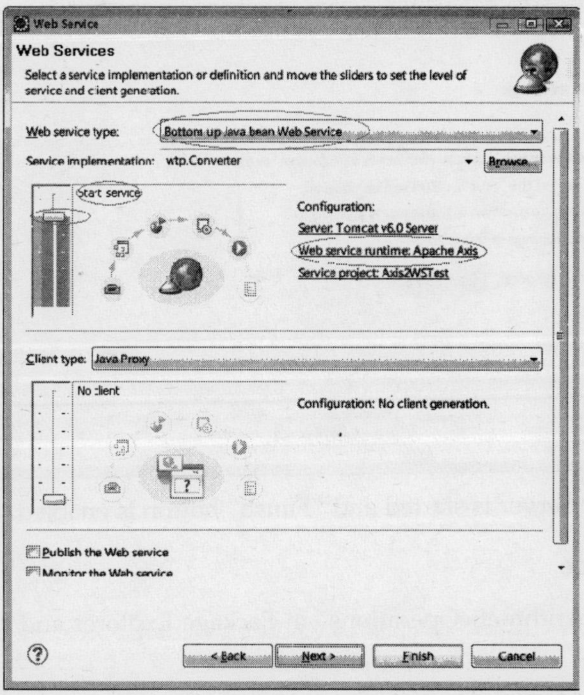

Click on "Next". Specify if you are using won services.xml file. In this demo, accept the default setting and let Eclipse generate a default services.xml file.

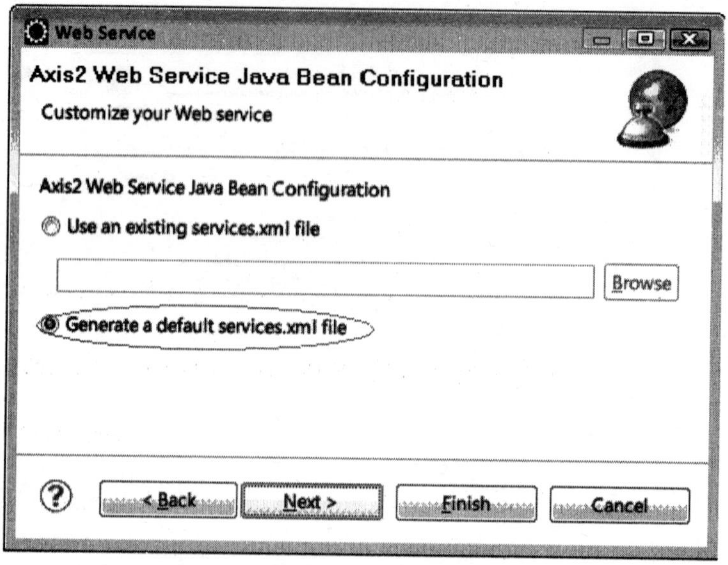

Start the server (Apache Tomcat, which is already configured) if not started.

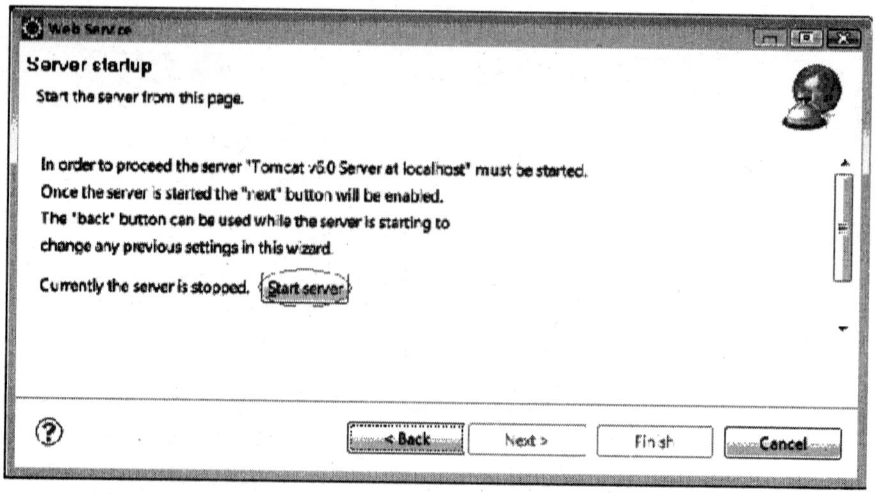

Click on "Finish" after Server is started and "Finish" button is enabled.

Executing Web Service

Select the project name "ArithmeticOperations" in Package Explorer and right click and choose Run As → Run on Server.

Eclipse will prompt for server. The already created runtime (Tomcat) will be selected. Accept the default and click on "Next".

Make sure that our web project "ArithmeticOperations is added in "Configured" list box (right-hand side) and click on "Finish".

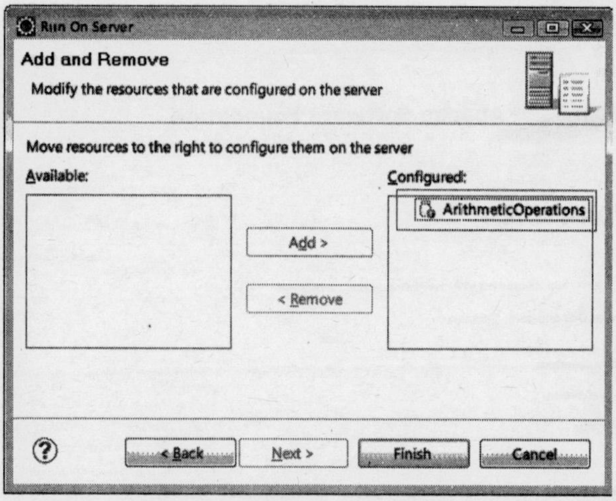

Then, the default web page will be opened with default browser of Eclipse.

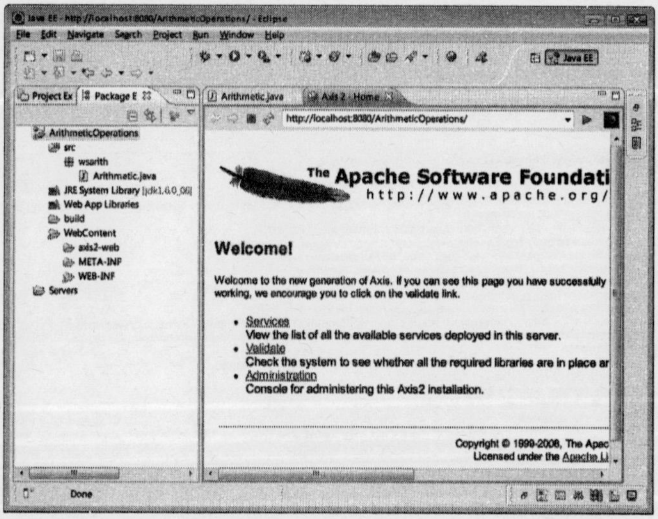

This is the default page specified in the generated web.xml file. You can invoke this page with any browser as shown below .

(URL: http://localhost:8080/ArithmeticOperations/axis2-web/index.jsp)

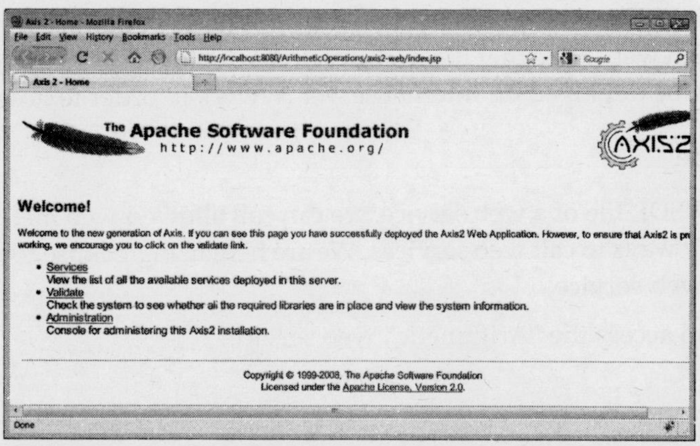

Click on the link "Services".

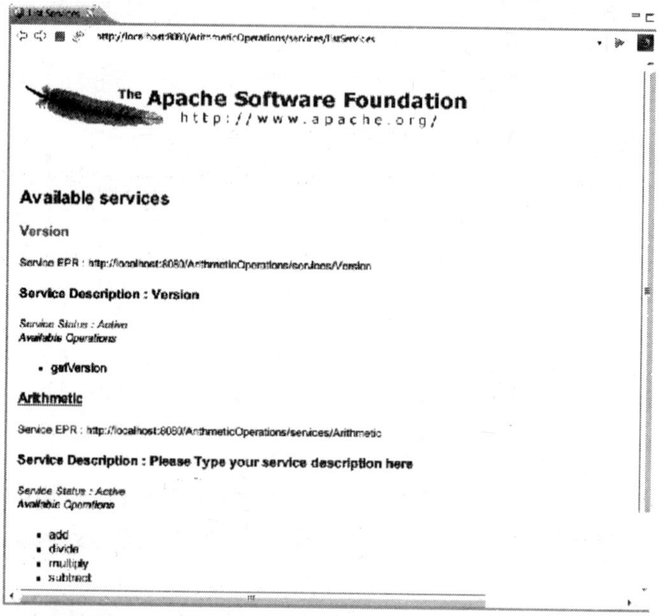

Click on the link "Arithmetic" to get the WSDL.

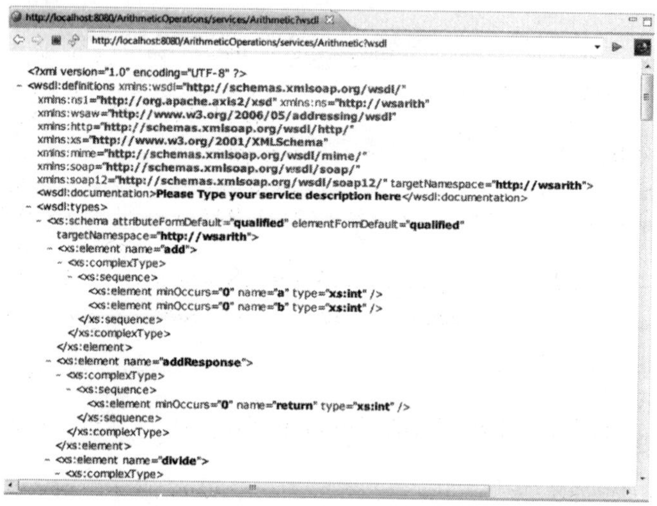

Any one can use this WSDL file and call the web methods (add(), subtract(), multiply(), divide()) from any where through web. Note that this web service is deployed in local server (localhost) for demo purpose; should be deployed on Internet server (www), in order to access world wide.

Calling Web Service

Once we have given WSDL file of a web service, we can call allowed web methods defined in the WSDL. There are many ways to call web services. We are here using Eclipse tools to call the above created "Arithmetic" web service.

Let the server run to access the "Arithmetic" web service.

Create a Dynamic web Project.

File → New → Other → Java Project.

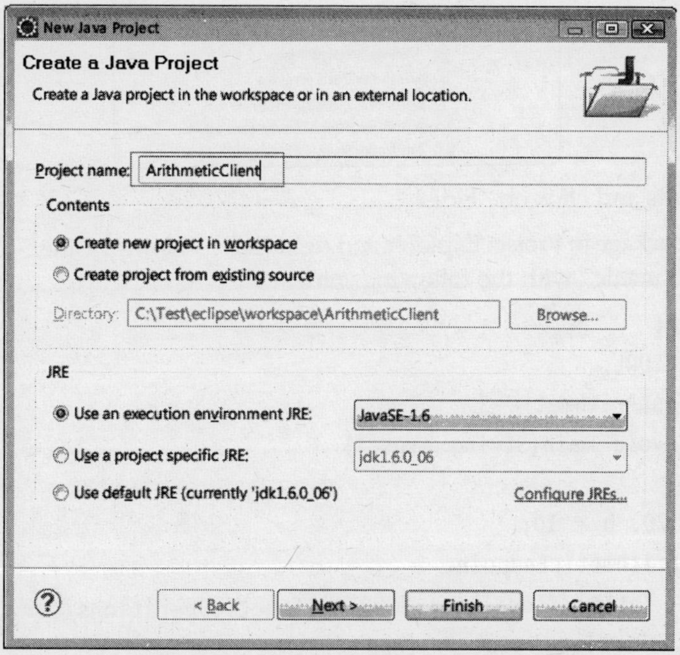

Specify "ArithmeticClient" as Project name and click on "Finish".

Select "ArithmeticClient" in Package Explorer and right click → choose New → Other → Web Service Client. Specify the WSDL file of web service as Service definition.

In our case, it is http://localhost:8080/ArithmeticOperations/services/Arithmetic?wsdl

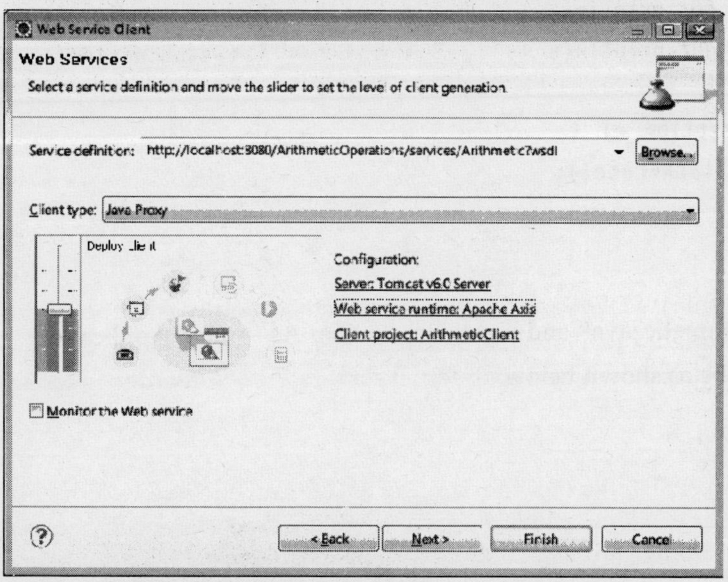

Click on "Finish". Then, web service bindings for client side will be automatically generated. A look at Project Explorer is as below.

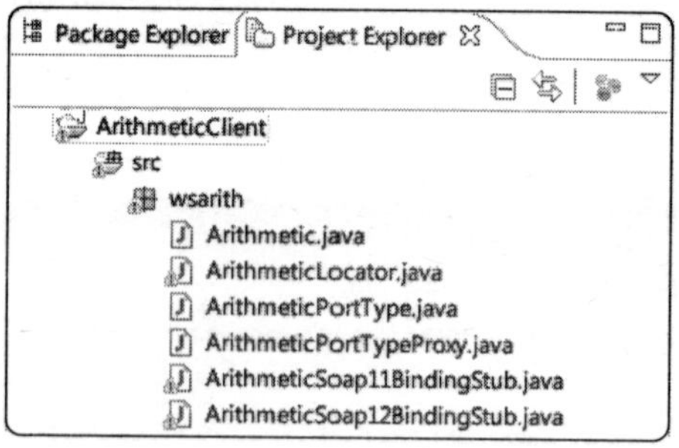

Accept the defaults and click on "Finish".

Select "wsarith" package in Project Explorer and right click → New → Other → Class. Create a class with name "TestArithmetic" with the following content.

```
package wsarith;
import java.net.URL;
public class TestArithmetic {
 public static void main(String args[]) {
  try {
      int a = 20, b = 10;
      String arithmeticEndpoint =
              "http://localhost:8080/ArithmeticOperations/services/Arithmetic";
      ArithmeticPortType stub = (new ArithmeticLocator())
                  .getArithmeticHttpSoap12Endpoint(new URL(arithmeticEndpoint));
      int c = stub.add(a, b);
      System.out.println(a + " + " + b + " = " + c);
      System.out.println(a + " - " + b + " = " + stub.subtract(a, b));
      System.out.println(a + " * " + b + " = " + stub.multiply(a, b));
      System.out.println(a + " / " + b + " = " + stub.divide(a, b));
}
   catch (Exception e) {
     e.printStackTrace();
  }
 }
}
```

Select "TestArithmetic.java" and right click → Run As → Java Application.

The result will be as shown below.

```
20 + 10 = 30
20 - 10 = 10
20 * 10 = 200
20 / 10 = 2
```

SUMMARY

The Service Oriented Architecture makes easy the Enterprise Application Integration. This chapter started with the architecture of SOA and its importance. Further, it explained how Web Services became as developer's choice as SOA implementation. An example Web Service creation and its client call are given for illustration.

9

Message Oriented Middleware and Java Messaging Service (JMS)

9.0 INTRODUCTION

The Java Messaging Service is one of he Message Oriented Middleware implementation, supporting asynchronous communication between client and server in a Client-Server application. This chapter introduces the importance and working principle of Message Oriented Middleware with Java Messaging Service examples.

9.1 MESSAGE ORIENTED MIDDLEWARE (MOM)

The Message Oriented Middleware (MOM) is for message oriented communications on client/server applications typically in asynchronous mode. The messages carry data and MOM uses store-and-forward mechanism for messages in which they are sent to queues and held for the recipient application to pick up.

In synchronous interaction (on client-server application), both caller and receiver application should be 'on-line'. The synchronous communication works as: (i) the caller request, (ii) the receiver receives the request, (iii) the receiver processes the request, (iv) the receiver sends the response, and (v) the caller receives the response. Note that his communication should be performed with in the pre-defined session timeout. Also, the caller application has to wait to proceed further until it receives response for its request.

In asynchronous interaction (on client-server application), both caller and receiver applications are no need to be 'on-line'. The asynchronous communication works as: (i) the caller sends a message (request), (ii) the message (request) is stored on he message queue, (iii) the receiver picks up the message (request), (iv) the receiver process the message (request), (v) the receiver sends response as a message (response), (vi) the response message is stored on the message queue, and (vii) the caller picks up the response message. Note that his communication is also works on offline and not based on session timeout. The caller is no need to wait for response of its request.

9.2 JAVA MESSAGING SERVICE (JMS)

The Java Messaging Service (JMS) is a Java API for accessing enterprise messaging systems. JMS implements MOM concept. The latest specification is JMS 1.1. JMS actually defines Java classes and interfaces, through which Java applications can use message service. A JMS implementation (which follows JMS specification and in simple terms, the code implementation for JMS classes and interfaces) is known as "JMS Provider". For example, Apache Active MQ is a (also open-source) JMS provider. The following are other JMS related key words.

- JMS Message: Message carrying data between JMS Clients.
- JMS Producer: An application that creates and sends the JMS messages.
- JMS Consumer: An application that receives and processes the JMS messages.
- JMS Client: Java application to send and receive the JMS messages.

9.3 JMS MESSAGE DELIVERY MODES (JMS DOMAINS)

JMS supports the following two message delivery modes. They decide how to deliver messages from message producer to message consumer.

9.3.1 Point-to-Point (PTP – One to One Mechanism)

In this model, the messages are sent to and received from a destination called "Queue". Each message from the message producer will be delivered to only one consumer (once-and-only-once), and the message delivery is guaranteed.

9.3.2 Publish/Subscribe (pub/sub – One to Many Mechanism)

In this model, the messages are sent to and received from a destination called "Topic". The Message producers (called as Publishers) send messages to the topic, and the Message consumers (called as Subscribers) register with topic to receive messages from the topic. A message may be delivered to zero, one, or more subscribers (at-most-once), and the message delivery is not guaranteed but the message will not be delivered more than one time to a single subscriber. The message deliver is not guaranteed due to the subscribers are not on-line and the message may be lost during the time; however JMS allows us to configure his message durable setting.

Message Durability: The Message Subscriber (receiver) may establish 'Durable Subscription' with the topic, and then JMS Provider will preserve all messages for the subscriber when the subscriber is inactive (offline) and will deliver all the preserved messages when the subscriber became active (online). With 'Non-Durable Subscription', the JMS provider will not preserve any messages (that should be sent to the subscriber) when the subscriber is inactive, thus the subscriber will lose all the messages during it offline time.

9.4 JMS MESSAGE STRUCTURE

A JMS Message consists of (*i*) Message Header, (*ii*) Message Properties, and (*iii*) Message Payload (Message Body)

9.4.1 Message Header

Every JMS Message must have a message header and most of the values for the header are set by the JMS Provider, and there are some properties that can be set by JMS clients (applications). Some of the header properties are given below.

`JMSXUserID`	:	Identifies the user who is sending the message.
JMSDestination	:	The destination of the message.
JMSDeliveryMode	:	Defines message delivery mode: persistent or non-persistent. Default is persistent.
JMSExpiration	:	Specifies expiration time of the message. It is calculated by JMS Provider as current time plus specified `timeToLive` value. If its value is zero, then the message will not be expired, and it defaults to zero.
JMSPriority	:	It defines priority of the message for delivery; from level 0 to 9 where 0 is lowest and 9 is highest.
JMSTimeStamp	:	Specifies the time that the message was sent to JMS Provider by Message Producer client.
JMSMessageID	:	String value prefixed with '`ID:`' assigned by JMS Provider to uniquely identify the message.
JMSRedelivered	:	This property is used by JMS Provider, to ackle some situations like: JMS Provider sends a message to a JMC consumer, but not received reply.
JMSCorrelationID	:	Used to relate messages. For example, JMS Client "A" sends a request to JMS Client "B" as a message with Message ID '`ID: 123`'. The JMS Client "B" sends the response to JMS Client "A" as a message with Correlation ID as '`ID: 123`' *i.e.*, Message ID of its request. Through which, the sender can easily understand which response message is for which request message.
JMSReplyTo	:	Specifies the destination where (which Queue/Topic) the reply (if you want) is to be delivered. It defaults to null.
JMSType	:	Type of Message (such as text, Bytes, Map, Stream)

The properties JMSCorrelationID, JMSReplyTo, and JMSType can be set by JMS client applications.

9.4.2 Message Properties

These Message properties specify additional information to the JMS message with header info. These properties may differ to JMS Providers (such as ActiveMQ, JBossMQ, OpenJMS, and JORAM). However, few standard properties are given below for reference.

`JMSXUserID`	:	Identifies the user who is sending the message.
`JMSXAppID`	:	Identifies the application which is sending the message.
`JMSXDeliveryCount`	:	Defines the number of times the message delivery had been attempted in order to deliver the message.

9.4.3 Message Payload (Message Body)

This Message Body contains the actual data that are to be exchanged. JMS Providers supports the following types of data.

`Message`	:	Message without message body.
`TextMessage`	:	Message whose message body contains text (String data type) data. Used to transfer Alert text, XML text ...
`BytesMessage`	:	Message whose message body contains sequence of bytes.
`StreamMessage`	:	Message whose message body contains stream of primitive data (data of Java primitive data types such as Integer, Double, ... including String).
`MapMessage`	:	Message whose message body contains a set of name-value pairs (Map) data.
`ObjectMessage`	:	Message whose message body contains an object (The object of the Java Class should be Serialized).

9.5 APACHE ACTIVEMQ

ActiveMQ is an open source product from Apache Software Foundation, provides full support for JMS and it a complete JMS provider.

Download the latest release of ActiveMQ from its official web site (http://activemq.apache.org/download.html). I downloaded ActiveMQ 5.3.0 Release in .zip format (MS Windows platform). Extract the .zip file (apache-activemq-5.3.0-bin.zip) and it results in creation of apache-activemq-5.3.0 directory.

9.5.1 Setting ActiveMQ

Take a look at the ActiveMQ home directory. The "`bin`" directory contains start-up scripts. The "`conf`" directory contains all configuration details. The "`data`" directory contains the log files and Message Persistence data (default for `kahadb`). The "`webapps`" directory contains ActiveMQ web console. The "`lib`" directory contains all the library files that are needed for ActiveMQ, any additional lib files (such as JDBC Connector) can be included in "`optional`" directory under this "`lib`" directory (`lib/optional`). The jar file (activemq-all-5.3.0.jar) in the home directory should be included in CLASSPATH environment so that JMS Client applications (Java applications which uses JMS features) can use ActiveMQ, and this jar file is the code implementation of JMS for ActiveMQ JMS Provider.

The "conf" directory contains many XML files, carrying default configurations and we can alter them whenever required. The parent file is "activemq.xml".

Open activemq.xml file and change the Broker Name to any meaningful name, from the default string "`localhost`". You can keep the default string also, and it is not necessary to change the name.

```
<broker xmlns="http://activemq.apache.org/schema/core"
        brokerName="localhost" dataDirectory="${activemq.base}/data">
```

Do the following configuration, if you want use Message Persistence. Here, the configuration is set to use MySQL database for message persistence. However, it is also allowed to use other

RDBMS, change the database connection parameters and add the JDBC Connector jar file according to the chosen database. (Assumed that MySQL is installed and the 'root' user password is 'ibrahim')

Login as 'root':

```
C:\Users\Ibrahim> mysql -u root -pibrahim
Welcome o he MySQL monitor. Commands end with ; or \g.
Your MySQL connection id is 1
Server version: 5.1.32-community MySQL Community Server (GPL)
Type 'help;' or '\h' for help. type '\c' to clear the buffer.
mysql> create database activemq;
Query OK, 1 row affected (0.06 sec)
mysql> grant all privileges on activemq.* to activemquser@localhost
    -> identified by 'activemqpword';
Query OK, 0 rows affected (0.13 sec)
mysql> exit
Bye
```

Login as 'activemquser':

```
C:\Users\Ibrahim> mysql -u activemquser -pactivemqpword activemq
Welcome to the MySQL monitor. Commands end with ; or \g.
Your MySQL connection id is 2
Server version: 5.1.32-community MySQL Community Server (GPL)
Type 'help;' or '\h' for help. type '\c' to clear the buffer.
mysql> show ables;
Empty set (0.06 sec)
```

Configuring ActiveMQ:

Open activemq.xml file, and configure as shown below.

Change the default persistence data store from 'derby' to 'mysql'

```
<persistenceAdapter>
  <jdbcPersistenceAdapter dataDirectory="${activemq.base}/data"
                          dataSource="#mysql-ds"/>
</persistenceAdapter>
```

Delete kahaDB configuration

Delete the following segment.

```
<persistenceAdapter>
  <kahaDB directory="${activemq.base}/data/kahadb"/>
</persistenceAdapter>
```

Defining 'mysql data source

Add the following segment within the </beans> ag.

```
   <bean id="mysql-ds" class="org.apache.commons.dbcp.BasicDataSource"
         destroy-method="close">
```

```
    <property name="driverClassName" value="com.mysql.jdbc.Driver"/>
    <property name="url"
         value="jdbc:mysql://localhost/activemq?relaxAutoCommit=true"/>
    <property name="username" value="activemquser"/>
    <property name="password" value="activemqpword"/>
    <property name="maxActive" value="200"/>
    <property name="poolPreparedStatements" value="true"/>
  </bean>
```

A partial content of activemq.xml file in editor is as shown below.

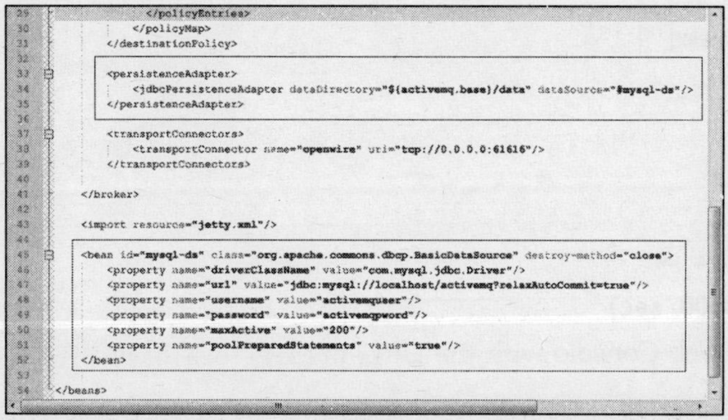

Include MySQL Connector/J library file in 'conf' directory

Download JDBC Driver for MySQL (Connector/J) from MySQL web site (http://www.mysql.com/products/connector/) in .zip format and extract it. I downloaded Connector/J version 5.1.12 (mysql-connector-java-5.1.12.zip).

Copy the jar file (mysql-connector-java-5.1.12-bin.jar) from the extracted one, and paste it in `ActiveMQ_Home/lib/optional` directory.

Create ACTIVEMQ_HOME Environment Variable

Select My Computer → Right Click → Properties → Advanced system settings → Environment Variables → Add a new System variable "ACTIVEMQ_HOME" with he value "C:\Test\apache-activemq-5.3.0" (Home directory of ActiveMQ, I installed ActiveMQ in C:\Test directory).

9.5.2 Running ActiveMQ

Go to "bin" directory of ActiveMQ Home directory in a DOS window. And invoke "activemq.bat".

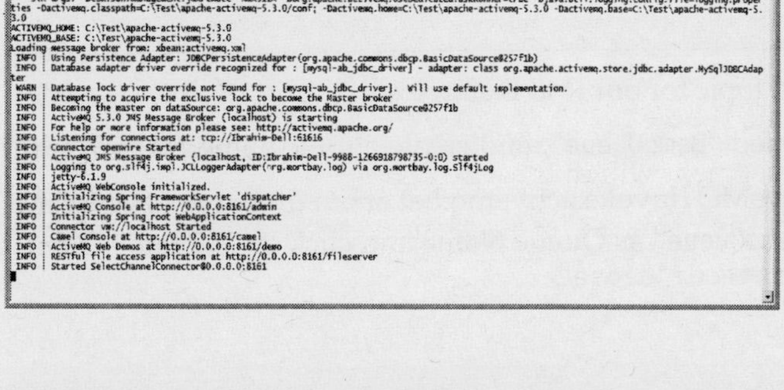

Press Ctrl+C (^C) o stop ActiveMQ execution in DOS window.

Now check with underlying MySQL database, necessary tables are created by ActiveMQ.

```
C:\Users\Ibrahim> mysql -u activemquser -pactivemqpword activemq
Welcome to the MySQL monitor. Commands end with ; or \g.
Your MySQL connection id is 21
Server version: 5.1.32-community MySQL Community Server (GPL)
Type 'help;' or '\h' for help. type '\c' to clear the buffer.
mysql> show tables;
+- - - - - - - - - - -+
| tables_in_activemq |
+- - - - - - - - - - -+
| activemq_acks |
| activemq_lock |
| activemq_msgs |
+- - - - - - - - - - -+
3 rows in set (0.00 sec)
```

Invoke ActiveMQ Web Console with the URL: `http://localhost:8161/admin/`

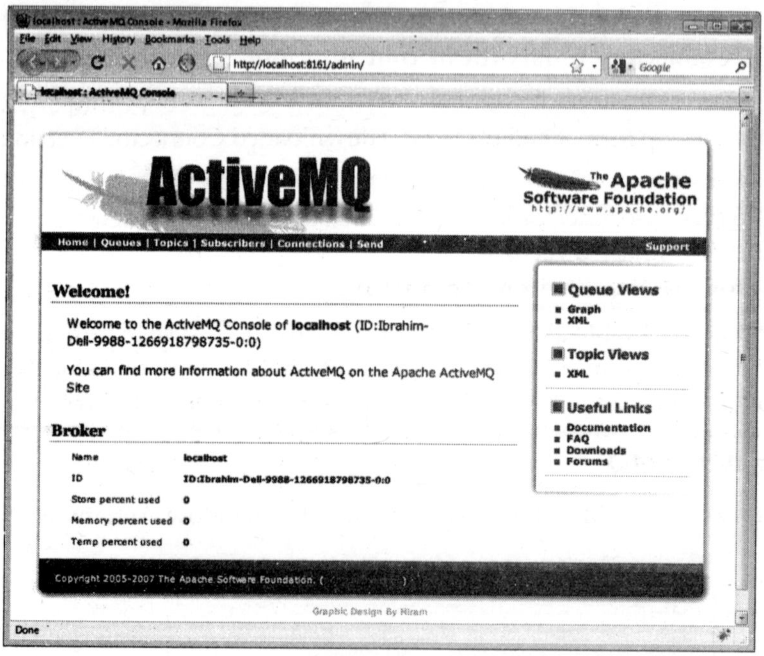

Creating Queue and topic for our JMS Examples:

Create a Queue named "`DemoQueue`", and create a topic named "`DemoTopic`" in ActiveMQ.

To do, start the ActiveMQ (invoke activemq.bat at bin directory of ActiveMQ installation. Click on "Queues", type "`DemoQueue`" as Queue Name and click on "Create". Then, the specified queue will be created.

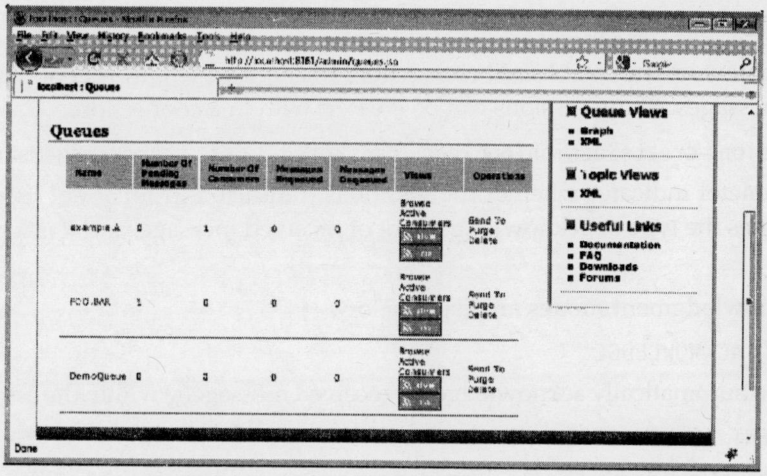

Click on "Topics", type "`DemoTopic`" as opic Name and click on "Create". Then, the specified topic will be created.

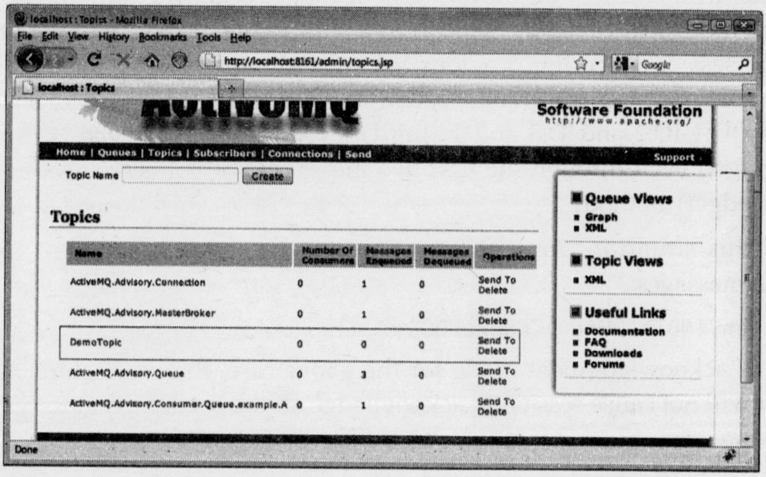

9.5.3 Creating ActiveMQ Connection

A connection should be created with JMS Provider (ActiveMQ) in order to communicate with it.

```
ActiveMQConnectionFactory connectionFactory =
        new ActiveMQConnectionFactory("tcp://localhost:61616");
Connection connection = connectionFactory.createConnection();
connection.start();
```

Assumed that the ActiveMQ is running on local machine and listen for the default port 61616.

Some methods in `Connection` Interface:

`void start()`

Starts (or restarts) a connection's delivery of incoming messages.

`void close()`

Closes the connection.

9.5.4 Creating ActiveMQ Session

A session is a context on the established connection, through which JMS clients can produce and consume JMS messages. Many sessions can be created with in a connection.

```
Session createSession(boolean ransacted, int acknowledgeMode)
```

The first parameter indicates whether the session is transacted (true) or not (false). The second parameter specifies the type of acknowledgement of received message, and it is ignored if session is transacted.

Allowed acknowledgment modes are listed below.

`Session.AUTO_ACKNOWLEDGE`

The session automatically acknowledge for received message(s) within the associated session.

`Session.CLIENT_ACKNOWLEDGE`

The JMS client (Java application) acknowledges a consumed message by calling acknowledge() method available in the Message.

Important Note: In this Client Acknowledgment mode, acknowledging a message (through acknowledge() method) will cause the session to acknowledge all the messages that have been consumed by the session since the previous acknowledgment of any message (the previous invocation of the acknowledgment() method) within the session. For example, If a client received three messages say ID:1, ID:2, and ID:3, and the third message is acknowledged, then all the messages will be acknowledged even through the first two messages are not acknowledged by the client (through acknowledge() method).

To overcome this situation, ActiveMQ provide the following constant to individually acknowledge JMS messages.

`ActiveMQSession.INDIVIDUAL_ACKNOWLEDGE`

If we apply this acknowledgment mode for the above case, then only third message will be acknowledged. It will not cause session to acknowledge all the consumed messages.

`Session.DUPS_OK_ACKNOWLEDGE`

The session acknowledges messages batch by batch lazily, instead of acknowledging immediately for a received message acknowledging before receiving next message. However, this acknowledges mode result in duplicate delivery of messages as JMS Provider will not get acknowledgment for a message immediately.

Example:

```
Session session = connection.createSession(false, Session.AUTO_ACKNOWLEDGE);
```

9.6 JMS API

The following section describes some JMS API for AciveMQ JMS Provider/

9.6.1 Session Interface

Some important methods in Session interface are given below.

```
Queue createQueue(String queue-name)
```

Returns Queue object for the specified queue-name in ActiveMQ. The interface Queue entends Destination interface.

`Topic createTopic(String topic-name)`

Returns topic object for the specified opic-name. The interface topic extends Destination interface.

`MessageProducer createProducer(Destination destination)`

Creates a `MessageProducer` to send messages to the specified destination.

`MessageConsumer createConsumer(Destination destination)`

Creates a `MessageConsumer` for the specified destination.

`Message createMessage()`

Creates a `Message` object.

`TextMessage createTextMessage()`

Creates a `TextMessage` object. The interface `TextMessage` extends `Message` interface.

`TextMessage createTextMessage(String text)`

Creates an initialized `TextMessage` object.

`BytesMessage createBytesMessage()`

Creates a `BytesMessage` object. The interface `BytesMessage` extends `Message` interface.

`MapMessage createMapMessage()`

Creates a `MapMessage` object. The interface `MapMessage` extends `Message` interface.

`ObjectMessage createObjectMessage()`

Creates an `ObjectMessage` object. The interface `ObjectMessage` extends Message interface.

`ObjectMessage createObjectMessage(Serializable object)`

Creates an initialized `ObjectMessage` object.

`StreamMessage createStreamMessage()`

Creates a `StreamMessage` object. The interface `StreamMessage` extends Message interface.

`TopicSubscriber createDurableSubscriber(Topic topic, String name)`

Creates a durable subscriber to the specified topic. The `topicSubscriber` extends `Message Consumer` interface.

`void commit()`

Commits all messages done in this transaction and releases any locks currently held.

`void rollback()`

Rolls back any messages done in this transaction and releases any locks currently held.

`void close()`

Closes the session.

9.6.2 MessageProducer Interface

Some methods under MessageProducer interface are given below.

A client uses a `MessageProducer` object to send messages to a destination. This `MessageProducer` is the parent interface for all message producers.

`void send(Message message)`

Sends a message using the `MessageProducer`'s default delivery mode, priority, and time to live.

`public void setDeliveryMode(int deliveryMode) throws JMSException`

Sets the producer's default delivery mode. Delivery mode is set to PERSISTENT by default. the attribute deliveryMode defines the message delivery mode for his message producer; legal values are `DeliveryMode.NON_PERSISTENT` and `DeliveryMode.PERSISTENT`

`void setPriority(int defaultPriority)`

Sets the producer's default priority.

`void setTimeToLive(long timeToLive)`

Sets the default length of time in milliseconds from its dispatch time that a produced message should be retained by the message system.

`void send(Message message, int deliveryMode, int priority, long timeToLive)`

Sends a message to the destination, specifying delivery mode, priority, and time to live.

9.6.3 MessageConsumer Interface

A client uses a `MessageConsumer` object to receive messages from a destination. `MessageConsumer` is the parent interface for all message consumers.

For synchronous receipt, a client can request the next message from a message consumer using one of it's `receive` methods.

For asynchronous delivery, a client can register a `MessageListener` object with a message consumer. As messages arrive at the message consumer, it delivers them by calling the `MessageListener`'s `onMessage` method.

`Message receive()`

Receives the next message produced for this message consumer. The meaning of "next message" is, if the Queue already having messages, those messages will be consumed by this method one by one on each call. This call blocks indefinitely until a message is produced or until this message consumer is closed.

`Message receive(long timeout)`

Receives the next message that arrives within the specified timeout interval (milliseconds). A `timeout` of zero never expires, and the call blocks indefinitely. It is same as `receive()`, but if there is no message in the queue, then it will wait for the specified milliseconds for new messages adding to queue. If the specified timeout period is expired, then it simply exists its listening to messages.

`Message receiveNoWait()`

Receives the next message if one is immediately available.

`void setMessageListener(MessageListener listener)`

Sets the message consumer's MessageListener. Pass as argument to this method the object of the class which implements MessageListener interface and defines "void onMessage (Message message)" method.

9.6.4 Message Interface

Some methods in Message interface are given below.

`void acknowledge()`

Acknowledges all consumed messages of the session of this consumed message.

`String getJMSCorrelationID()`

Gets the correlation ID for the message.

`String getJMSMessageID()`

Gets the message ID.

`int getJMSPriority()`

Gets the message priority level.

`void setJMSPriority(int priority)`

Sets the priority level for this message.

`void setJMSMessageID(String id)`

Sets the message ID.

`void setJMSExpiration(long expiration)`

Sets the message's expiration value.

`void setJMSDeliveryMode(int deliveryMode)`

Sets the DeliveryMode value for this message.

`void setJMSDestination(Destination destination)`

Sets the Destination object for this message.

`void setJMSCorrelationID(String correlationID)`

Sets the correlation ID for the message.

Constants in Message Interface:

`Message.DEFAULT_DELIVERY_MODE`

The message producer's default delivery mode is Persistent.

`Message.DEFAULT_PRIORITY`

The message producer's default priority is 4.

`Message.DEFAULT_TIME_TO_LIVE`

The message producer's default time to live is unlimited; the message never expires.

9.6.5 TextMessage Interface

A `TextMessage` object is used to send a message containing a `String`. This interface extends `Message` interface.

`String getText()`

Gets the string containing this message's data.

`void setText(String string)`

Sets the string containing this message's data.

9.6.6 BytesMessage Interface

A `BytesMessage` object is used to send a message containing a stream of uninterpreted bytes. `This interface extends Message interface.`

`boolean readBoolean()`

Reads a boolean from the bytes message stream.

`byte readByte()`

Reads a signed 8-bit value from the bytes message stream.

`int readBytes(byte[] value)`

Reads a byte array from the bytes message stream.

`int readBytes(byte[] value, int length)`

Reads a portion of the bytes message stream.

`char readChar()`

Reads a character value from the bytes message stream.

`double readDouble()`

Reads a double from the bytes message stream.

`float readFloat()`

Reads a float from the bytes message stream.

`int readInt()`

Reads an integer from the bytes message stream.

`long readLong()`

Reads a long from the bytes message stream.

`short readShort()`

Reads a short from the bytes message stream.

`String readUTF()`

Reads a string from the bytes message stream.

`void writeBoolean(boolean value)`

Writes a boolean to the bytes message stream as a 1-byte value.

`void writeByte(byte value)`

Writes a byte to the bytes message stream as a 1-byte value.

`void writeBytes(byte[] value)`

Writes a byte array to the bytes message stream.

`void writeBytes(byte[] value, int offset, int length)`

Writes a specified portion of a byte array to the bytes message stream.

`void writeChar(char value)`

Writes a chart to the bytes message stream as a 2-byte value.

`void writeDouble(double value)`

Writes a double to the bytes message stream by using internal conversion.

`void writeFloat(float value)`

Writes a float to the bytes message stream by using internal conversion.

`void writeInt(int value)`

Writes an int to the bytes message stream.

`void writeLong(long value)`

Writes a long to the bytes message stream.

`void writeObject(Object value)`

Writes an object to the bytes message stream.

`void writeShort(short value)`

Writes a short to the bytes message stream.

`void writeUTF(String value)`

Writes a string to the bytes message.

9.6.7 MapMessage Interface

A MapMessage object is used to send a set of name-value pairs. The names are String objects, and the values are primitive data types in the Java programming language. This interface extends Message interface.

When a client receives a MapMessage, it is in read-only mode. If a client attempts to write to the message at this point, a MessageNotWriteableException is thrown. If clearBody is called, the message can now be both read from and written to.

`boolean getBoolean(String name)`

Returns the boolean value with the specified name.

`byte getByte(String name)`

Returns the byte value with the specified name.

`byte[] getBytes(String name)`

Returns the byte array value with the specified name.

`char getChar(String name)`

Returns the character value with the specified name.

`double getDouble(String name)`

Returns the double value with the specified name.

`float getFloat(String name)`

Returns the float value with the specified name.

`int getInt(String name)`

Returns the int value with the specified name.

`long getLong(String name)`

Returns the long value with the specified name.

`Object getObject(String name)`

Returns the value of the object with the specified name.

`short getShort(String name)`

Returns the short value with the specified name.

`String getString(String name)`

Returns the String value with the specified name.

`void setBoolean(String name, boolean value)`

Sets a boolean value with the specified name into the Map.

`void setByte(String name, byte value)`

Sets a byte value with the specified name into the Map.

`void setBytes(String name, byte[] value)`

Sets a byte array value with the specified name into the Map.

`void setBytes(String name, byte[] value, int offset, int length)`

Sets a portion of the byte array value with the specified name into the Map.

`void setChar(String name, char value)`

Sets a character value with the specified name into the Map.

`void setDouble(String name, double value)`

Sets a double value with the specified name into the Map.

`void setFloat(String name, float value)`

Sets a float value with the specified name into the Map.

`void setInt(String name, int value)`

Sets an int value with the specified name into the Map.

`void setLong(String name, long value)`

Sets a long value with the specified name into the Map.

`void setObject(String name, Object value)`

Sets an object value with the specified name into the Map.

`void setShort(String name, short value)`

Sets a short value with the specified name into the Map.

`void setString(String name, String value)`

Sets a String value with the specified name into the Map.

`Enumeration getMapNames()`

Returns an Enumeration of all the names in the `MapMessage` object.

`boolean itemExists(String name)`

Indicates whether an item exists in this `MapMessage` object.

9.6.8 StreamMessage Interface

A `StreamMessage` object is used to send a stream of primitive types in the Java programming language. This interface extends `Message` interface.

Some of the methods in this interface are listed below.

`boolean readBoolean()`

Reads a boolean from the stream message.

`byte readByte()`

Reads a byte value from the stream message.

`int readBytes(byte[] value)`

Reads a byte array field from the stream message into the specified byte[] object.

`char readChar()`

Reads a character value from the stream message.

`double readDouble()`

Reads a double from the stream message.

`float readFloat()`

Reads a float from the stream message.

`int readInt()`

Reads an integer from the stream message.

`long readLong()`

Reads a long from the stream message.

`Object readObject()`

Reads an object from the stream message.

`short readShort()`

Reads a short from the stream message.

`String readString()`

Reads a String from the stream message.

`void writeBoolean(boolean value)`

Writes a boolean to the stream message.

`void writeByte(byte value)`

Writes a byte to the stream message.

`void writeBytes(byte[] value)`

Writes a byte array field to the stream message.

`void writeBytes(byte[] value, int offset, int length)`

Writes a portion of a byte array as byte[] field to the stream message.

`void writeChar(char value)`

Writes a char to the stream message.

`void writeDouble(double value)`

Writes a double to the stream message.

`void writeFloat(float value)`

Writes a float to the stream message.

`void writeInt(int value)`

Writes an int to the stream message.

`void writeLong(long value)`

Writes a long to the stream message.

`void writeObject(Object value)`

Writes an object to the stream message.

`void writeShort(short value)`

Writes a short to the stream message.

`void writeString(String value)`

Writes a String to the stream message.

9.6.9 ObjectMessage Interface

An `ObjectMessage` object is used to send a message that contains a serializable Java Object. This interface extends `Message` interface.

Some of the methods in this interface are listed below.

`Serializable getObject()`

Gets the serializable object containing this message's data.

`void setObject(Serializable object)`

Sets the serializable object containing this message's data.

9.7 JMS DEMO USING ACTIVEMQ

This section provides few examples, which illustrates JMS API.

9.7.1 Example: Point-To-Point Messaging

In Eclipse, File → New → Java Project → Project name: JMSDemo → Finish.

Select "src" of JMSDemo in Project Explorer → Right click → New → Package →

Package name: jmsexamples → Finish.

Copy "activemq-all-5.3.0.jar" file from ActiveMQ home directory and paste it in "JMSDemo" directory. Select "JMSDemo" → Right click → Properties → Java Build Path → Libraries tab → Add JARs button → Select activemq-all.5.3.0.jar under JMSDemo directory → OK → OK.

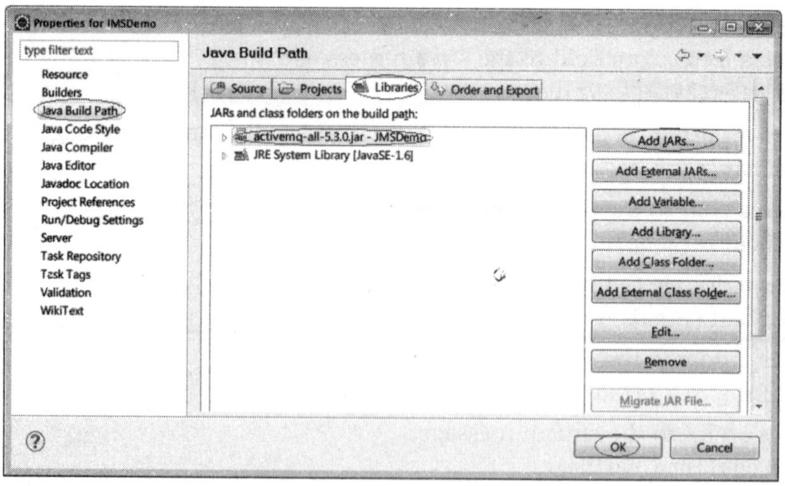

Message Producer:

Select "jmsexamples" → Right click → New → Class → Class name: MsgProducer → Finish.

Start the ActiveMQ (as described earlier sections) and note that we have created one queue named "DemoQueue" (otherwise create it).

The content of the MsgProducer.java is as below.

package jmsexamples;

```
import javax.jms.Connection;
import javax.jms.Destination;
import javax.jms.MessageProducer;
import javax.jms.Session;
import javax.jms.TextMessage;
import org.apache.activemq.ActiveMQConnection;
import org.apache.activemq.ActiveMQConnectionFactory;
import org.apache.activemq.util.IndentPrinter;
public class MsgProducer {
 public static void main(String args[]) {
  try {
      ActiveMQConnectionFactory connectionFactory =
                 new ActiveMQConnectionFactory("tcp://localhost:61616");
      Connection connection = connectionFactory.createConnection();
      Session session = connection.createSession(false, Session.AUTO_ACKNOWLEDGE);
      Destination destination = session.createQueue("DemoQueue");
      MessageProducer messageProducer = session.createProducer(destination);
      ActiveMQConnection c = (ActiveMQConnection) connection;
      c.getConnectionStats().dump(new IndentPrinter());
      TextMessage message = session.createTextMessage("This is a test message.");
      messageProducer.send(message);
      messageProducer.close();
      session.close();
      connection.close();
      System.out.println("Message successfully sent.");
  }
   catch (Exception e) {
      System.out.println("Error occurred while sending message.");
      e.printStackTrace();
  }
 }
}
```

Message Consumer:

Follow the above procedure to create the following Message Consumer class.

```
package jmsexamples;
import javax.jms.Connection;
import javax.jms.Destination;
import javax.jms.Message;
```

```
import javax.jms.MessageConsumer;
import javax.jms.Session;
import javax.jms.TextMessage;
import org.apache.activemq.ActiveMQConnectionFactory;
public class MsgConsumer {
 public static void main(String arg[]) {
  try {
      ActiveMQConnectionFactory connectionFactory =
            new ActiveMQConnectionFactory("tcp://localhost:61616");
      Connection connection = connectionFactory.createConnection();
      connection.start();
      Session session =
           connection.createSession(false, Session.AUTO_ACKNOWLEDGE);
      Destination destination = session.createQueue("DemoQueue");
      MessageConsumer consumer = session.createConsumer(destination);
      System.out.println("Waiting for message...");
      Message message = consumer.receive(10000);
      if (message == null) {
        System.out.println("No message produced for
                                 this Queue in last 10 seconds.");
      }
      else if (message instanceof textMessage) {
           TextMessage textMessage = (TextMessage) message;
           String msg = textMessage.getText();
           System.out.println("Received Message [" + msg + "]");
      }
      consumer.close();
      session.close();
      connection.close();
   }
   catch (Exception e) {
      System.out.println("Error occurred while receiving message.");
      e.printStackTrace();
  }
 }
}
```

Execute the Message Producer (select the MsgProducer.java → Right click → Run As Java Application).

ActiveMQ Web console show the message is produced.

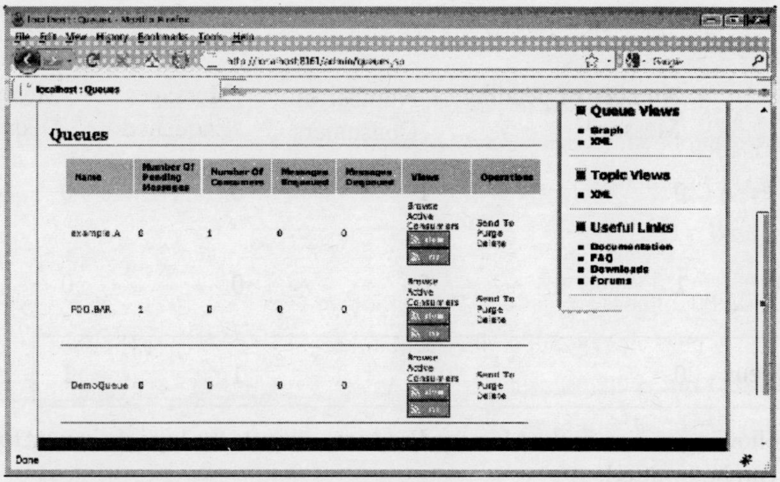

Our setting is to persist the messages in MySQL database.

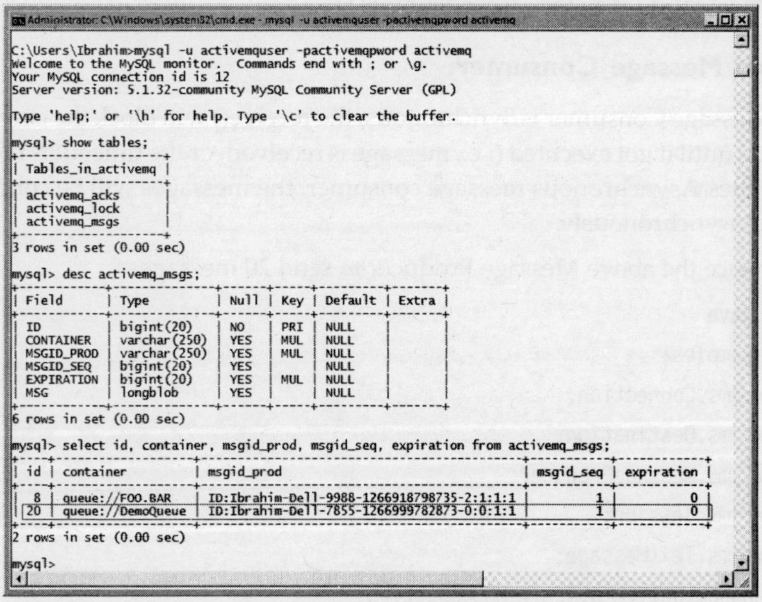

Note that the delivery mode for a JMS Message is persistent, and its expiration is zero, that is the message will not be expired at all. If you restart JMS Provider (ActiveMQ) will not destroy the message in the Queue.

Now, run the Message Consumer, then the output will be produced as below.

Waiting for message...

Received Message [This is a test message.]

After the message is consumed, now check with ActiveMQ web cosole.

Queues

Name	Number of pending Messages	Number of Consumers	Messages Enqueued	Messages Dequeued
example. A	0	1	0	0
FOO.BAR	1	0	0	0
DemoQueus	0	0	1	1

Note: The following section in the Message Producer outputs the log info in neat format with indentation, and it can be omitted.

```
ActiveMQConnection c = (ActiveMQConnection) connection;
c.getConnectionStats().dump(new IndentPrinter());
```

Asynchronous Message Consumer:

The above Message Consumer is Synchronous, the receive() will block the execution of the other parts of the code until it got executed (i.e., message is received, or the timeout is met). The following example illustrates Asynchronous message consumer, the messages will be continuously listened and consumed asynchronously.

We will enhance the above Message Producer to send 20 messages.

MsgProducer.java

```
package jmsexamples;
import javax.jms.Connection;
import javax.jms.Destination;
import javax.jms.MessageProducer;
import javax.jms.Session;
import javax.jms.TextMessage;
import org.apache.activemq.ActiveMQConnection;
import org.apache.activemq.ActiveMQConnectionFactory;
import org.apache.activemq.util.IndentPrinter;
public class MsgProducer {
  public static void main(String args[]) {
    try {
          ActiveMQConnectionFactory connectionFactory =
                     new ActiveMQConnectionFactory("tcp://localhost:61616");
          Connection connection = connectionFactory.createConnection();
          Session session =
                connection.createSession(false, Session.AUTO_ACKNOWLEDGE);
```

```
      Destination destination = session.createQueue("DemoQueue");
      MessageProducer messageProducer = session.createProducer(destination);
      ActiveMQConnection c = (ActiveMQConnection) connection;
      c.getConnectionStats().dump(new IndentPrinter());
      for (int i = 1; i <= 20; i++) {
        TextMessage message =
                  session.createTextMessage("This is a test message " + i);
        messageProducer.send(message);
      }
      messageProducer.close();
      session.close();
      connection.close();
      System.out.println("Message successfully sent.");
   }
   catch (Exception e) {
      System.out.println("Error occurred while sending message.");
      e.printStackTrace();
   }
  }
}
```

AsynchronousMsgConsumer.java

```
package jmsexamples;
import javax.jms.Connection;
import javax.jms.Destination;
import javax.jms.JMSException;
import javax.jms.Message;
import javax.jms.MessageConsumer;
import javax.jms.MessageListener;
import javax.jms.Session;
import javax.jms.TextMessage;
import org.apache.activemq.ActiveMQConnectionFactory;
public class AsynchronousMsgConsumer {
 Connection connection = null;
 Session session = null;
 MessageConsumer consumer = null;
 int msgCount = 0;
private void doListening() throws Exception {
 try {
  ActiveMQConnectionFactory connectionFactory =
```

```
                new ActiveMQConnectionFactory("tcp://localhost:61616");
  connection = connectionFactory.createConnection();
  connection.start();
  session = connection.createSession(false, Session.AUTO_ACKNOWLEDGE);
  Destination destination = session.createQueue("DemoQueue");
  System.out.println("Receiving messages...");
  consumer = session.createConsumer(destination);
  consumer.setMessageListener(new MessageListener() {
  public void onMessage(Message message) {
        if (message instanceof textMessage) {
          msgCount++;
          TextMessage extMessage = (TextMessage) message;
          String msg = "";
          try {
              msg = textMessage.getText();
          }
          catch (JMSException e) {
           System.out.println(msgCount + "] Error in parsing Text Message.");
           e.printStackTrace();
           return;
          }
          System.out.println(msgCount + "] Received Message [" + msg + "]");
        }
   } });
}
catch (Exception e) {
 System.out.println("Error occurred while listening for messages.");
 e.printStackTrace();
 throw e;
 }
}
private void stopListening() {
 try {
  if (session != null) session.close();
  if (connection != null) connection.close();
  if (consumer != null) consumer.close();
 }
catch (JMSException e) {
 e.printStackTrace();
 }
}
```

```
public static void main(String arg[]) {
 try {
 AsynchronousMsgConsumer msgConsumer = new AsynchronousMsgConsumer();
 msgConsumer.doListening();
 // Decide how much time to listen and receive messages
 // In our demo, let it run for 1 minute.
 // Specify duration in Milliseconds
 Thread.sleep(1 * 60 * 1000);
 // Stop listening
 msgConsumer.stopListening();
 }
 catch (Exception e) {
   System.out.println("Exception occurred. Error[" + e.getMessage() + "]");
   e.printStackTrace();
   }
  }
 }
```

Run the Message Consumer and then Message Producer. The output at Message Consumer side is as shown below.

```
Receiving messages...
1] Received Message [This is a Test message 1]
2] Received Message [This is a Test message 2]
3] Received Message [This is a Test message 3]
4] Received Message [This is a Test message 4]
5] Received Message [This is a Test message 5]
6] Received Message [This is a Test message 6]
7] Received Message [This is a Test message 7]
8] Received Message [This is a Test message 8]
9] Received Message [This is a Test message 9]
10] Received Message [This is a Test message 10]
11] Received Message [This is a Test message 11]
12] Received Message [This is a Test message 12]
13] Received Message [This is a Test message 13]
14] Received Message [This is a Test message 14]
15] Received Message [This is a Test message 15]
16] Received Message [This is a Test message 16]
17] Received Message [This is a Test message 17]
18] Received Message [This is a Test message 18]
19] Received Message [This is a Test message 19]
20] Received Message [This is a Test message 20]
```

9.7.2 Example: Publish/Subscribe Messaging

Create a topic in ActiveMQ named "DemoTopic" using ActiveMQ web console. Two Synchronous Message Consumers (MsgTopicConsumerClient1.java, MsgTopicConsumerClient2.java) and one Message Producer (MsgTopicProducer.java) are given below. Run the Message Clients and then run the Message Producer. then, you can observe that both clients receive the same message since both are subscribed to the Topic, to which the Message Producer sends message.

MsgTopicConsumerClient1.java

```
package jmsexamples;
import javax.jms.Connection;
import javax.jms.Destination;
import javax.jms.Message;
import javax.jms.MessageConsumer;
import javax.jms.Session;
import javax.jms.TextMessage;
import org.apache.activemq.ActiveMQConnectionFactory;
public class MsgTopicConsumerClient1 {
 public static void main(String arg[]) {
  try {
    ActiveMQConnectionFactory connectionFactory =
              new ActiveMQConnectionFactory("tcp://localhost:61616");
    Connection connection = connectionFactory.createConnection();
    connection.start();
    Session session = connection.createSession(false, Session.AUTO_ACKNOWLEDGE);
    Destination destination = session.createTopic("DemoTopic");
    MessageConsumer consumer = session.createConsumer(destination);
    System.out.println("Client1: Waiting for message...");
    Message message = consumer.receive(10000);
    if (message == null) {
       System.out.println("No message produced for this topic
                                             in last 10 seconds.");
    }
    else if (message instanceof TextMessage) {
        TextMessage TextMessage = (TextMessage) message;
        String msg = TextMessage.getText();
        System.out.println("Client1: Received Message [" + msg + "]");
    }
    consumer.close();
    session.close();
    connection.close();
```

```
  }
  catch (Exception e) {
    System.out.println("Caught: " + e);
    e.printStackTrace();
  }
 }
}
```

MsgTopicConsumerClient2.java

```
package jmsexamples;
import javax.jms.Connection;
import javax.jms.Destination;
import javax.jms.Message;
import javax.jms.MessageConsumer;
import javax.jms.Session;
import javax.jms.TextMessage;
import org.apache.activemq.ActiveMQConnectionFactory;
public class MsgTopicConsumerClient2 {
 public static void main(String arg[]) {
  try {
   ActiveMQConnectionFactory connectionFactory =
           new ActiveMQConnectionFactory("tcp://localhost:61616");
   Connection connection = connectionFactory.createConnection();
   connection.start();
   Session session = connection.createSession(false, Session.AUTO_ACKNOWLEDGE);
   Destination destination = session.createTopic("DemoTopic");
   MessageConsumer consumer = session.createConsumer(destination);
   System.out.println("Client2: Waiting for message...");
   Message message = consumer.receive(10000);
   if (message == null) {
      System.out.println("No message produced for this topic
                                              in last 10 seconds.");
   }
   else if (message instanceof TextMessage) {
       TextMessage TextMessage = (TextMessage) message;
       String msg = TextMessage.getText();
       System.out.println("Client2: Received Message [" + msg + "]");
   }
   consumer.close();
   session.close();
   connection.close();
```

```
    }
    catch (Exception e) {
     System.out.println("Caught: " + e);
     e.printStackTrace();
    }
  }
}
```

MsgTopicProducer.java

```
package jmsexamples;
import javax.jms.Connection;
import javax.jms.Destination;
import javax.jms.MessageProducer;
import javax.jms.Session;
import javax.jms.TextMessage;
import org.apache.activemq.ActiveMQConnection;
import org.apache.activemq.ActiveMQConnectionFactory;
import org.apache.activemq.util.IndentPrinter;
public class MsgTopicProducer {
 public static void main(String args[]) {
  try {
   ActiveMQConnectionFactory connectionFactory =
             new ActiveMQConnectionFactory("tcp://localhost:61616");
   Connection connection = connectionFactory.createConnection();
   Session session = connection.createSession(false, Session.AUTO_ACKNOWLEDGE);
   Destination destination = session.createTopic("DemoTopic");
   MessageProducer messageProducer = session.createProducer(destination);
   ActiveMQConnection c = (ActiveMQConnection) connection;
   c.getConnectionStats().dump(new IndentPrinter());
   TextMessage message =
                  session.createTextMessage("This is a test message.");
   messageProducer.send(message);
   messageProducer.close();
   session.close();
   connection.close();
   System.out.println("Message successfully sent.");
 }
 catch (Exception e) {
   System.out.println("Error occurred while sending message.");
   e.printStackTrace();
  }
```

```
  }
}
```

Output:

```
At Cient1:
Client1: Waiting for message...
Client1: Received Message [This is a Test message.]
At Cient2:
Client2: Waiting for message...
Client2: Received Message [This is a Test message.]
```

Asynchronous Topic Consumer:

We can use MessageListener; whenever message is added to topic, it immediately picks up (asynchronously).

```
package jmsexamples;
import javax.jms.Connection;
import javax.jms.Destination;
import javax.jms.JMSException;
import javax.jms.Message;
import javax.jms.MessageConsumer;
import javax.jms.MessageListener;
import javax.jms.Session;
import javax.jms.TextMessage;
import org.apache.activemq.ActiveMQConnectionFactory;
public class MsgTopicConsumer {
  Connection connection = null;
  Session  session  =  null;
  MessageConsumer consumer = null;
  int msgCount = 0;
  private void doListening() throws Exception {
  try {
        ActiveMQConnectionFactory connectionFactory =
                    new ActiveMQConnectionFactory("tcp://localhost:61616");
        connection = connectionFactory.createConnection();
        connection.start();
        session = connection.createSession(false, Session.AUTO_ACKNOWLEDGE);
        Destination destination = session.createTopic("DemoTopic");
        System.out.println("Receiving messages...");
        consumer = session.createConsumer(destination);
        consumer.setMessageListener(new MessageListener() {
```

```
        public void onMessage(Message message) {
         if (message instanceof TextMessage) {
              msgCount++;
              TextMessage TextMessage = (TextMessage) message;
              String msg = "";
              try {
                msg = TextMessage.getText();
              }
              catch (JMSException e) {
                System.out.println(msgCount +
                        "] Error in parsing Text Message.");
             e.printStackTrace();
             return;
         }
        System.out.println(msgCount +
                    "] Received Message [" + msg + "]");
      }
    } });
  }
  catch (Exception e) {
    System.out.println("Error occurred while listening for messages.");
    e.printStackTrace();
    throw e;
  }
}
private void stopListening() {
 try {
     if (session != null) session.close();
     if (connection != null) connection.close();
     if (consumer != null) consumer.close();
 }
 catch (JMSException e) {
     e.printStackTrace();
 }
}
public static void main(String arg[]) {
 try {
     MsgTopicConsumer msgConsumer = new MsgTopicConsumer();
     msgConsumer.doListening();
```

```
      // Decide how much time to listen and receive messages
      // In our demo, let it run for 1 minute.
      // Specify duration in Milliseconds
      Thread.sleep(1 * 60 * 1000);
      // Stop listening
      msgConsumer.stopListening();
    }
    catch (Exception e) {
      System.out.println("Exception occurred. Error[" +
                                        e.getMessage() + "]");
      e.printStackTrace();
    }
  }
}
```

Durable Subscriber:

If a JMS client makes a durable subscription with JMS Provider, then the messages added on JMS Provider during time that the JMS client was on-line will be kept in JMS Provider and delivered once JMS Client became on-line.

In the following example, the Client 1 (MsgTopicConsumerClient1.java) makes durable sub-scription and Client 2 (MsgTopicConsumerClient1.java) makes non-durable sub-scription. First run the Message Producer, and then run both the clients; the Client 1 will get that produced mes-sage, and the Client 2 will not get that message.

MsgTopicProducer.java

```
package jmsexamples;
import javax.jms.Connection;
import javax.jms.Destination;
import javax.jms.MessageProducer;
import javax.jms.Session;
import javax.jms.TextMessage;
import org.apache.activemq.ActiveMQConnection;
import org.apache.activemq.ActiveMQConnectionFactory;
import org.apache.activemq.util.IndentPrinter;
public class MsgTopicProducer {
  public static void main(String args[]) {
   try {
     ActiveMQConnectionFactory connectionFactory =
               new ActiveMQConnectionFactory("tcp://localhost:61616");
     Connection connection = connectionFactory.createConnection();
     Session session = connection.createSession(false, Session.AUTO_ACKNOWLEDGE);
```

```
    Destination destination = session.createTopic("DemoTopic");
    MessageProducer messageProducer = session.createProducer(destination);
    ActiveMQConnection c = (ActiveMQConnection) connection;
    c.getConnectionStats().dump(new IndentPrinter());
    TextMessage message =
                      session.createTextMessage("This is a Test message.");
    messageProducer.send(message);
    messageProducer.close();
    session.close();
    connection.close();
    System.out.println("Message successfully sent.");
   }
  catch (Exception e) {
    System.out.println("Error occurred while sending message.");
    e.printStackTrace();
   }
  }
}
```

MsgTopicConsumerClient1.java

```
package jmsexamples;
import javax.jms.Connection;
import javax.jms.Message;
import javax.jms.MessageConsumer;
import javax.jms.Session;
import javax.jms.TextMessage;
import javax.jms.Topic;
import org.apache.activemq.ActiveMQConnectionFactory;
public class MsgTopicConsumerClient1 {
 public static void main(String arg[]) {
  try {
      ActiveMQConnectionFactory connectionFactory =
              new ActiveMQConnectionFactory("tcp://localhost:61616");
      Connection connection = connectionFactory.createConnection();
      connection.setClientID("DurableSubClientId1");
      connection.start();
      Session session = connection.createSession(false, Session.AUTO_ACKNOWLEDGE);
      Topic destination = session.createTopic("DemoTopic");
      MessageConsumer consumer =
        session.createDurableSubscriber(destination, "DurableSubClient1");
```

```
        System.out.println("Client1: Waiting for message...");
        Message message = consumer.receive(10000);
        if (message == null) {
           System.out.println("No message produced for this topic
                                      in last 10 seconds.");
        }
        else if (message instanceof TextMessage) {
           TextMessage TextMessage = (TextMessage) message;
           String msg = TextMessage.getText();
           System.out.println("Client1: Received Message [" + msg + "]");
        }
        consumer.close();
        session.close();
        connection.close();
    }
    catch (Exception e) {
       System.out.println("Caught: " + e);
       e.printStackTrace();
    }
  }
}
```

MsgTopicConsumerClient2.java

```
import javax.jms.Connection;
import javax.jms.Destination;
import javax.jms.Message;
import javax.jms.MessageConsumer;
import javax.jms.Session;
import javax.jms.TextMessage;
import org.apache.activemq.ActiveMQConnectionFactory;
public class MsgTopicConsumerClient2 {
 public static void main(String arg[]) {
  try {
      ActiveMQConnectionFactory connectionFactory =
               new ActiveMQConnectionFactory("tcp://localhost:61616");
      Connection connection = connectionFactory.createConnection();
      connection.start();
      Session session = connection.createSession(false, Session.AUTO_ACKNOWLEDGE);
      Destination destination = session.createTopic("DemoTopic");
      MessageConsumer consumer = session.createConsumer(destination);
```

```
        System.out.println("Client2: Waiting for message...");
        Message message = consumer.receive(10000);
        if (message == null) {
            System.out.println("No message produced for this topic
                                                in last 10 seconds.");
        }
        else if (message instanceof TextMessage) {
            TextMessage TextMessage = (TextMessage) message;
            String msg = TextMessage.getText();
            System.out.println("Client2: Received Message [" + msg + "]");
        }
        consumer.close();
        session.close();
        connection.close();
    }
    catch (Exception e) {
      System.out.println("Caught: " + e);
      e.printStackTrace();
    }
  }
}
```

Output:

Client1: Waiting for message...

Client1: Received Message [This is a Test message.]

Client2: Waiting for message...

No message produced for this topic in last 10 seconds.

SUMMARY

The Message Oriented Middleware provides asynchronous communication for Enterprise Application Integration. The Java Messaging Service is a specification that is developed by Sun Microsystems. Many JMS implementations are available in the market, known as JMS Providers. One of the open-source JMS Provider is Apache ActiveMQ. This chapter explained briefly the working principle of MOM, and illustrated JMS concepts with ActiveMQ.

10

Project Management with Apache Maven

10.0 INTRODUCTION

The Maven is an open source Apache Software Foundation project. It is a Project Management tool, which is used to manage entire software project development and maintenance such as creating a project, testing, building the project, preparing reports and documentation. This chapter explains the important usages of Maven with demonstration code.

10.1 ANT VERSUS MAVEN

Apache Ant (Another Neat Tool) is a platform independent Java-based build tool. Apache Maven is also platform independent Java-based tool, but it is beyond build tools. It also supports project management activates such as creation of project structures, preparation of reports and documents along with the role of a build tool.

What is "build"? In a programming context, a build is a version of an application. It is not necessary to be the final version of the application to release. During the development (implementation) phase of software development, all the Java classes should be compiled and should be packed (packaged) with required resources, and should be unit tested for end-user esting. This process is called "building" an application and repeated by the developer as long as errors remain in the application. If all the functionalities of the application are tested properly, the packed version is ready for release. Instead of doing these build process every time of error correction by himself, the can automate this build process using a build tool such as Ant (used by Java developers), Make (mostly used by C++ developers).

Maven is not developed as a replacement of Ant or any other build tool. However, Maven does the build jobs as Ant does, and we can even call Ant's "target" in Maven.

Maven provides uniform structure for each type of project so that all other developers using Maven can easily understand the project, and Maven also facilitates communication among the eam members of a Project over the web. Maven works based on "Convention over Configuration" concept. It defines reasonable default values for properties and it enforces that which type of files should be placed which directory. For example, all Java sources codes should be stored in `/src/main/java` directory, and the test case Java files should be stored in `/src/test/java`.

Maven introduces excellent concept "Reusable Plug-ins and Repositories" for centralised access of plug-ins and libraries by projects; no need to download, locate, copy and paste library files for each project. All the dependencies (required libraries) are downloaded automatically from remote repository for the projects by Maven.

10.2 INSTALLING MAVEN

The Maven software can be downloaded from Maven's website *http://maven.apache.org/*. Click on "Download" link from the Maven's home page and download latest stable version. Download Maven in .zip format (in our demonstrations, *apache-maven-2.0.10-bin.zip* is used) for Window OS installation, and download maven in .gz format (in our case, *apache-maven-2.0.10-bin.tar.gz*) for UNIX based operating systems (UNIX, Linux).

Installing Maven on Windows:

Unzip he downloaded *apache-maven-2.0.10-bin.zip* file and set the path of the extracted folder to the environment variable M2_HOME.

On Windows Vista,

Choose "Computer" icon on Desktop and Right click → Properties → Advanced system settings → Environment Variables in child window → System Variables New → Set M2_HOME to C:\Development\apache-maven-2.0.10 (in our case, Maven files are extracted here) → OK

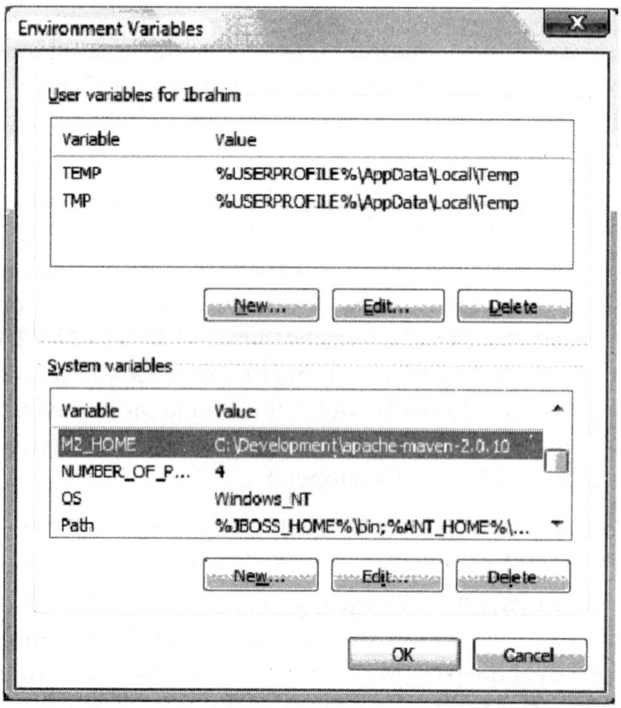

Edit "Path" System variable and add Maven's bin directory to it to make available "mvn.bat" file to all directories.

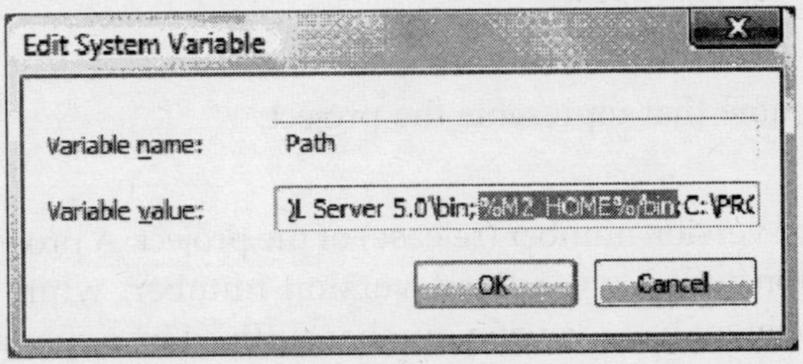

Open DOS window, and give the following command (from any directory, no need to go to bin directory of Maven installation).

```
mvn -version
```

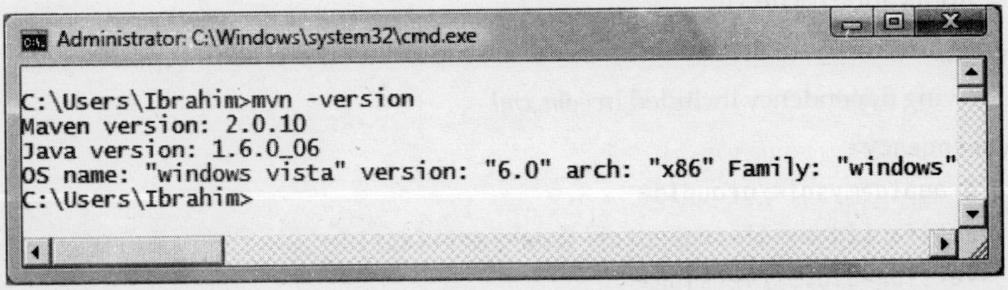

Note that Maven automatically creates one directory (first time only, when you invoke mvn) named .m2 under your HOME directory (It is C:\Users\<UserName> in Windows Vista). This directory contains Maven's local repository; when you download a dependency (library) for a project, Maven stores a copy of the dependency in this directory which will be served to other projected when required. This directory also contains one XML file named *settings.xml,* which defines configurations to customize the behaviour of Maven such as authentication of users, remote repository settings.

10.3 MAVEN COORDINATES

A Maven coordinate is a "composite" of values, which uniquely identifies an artefact (software component). These coordinated "composite" values are delimited by colon while referring a Maven coordinate as below.

```
groupId:artifactId:version:packaging
```

`groupId:`

The organisation/group/project/team/entity (any one) responsible for producing the artefact.

For example,

Use the reverse domain name while specifying the organisation's domain name as *groupId,* this is one convention followed.

```
<groupId>org.apache.tomcat</groupId>
<groupId>com.oracle</groupId>
```

We can just specify the project name only as below.

<groupId>mysql</groupId>

`artifactId:`

The artifact name that represents the project.

`version:`

Represents the version number (release) of the project. A project which is to be released for production will have a fixed version number, while the project still under active development has a version number suffixed by a special value "-SNAPSHOT".

`packaging:`

Represents the type of project (Java application - jar, Web application – war ...). Default is "jar". A value "jar" produces a JAR archive; a value "war" produces a WAR (web application) achieve.

The same directory structure is followed when a product is stored in repository.

The following dependency included in *pom.xml*

```
<dependency>
   <groupId>mysql</groupId>
   <artifactId>mysql-connector-java</artifactId>
   <version>5.0.5</version>
</dependency>
```

refers a product in repository as follows.

```
Home Dirctory\.m2\repository\mysql\mysql-connector-java\5.0.5
                                  \mysql-connector-java-5.0.5.jar
```

That is, in the format of

```
Home Dirctory\.m2\repository\groupId\artifactId\version\
artifactId-version.packaging
```

If our project requires one dependency which in turn requires many dependencies (Transitive dependencies), then in this case, just add the dependency required for our project, Maven will take care of adding the dependencies required for the added dependency implicitly.

Note: If one element (first element) is in relation two second element and the second element is in relation to third element, then the first element will be in relation to third element. This is called "Transitive" relationship.

10.4 MAVEN LIFE-CYCLE PHASES

Maven's default build life cycle consists of many distinct phases. Some of them are descried below.

`validate`

Validates the project configurations and POM are correct.

`initialize`

Initializes build state, such as creation of required directories.

`generate-sources`
: Generates source code, if code generators are used.

`process-sources`
: Processes the source code for parsing, modification, filtration of values ...

`generate-resources`
: Generates resources like configuration and meta-data files.

`process-resources`
: Processes the resource files for modification, and relocating to destination (output) directory.

`compile`
: Compiles the source code of the project and places compiled class files to the target directory.

`process-classes`
: Processes generated class files for byte code optimisation.

`generate-test-sources`
: Generates test source code (unit test case Java files), if code generators are used.

`process-test-sources`
: Processes the test source code for parsing, modification, filtration of values ...

`generate-test-resources`
: Generates resources like configuration resource files for testing.

`process-test-resources`
: Processes resources for test such as copying these resources to the test output directory.

`test-compile`
: Compiles the test source code into the test destination directory.

`process-test-classes`
: Processes generated test class files for byte code optimisation.

`test`
: Runs the compiled (unit) tests. By default, this goal will terminate a build if any test fails.

`prepare-package`
: Performs any operations necessary to prepare a package (jar, war ...) before the actual packaging.

`package`
: Packages (bundles) the project (compiled code and resources) in its distributable format, such as a JAR, WAR, ...

`pre-integration-test`
: Prepares for integration testing. It sets up the actual development environment for testing.

`integration-test`
: Deploys the package in to the actual development environment for performing integration tests.

`post-integration-test`

Performs actions required after integration tests have been executed such as cleaning up the testing environment.

`verify`

Verifies the validity and integrity of the generated deployable archive (jar, war …).

`install`

Installs the package into the local repository. So that other project can use this package (software) as dependency.

`deploy`

Copies the archive to a remote Maven repository so that other developers can use his package (software) as dependency for their projects.

10.5 MAVEN DIRECTORY STRUCTURE

Maven creates projects with the following directory structures.

`/artifactId/pom.xml` → Maven2 Project Object Model file

`/artifactId/src/main/java/` → Java source files

`/artifactId/src/test/java/` → Java unit tests files

`/artifactId/src/main/resources/` → CLASSPATH resources for Java source files

`/artifactId/src/test/resources/` → CLASSPATH resources for Java unit test files

`/artifactId/target/classes/` → Compiled Java classes

`/artifactId/target/test-classes/` → Compiled Java unit test classes

`/artifactId/src/main/webapp/` → root of webapp of web project

10.6 DEVELOPING A STAND-ALONE JAVA APPLICATION: DEMONSTRATION

We will now develop a stand-alone Java application using Maven. The application is to process Employee data.

Create a Java Project:

We are using Eclipse as Java IDE, download from *http://www.eclipse.org/* (in our case Eclipse Ganymede Version: 3.4.0) and install if you are not installed. I installed Eclipse at C:\Development\eclipse-jee-ganymede-win32 and created a workspace directory "workspace" under it.

Go to the "workspace" directory of Eclipse and issue the following command.

```
mvn archetype:generate
```

Note: User input is highlighted in bold. Some parts of the output text are removed and some of them are indicated by "...".

```
C:\Development\eclipse-jee-ganymede-win32\workspace> mvn archetype:generate
[INFO] Scanning for projects...
...
Choose archetype:
```

```
1: internal -> appfuse-basic-jsf (AppFuse archetype for creating a web application
with Hibernate, Spring and JSF)
...
15: internal -> maven-archetype-quickstart ()
...
41: internal -> gmaven-archetype-mojo (Groovy mojo archetype)
Choose a number: (1/2/3/4/5/6/7/8/9/10/11/12/13/14/15/16/17/18/19/20/21/22/23/24/
25/26/27/28/29/30/31/32/33/34/35/36/37/38/39/40/41) 15: : 15
Define value for groupId: : payroll
Define value for artifactId: : EmployeeApp
Define value for version: 1.0-SNAPSHOT: : ← Press Enter Key
Define value for package: payroll: : com.empapp
Confirm properties configuration:
groupId: payroll
artifactId: EmployeeApp
version: 1.0-SNAPSHOT
package: com.empapp
 Y: : ← Press Enter Key
...
[INFO] Parameter: groupId, Value: payroll
[INFO] Parameter: packageName, Value: com.empapp
[INFO] Parameter: package, Value: com.empapp
[INFO] Parameter: artifactId, Value: EmployeeApp
[INFO] Parameter: basedir, Value: C:\Development\eclipse-jee-ganymede-win32\workspace
[INFO] Parameter: version, Value: 1.0-SNAPSHOT
...
[INFO] BUILD SUCCESSFUL
...
```

Change Project editable in Eclipse:

Go to the created "EmployeeApp" directory, and use the following command to make project that can be editable with Eclipse.

```
mvn eclipse:eclipse
C:\Development\eclipse-jee-ganymede-win32\workspace> cd EmployeeApp
C:\Development\eclipse...win32\workspace\EmployeeApp> mvn eclipse:eclipse
[INFO] Scanning for projects...
[INFO] Building EmployeeApp
[INFO] task-segment: [eclipse:eclipse]
[INFO] [eclipse:eclipse]
...
[INFO] BUILD SUCCESSFUL
```

Import the Project to Eclipse IDE:

Invoke Eclipse IDE, Right click on Package Explorer tab, choose "Import" menu item. Select "Existing Projects into Workspace" and click "Next". Select the workspace directory (our EmployeeApp application resides) as root directory and tick the EmployeeApp project. Then, click "Finish".

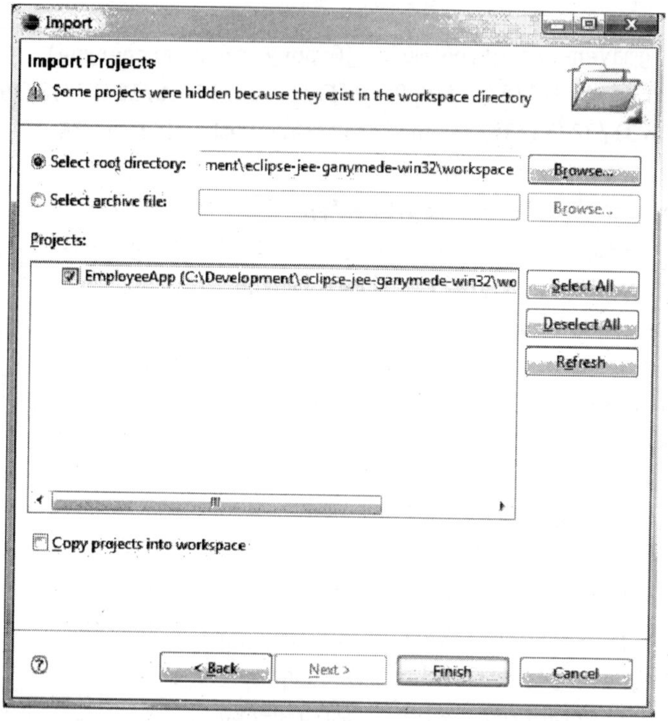

Then, you can see the directory structure in Package Explorer tab as below.

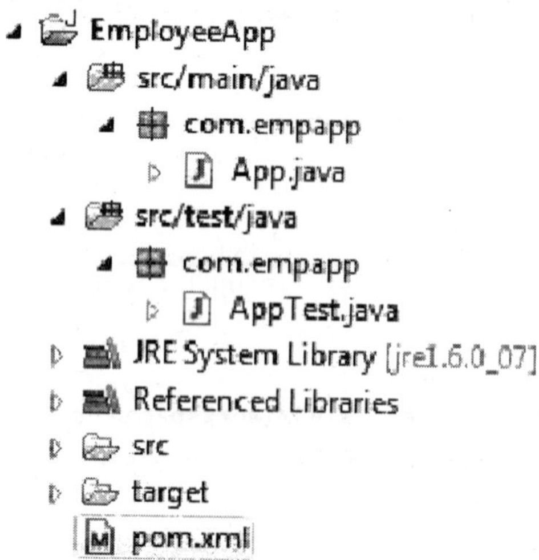

The content of the generated pom.xml (Project Object Model) file is as below.

```
<project xmlns="http://maven.apache.org/POM/4.0.0"
        xmlns:xsi="http://www.w3.org/2001/XMLSchema-instance"
```

```
        xsi:schemaLocation="http://maven.apache.org/POM/4.0.0
        http://maven.apache.org/maven-v4_0_0.xsd">
  <modelVersion>4.0.0</modelVersion>
  <groupId>payroll</groupId>
  <artifactId>EmployeeApp</artifactId>
  <packaging>jar</packaging>
  <version>1.0-SNAPSHOT</version>
  <name>EmployeeApp</name>
  <url>http://maven.apache.org</url>
  <dependencies>
   <dependency>
      <groupId>junit</groupId>
      <artifactId>junit</artifactId>
      <version>3.8.1</version>
      <scope>test</scope>
   </dependency>
  </dependencies>
</project>
```

Add Maven 2 Repository o CLASSPATH for Eclipse by choosing Window → Preferences menu items.

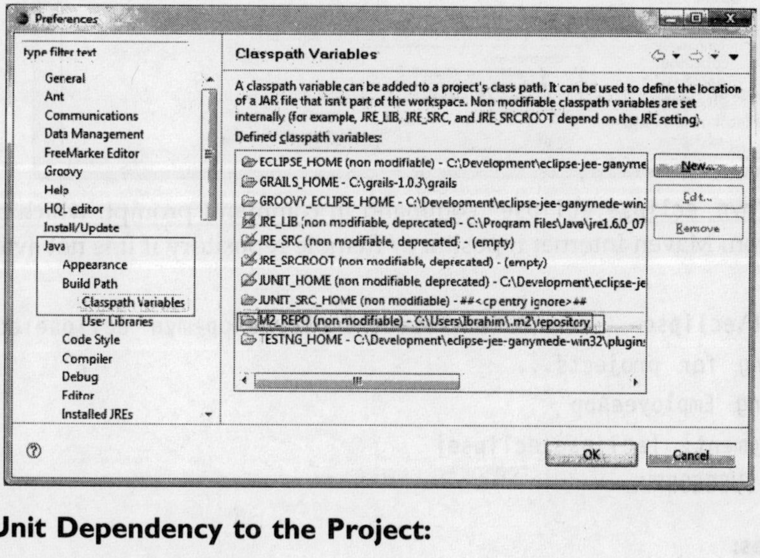

Add Latest JUnit Dependency to the Project:

Add JUnit 4.5 dependency to the project.

Edit the pom.xml and change "junit" version to 4.5 (which supports Java Annotations) as below.

```
<dependencies>
    <dependency>
      <groupId>junit</groupId>
```

```
      <artifactId>junit</artifactId>
      <version>4.5</version>
      <scope>test</scope>
    </dependency>
</dependencies>
```

You can find dependency information for each available dependency in *http://mvnrepository.com*.

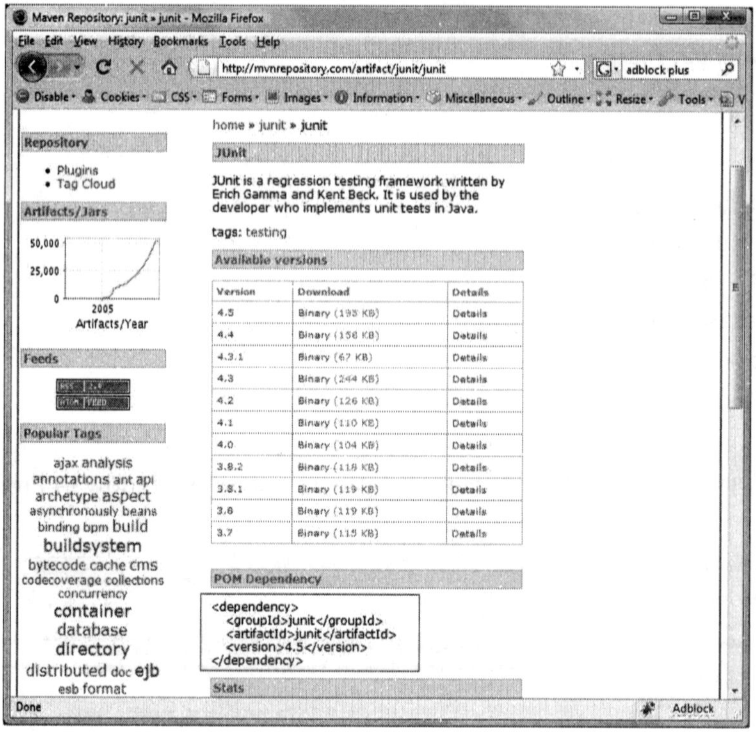

Then, use the "`mvn eclipse:eclipse`" command in command prompt, which download the required library from Maven Internet repository / Remote repository if it is not available in local repository.

```
C:\Development\eclipse-...-win32\workspace\EmployeeApp>mvn eclipse:eclipse
[INFO] Scanning for projects...
[INFO] Building EmployeeApp
[INFO] ask-segment: [eclipse:eclipse]
[INFO] BUILD SUCCESSFUL
```

Add Source Files:

Delete "*App.java*" and "*AppTest.java*" files, as they are generated automatically.

Add the following three classes in the package "com.empapp" under src/main/java. Select this package in Eclipse IDE, and right click New → Class.

```
// File Name: Employee.java
package com.empapp;
```

```
public class Employee {
    private int empNumber;
    private String empName;
    private double basicpay;
    private double allowances;
    private double deductions;
    private double netpay;
    public int getEmpNumber() {
    return empNumber;
    }
    public void setEmpNumber(int empNumber) {
    this.empNumber = empNumber;
    }
    public String getEmpName() {
    return empName;
    }
    public void setEmpName(String empName) {
    this.empName = empName;
    }
    public double getBasicpay() {
    return basicpay;
    }
    public void setBasicpay(double basicpay) {
    this.basicpay = basicpay;
    }
    public double getAllowances() {
    return allowances;
    }
    public void setAllowances(double allowances) {
    this.allowances = allowances;
    }
    public double getDeductions() {
    return deductions;
    }
    public void setDeductions(double deductions) {
    this.deductions = deductions;
    }
    public double getNetpay() {
```

```
        return netpay;
        }
        public void setNetpay(double netpay) {
        this.netpay = netpay;
        }
}
// File Name: ProcessEmployee.java
package com.empapp;
public class ProcessEmployee {
  public void calculateNetpay(Employee e) {
        e.setNetpay(e.getBasicpay() + e.getAllowances() - e.getDeductions());
  }
}
// File Name: EmployeeManipulation.java
package com.empapp;
import java.util.Scanner;
public class EmployeeManipulation {
  public static void main(String args[]) throws Exception {
        Employee emp = new Employee();
        // Get Employee data from user
        readEmployee(emp);
        // Find Net pay
        ProcessEmployee processEmployee = new ProcessEmployee();
        processEmployee.calculateNetpay(emp);
        // Display the Employee data
        printEmployee(emp);
}
static void readEmployee(Employee e) {
        Scanner s = new Scanner(System.in);
        System.out.println("Enter Employee Number ==> ");
        e.setEmpNumber(s.nextInt());
        System.out.println("Enter Employee Name ==> ");
        s.nextLine(); // Clearing new-line character
        e.setEmpName(s.nextLine());
        System.out.println("Enter Basic pay ==> ");
        e.setBasicpay(s.nextDouble());
        System.out.println("Enter Allowances ==> ");
        e.setAllowances(s.nextDouble());
        System.out.println("Enter Deductions ==> ");
```

```
        e.setDeductions(s.nextDouble());
        }
    static void printEmployee(Employee e) {
        System.out.println("\n ================================");
        System.out.printf("\n Employee Number : %d", e.getEmpNumber());
        System.out.printf("\n Employee Name   : %s", e.getEmpName());
        System.out.printf("\n Basic pay       : %.2f", e.getBasicpay());
        System.out.printf("\n Allowances      : %.2f", e.getAllowances());
        System.out.printf("\n Deductions      : %.2f", e.getDeductions());
        System.out.printf("\n Net pay         : %.2f", e.getNetpay());
        System.out.println("\n ================================");
    }
}
```

Add JUnit Test File(s):

Add the following JUnit test class in the package "com.empapp" under src/test/java.

```
// File Name: EmployeeTest.java
package com.empapp;
import org.junit.*;
import static org.junit.Assert.*;
public class EmployeeTest {
  @Test
  public void TestNetpay() {
     System.out.println("Test for Net pay");
     ProcessEmployee processEmployee = new ProcessEmployee();
     Employee emp = new Employee();
     emp.setBasicpay(10000.0);
     emp.setAllowances(3000.0);
     emp.setDeductions(1400.0);
     processEmployee.calculateNetpay(emp);
     assertEquals(11600, emp.getNetpay(), 0); // (Expected, Actual, Delta)
  }
}
```

Install the Application:

Install the application as shown below.

```
C:\Development\eclipse-...-win32\workspace\EmployeeApp> mvn install
[INFO] Scanning for projects...
[INFO] Building EmployeeApp
[INFO] task-segment: [install]
```

```
[INFO] [resources:resources]
[INFO] [compiler:compile]
[INFO] [resources:testResources]
[INFO] [compiler:testCompile]
[INFO] [surefire:test]
- - - - - - - - - - - - - - - - - - - - - - - - - - -
 T E S T S
- - - - - - - - - - - - - - - - - - - - - - - - - - -
Running com.empapp.EmployeeTest
Test for Net pay
Tests run: 1, Failures: 0, Errors: 0, Skipped: 0, time elapsed: 0.031 sec
Results :
Tests run: 1, Failures: 0, Errors: 0, Skipped: 0
[INFO] [jar:jar]
[INFO] [install:install]
[INFO] BUILD SUCCESSFUL
```

Note that a JAR file (as we specified in *pom.xml* file <packaging>jar</packaging>) is created and installed in the local repository as other applications can use it.

```
C:\Users\Ibrahim\.m2\repository\payroll>tree /F
Folder PATH listing for volume IBRAHIM DISK
Volume serial number is 0015F298 E641:D213
C:.
└───EmployeeApp
    │   maven-metadata-local.xml
    │
    └───1.0-SNAPSHOT
            EmployeeApp-1.0-SNAPSHOT.jar
            EmployeeApp-1.0-SNAPSHOT.pom
            maven-metadata-local.xml
```

Run the Application:

To execute this Java application with Eclipse IDE: Select the EmployeeManipulation.java file, Right click on his content → Run As → Java Application.

To execute this Java application with Command Window: Change to the "target", where the generated JAR file presents. And issue the following command.

```
C:\Development\eclipse-jee-ganymede-win32\workspace\EmployeeApp\target>
   java -cp EmployeeApp-1.0-SNAPSHOT.jar com.empapp.EmployeeManipulation
Enter Employee Number ==>
1000
Enter Employee Name ==>
Mohamed Ibrahim
Enter Basic pay ==>
8000.0
Enter Allowances ==>
2000.0
```

```
Enter Deductions ==>
1000.0
 ================================
 Employee Number : 1000
 Employee Name   : Mohamed Ibrahim
 Basic pay       : 8000.00
 Allowances      : 2000.00
 Deductions      : 1000.00
 Net pay         : 9000.00
 ================================
```

10.7 DEVELOPING A WEB-BASED JAVA APPLICATION: DEMONSTRATION

We will develop a web-based application, which manipulates Employee data.

Create a Java Project:

Go to the "workspace" directory of Eclipse and issue the following command.

```
mvn archetype:generate
C:\Development\eclipse-jee-ganymede-win32\workspace> mvn archetype:generate
[INFO] Scanning for projects...
Choose archetype:
1: internal -> appfuse-basic-jsf (AppFuse archetype for creating a web application
with Hibernate, Spring and JSF)
...
18: internal -> maven-archetype-webapp (A simple Java web application)
...
41: internal -> gmaven-archetype-mojo (Groovy mojo archetype)
Choose a number: (1/2/3/4/5/6/7/8/9/10/11/12/13/14/15/16/17/18/19/20/21/22/23/24/
25/26/27/28/29/30/31/32/33/34/35/36/37/38/39/40/41) 15: : 18
[INFO] artifact org.apache.maven.archetypes:maven-archetype-webapp: checking for
updates from central
Define value for groupId: : payrollWeb
Define value for artifactId: : EmployeeAppWeb
Define value for version: 1.0-SNAPSHOT: :
Define value for package: payrollWeb: : com.empapp
Confirm properties configuration:
groupId: payrollWeb
artifactId: EmployeeAppWeb
version: 1.0-SNAPSHOT
package: com.empapp
 Y: :
[INFO] BUILD SUCCESSFUL
```

Change Project editable in Eclipse:

Go to the created "EmployeeAppWeb" directory, and use the following command to make project that can be editable with Eclipse.

```
      mvn eclipse:eclipse
C:\Development\eclipse-...\workspace\EmployeeAppWeb> mvn eclipse:eclipse
[INFO] Scanning for projects...
[INFO] Building EmployeeAppWeb Maven Webapp
[INFO] ask-segment: [eclipse:eclipse]
[INFO] Preparing eclipse:eclipse
[INFO] [eclipse:eclipse]
[INFO] BUILD SUCCESSFUL
```

Import the Project to Eclipse IDE:

Invoke Eclipse IDE, Right click on Package Explorer tab, choose "Import" menu item. Select "Existing Projects into Workspace" and click "Next". Select the workspace directory (our EmployeeAppWeb application resides) as root directory and tick the EmployeeAppWeb project. Then, click "Finish".

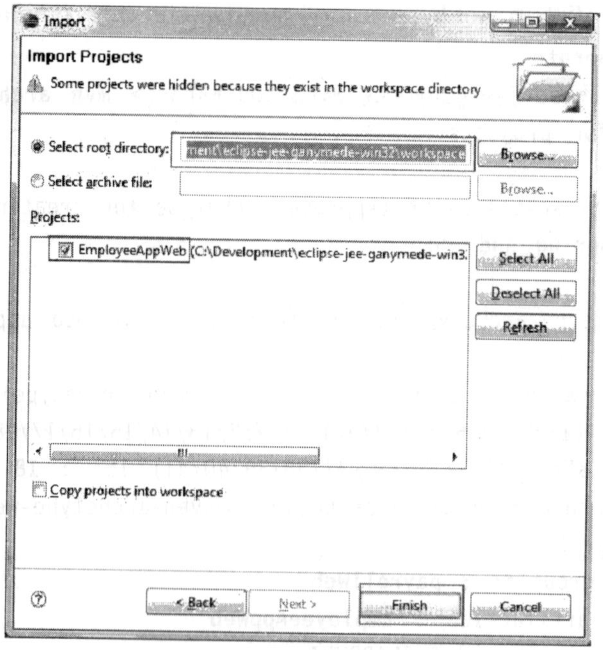

Then, you can see the directory structure in Package Explorer tab as below.

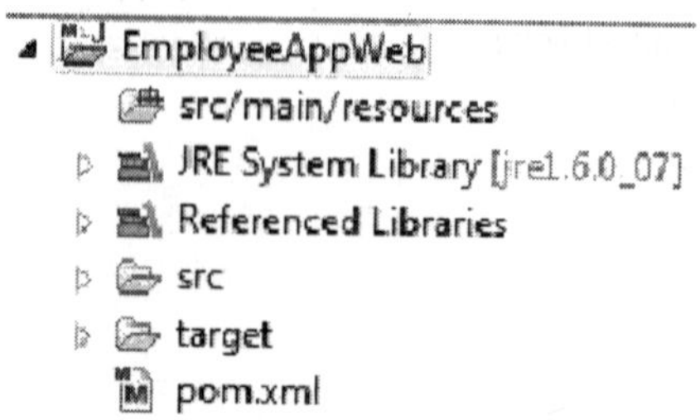

The content of the generated pom.xml (Project Object Model) file is as below.

```
<project  xmlns="http://maven.apache.org/POM/4.0.0"
     xmlns:xsi="http://www.w3.org/2001/XMLSchema-instance"
     xsi:schemaLocation="http://maven.apache.org/POM/4.0.0
     http://maven.apache.org/maven-v4_0_0.xsd">
   <modelVersion>4.0.0</modelVersion>
   <groupId>payrollWeb</groupId>
   <artifactId>EmployeeAppWeb</artifactId>
   <packaging>war</packaging>
   <version>1.0-SNAPSHOT</version>
   <name>EmployeeAppWeb  Maven  Webapp</name>
   <dependencies>
      <dependency>
           <groupId>javax.servlet</groupId>
           <artifactId>servlet-api</artifactId>
           <version>2.4</version>
           <scope>provided</scope>
      </dependency>
      <dependency>
           <groupId>junit</groupId>
           <artifactId>junit</artifactId>
           <version>4.5</version>
           <scope>test</scope>
      </dependency>
    </dependencies>
    <build>
           <finalName>EmployeeAppWeb</finalName>
           <plugins>
               <plugin>
                    <groupId>org.mortbay.jetty</groupId>
                    <artifactId>maven-jetty-plugin</artifactId>
               </plugin>
           </plugins>
     </build>
</project>
```

Note hat he packaging becomes war (<packaging>war</packaging>).

Add Maven 2 Repository o CLASSPATH for Eclipse by choosing Window → Preferences menu items, if not added earlier.

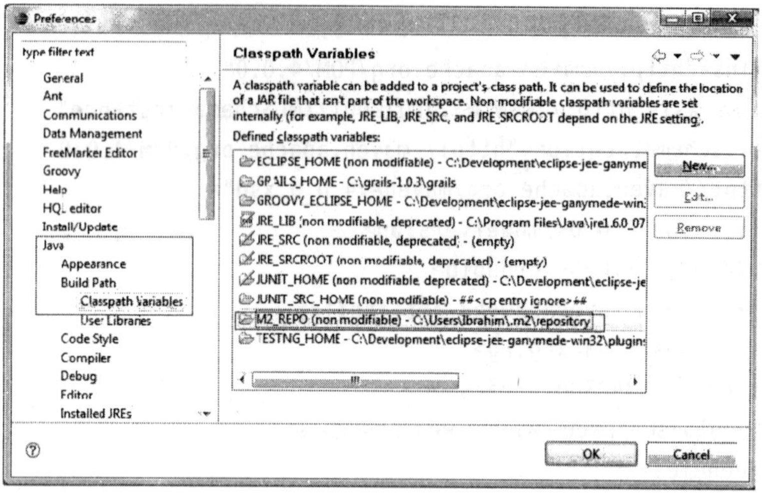

Add dependencies to the Project:

Add JUnit 4.5 dependency to the project: Edit the pom.xml and change "junit" version to 4.5 (which supports Java Annotations) as below.

```
<dependency>
   <groupId>junit</groupId>
   <artifactId>junit</artifactId>
   <version>4.5</version>
   <scope>test</scope>
</dependency>
```

Add Servlet 2.4 Specification dependency to the project: Add the following dependency tag inside the <dependencies> element.

```
<dependency>
      <groupId>javax.servlet</groupId>
      <artifactId>servlet-api</artifactId>
      <version>2.4</version>
      <scope>provided</scope>
</dependency>
```

Configuring Jetty Plug-in:

Once the project is installed, we are required one Servlet container such as *omcat* to test the application. Then you need to copy the *war* file to the deployment directory along with the required library files (when <scope>provided</scope>). Instead, we can use the Maven Jetty plug-in to run our web application within Maven. To do this, we will need to configure the Maven Jetty plug-in in pom.xml as below.

```
<build>
   <finalName>EmployeeAppWeb</finalName>
   <plugins>
```

```
            <plugin>
                    <groupId>org.mortbay.jetty</groupId>
                    <artifactId>maven-jetty-plugin</artifactId>
            </plugin>
      </plugins>
   </build>
```

The following plug-in forces Maven compiler to use Java 1.5 version.

```
<plugin>
      <groupId>org.apache.maven.plugins</groupId>
<artifactId>maven-compiler-plugin</artifactId>
      <configuration>
            <source>1.5</source>
            <target>1.5</target>
      </configuration>
</plugin>
```

At this stage, the content of *pom.xml* file is as below.

```
<project  xmlns="http://maven.apache.org/POM/4.0.0"
          xmlns:xsi="http://www.w3.org/2001/XMLSchema-instance"
          xsi:schemaLocation="http://maven.apache.org/POM/4.0.0
          http://maven.apache.org/maven-v4_0_0.xsd">
      <modelVersion>4.0.0</modelVersion>
      <groupId>payrollWeb</groupId>
      <artifactId>EmployeeAppWeb</artifactId>
      <packaging>war</packaging>
      <version>1.0-SNAPSHOT</version>
      <name>EmployeeAppWeb  Maven  Webapp</name>
   <dependencies>
   <dependency>
          <groupId>javax.servlet</groupId>
          <artifactId>servlet-api</artifactId>
          <version>2.4</version>
          <scope>provided</scope>
   </dependency>
   <dependency>
          <groupId>junit</groupId>
          <artifactId>junit</artifactId>
          <version>4.5</version>
          <scope>test</scope>
   </dependency>
```

```
</dependencies>
<build>
        <finalName>EmployeeAppWeb</finalName>
        <plugins>
                  <plugin>
                       <groupId>org.apache.maven.plugins</groupId>
                       <artifactId>maven-compiler-plugin</artifactId>
                       <configuration>
                             <source>1.5</source>
                             <target>1.5</target>
                       </configuration>
                 </plugin>
                 <plugin>
                       <groupId>org.mortbay.jetty</groupId>
                       <artifactId>maven-jetty-plugin</artifactId>
                 </plugin>
           </plugins>
      </build>
</project>
```

Then, use the "mvn eclipse:eclipse" command in command prompt, which updates dependencies to the project automatically. The "eclipse:clean" option used with mvn command removes old settings.

```
C:\Development\eclipse-jee-ganymede-win32\workspace\EmployeeAppWeb>
 mvn eclipse:clean eclipse:eclipse
[INFO] Scanning for projects...
[INFO] Building EmployeeAppWeb Maven Webapp
[INFO] ask-segment: [eclipse:clean, eclipse:eclipse]
[INFO] [eclipse:clean]
...
[INFO] [eclipse:eclipse]
...
[INFO] BUILD SUCCESSFUL
```

Create necessary directories:

Create /src/main/java and /src/test/java directories under Project root (EmployeeAppWeb) and make sure that the directory src/main/resources exists (already created by Maven). Use "mvn eclipse:eclipse" command in command prompt and refresh the project in Eclipse IDE.

The project structure in Eclipse IDE looks below.

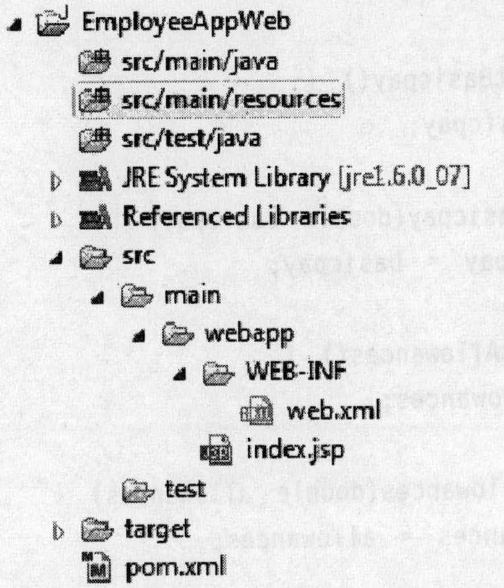

Add Source Files:

Add the following three classes in the package "com.empapp" under src/main/java.

Select "`src/main/java`" folder, and right click → New → Package.

Select this package in Eclipse IDE, and right click → New → Class.

```
// File Name: Employee.java
package com.empapp;
public class Employee {
      private int empNumber;
      private String empName;
      private double basicpay;
      private double allowances;
      private double deductions;
      private double netpay;
      public int getEmpNumber() {
            return empNumber;
      }
      public void setEmpNumber(int empNumber) {
            this.empNumber = empNumber;
      }
      public String getEmpName() {
            return empName;
      }
      public void setEmpName(String empName) {
            this.empName = empName;
```

```
        }
        public double getBasicpay() {
                return basicpay;
        }
        public void setBasicpay(double basicpay) {
                this.basicpay = basicpay;
        }
        public double getAllowances() {
                return allowances;
        }
        public void setAllowances(double allowances) {
                this.allowances = allowances;
        }
        public double getDeductions() {
                return deductions;
        }
        public void setDeductions(double deductions) {
                this.deductions = deductions;
        }
        public double getNetpay() {
                return netpay;
        }
        public void setNetpay(double netpay) {
                this.netpay = netpay;
        }
}
// File Name: ProcessEmployee.java
package com.empapp;
public class ProcessEmployee {
    public void calculateNetpay(Employee e) {
      e.setNetpay(e.getBasicpay() + e.getAllowances() - e.getDeductions());
    }
}
// File Name: EmployeeServlet.java
package com.empapp;
import java.io.IOException;
import java.io.PrintWriter;
import javax.servlet.ServletException;
import javax.servlet.http.HttpServlet;
```

```
import javax.servlet.http.HttpServletRequest;
import javax.servlet.http.HttpServletResponse;
public class EmployeeServlet extends HttpServlet {
  public void doGet(HttpServletRequest request,
                HttpServletResponse response)
                throws ServletException, IOException {
    doPost(request, response);
  }
  public void doPost(HttpServletRequest request,
                HttpServletResponse response)
                throws ServletException, IOException {
    try {
    Employee emp = new Employee();
    // Get Employee data from user (from browser)
    readEmployee(request, emp);
    // Find Net pay
    ProcessEmployee processEmployee = new ProcessEmployee();
    processEmployee.calculateNetpay(emp);
   // Display the Employee data on the browser (Send as response)
   printEmployee(emp, response);
  }
  catch (Exception e) {
   e.printStackTrace();
  }
}
static void readEmployee(HttpServletRequest request, Employee e)
                                             throws Exception {
   // Assumed that Javascript validation is performed
   // to ensure valid data are entered in the form
   e.setEmpNumber(Integer.parseInt(request.getParameter("empNumber")));
   e.setEmpName(request.getParameter("empName"));
   e.setBasicpay(Double.parseDouble(request.getParameter("basicpay")));
   e.setAllowances(Double.parseDouble(request.getParameter("allowances")));
   e.setDeductions(Double.parseDouble(request.getParameter("deductions")));
}
static void printEmployee(Employee e, HttpServletResponse response)
                                             throws Exception {
   PrintWriter out = response.getWriter();
   out.println("<html> <body>");
```

```
        out.println("<table> <caption><b><u> Employee Salary Information
                                               </u></b></caption>");
        out.println("<tr> <td> Employee Number </td> <td> " +
                                        e.getEmpNumber() + " </td> </tr>");
        out.println("<tr> <td> Employee Name </td> <td> " +
                                        e.getEmpName() + " </td> </tr>");
        out.println("<tr> <td> Basic pay </td> <td> " +
            String.format("%.2f", new Double(e.getBasicpay())) + " </td> </tr>");
        out.println("<tr> <td> Allowances </td> <td> " +
            String.format("%.2f", e.getAllowances()) + " </td> </tr>");
        out.println("<tr> <td> Deductions </td> <td> " +
            String.format("%.2f", e.getDeductions()) + " </td> </tr>");
        out.println("<tr> <td> Net pay </td> <td> " +
            String.format("%.2f", e.getNetpay()) + " </td> </tr>");
        out.println("</table> </body> </html>");
        out.flush();
        out.close();
    }
}
```

Add JUnit test File(s):

Add the following JUnit test class in the package "`com.empapp`" (create this package) under `src/test/java`.

```
// File Name: EmployeeTest.java
package com.empapp;
import org.junit.*;
import static org.junit.Assert.*;
public class EmployeeTest {
  @Test
  public void testNetpay() {
      System.out.println("Test for Net pay");
      ProcessEmployee processEmployee = new ProcessEmployee();
      Employee emp = new Employee();
      emp.setBasicpay(10000.0);
      emp.setAllowances(3000.0);
      emp.setDeductions(1400.0);
      processEmployee.calculateNetpay(emp);
      assertEquals(11600, emp.getNetpay(), 0); // (Expected, Actual, Delta)
  }
}
```

Add Deployment Descriptors in *web.xml* file:

Include `<servlet>` and `<servlet-mapping>` code for EmployeeServlet servlet in *web.xml* file.

Then, the content of `/src/main/webapp/WEB-INF/web.xml` file is as below.

```
<!DOCTYPE web-app PUBLIC
        "-//Sun Microsystems, Inc.//DTD Web Application 2.3//EN"
        "http://java.sun.com/dtd/web-app_2_3.dtd" >
<web-app>
    <display-name>Employee Manipulation</display-name>
    <servlet>
          <servlet-name>employee</servlet-name>
          <servlet-class>com.empapp.EmployeeServlet</servlet-class>
    </servlet>
    <servlet-mapping>
          <servlet-name>employee</servlet-name>
          <url-pattern>/EmpSal</url-pattern>
    </servlet-mapping>
</web-app>
```

Add required HTML/JSP files:

To get the Employee data from user, use a JSP file which will submit data to the EmployeeServlet. Store the JSP file named *"empdetails.jsp"* with the following content in the */src/main/webapp* directory.

```
<html>
  <head>
      <title>Employee Manipulation</title>
      <!– Write Javascript for validating data on input fields,
         before form submission. –>
  </head>
  <body>
      <form name="form" method="post" action="/EmployeeAppWeb/EmpSal">
      <h2>Enter Employee Details<h2>
  <table>
      <tr>
            <td>Employee Number</td>
            <td><input type="text" name="empNumber"></td>
     </tr>
     <tr>
            <td>Employee Name</td>
            <td><input type="text" name="empName"></td>
     </tr>
     <tr>
```

```
                <td>Basic pay</td>
                <td><input type="text" name="basicpay"></td>
        </tr>
        <tr>
                <td>Allowances</td>
                <td><input type="text" name="allowances"></td>
        </tr>
        <tr>
                <td>Deductions</td>
                <td><input type="text" name="deductions"></td>
        </tr>
        <tr align="center">
                <td colspan=2><input type="submit" value="Submit"></td>
        </tr>
      </table>
      </form>
    </body>
  </html>
```

Install the Application:

Install the application as shown below.

```
C:\Development\eclipse-...win32\workspace\EmployeeAppWeb> mvn clean install
[INFO] Scanning for projects...
[INFO] Building EmployeeAppWeb Maven Webapp
[INFO] task-segment: [clean, install]
[INFO] [clean:clean]
[INFO] [resources:resources]
[INFO] [compiler:compile]
[INFO] [resources:testResources]
[INFO] [compiler:testCompile]
[INFO] [surefire:test]
_______________________________
  TESTS
_______________________________
Running com.empapp.EmployeeTest
Test for Net pay
Tests run: 1, Failures: 0, Errors: 0, Skipped: 0, time elapsed: 0.025 sec
Results :
Tests run: 1, Failures: 0, Errors: 0, Skipped: 0
[INFO] [war:war]
```

```
[INFO] [install:install]
[INFO] BUILD SUCCESSFUL
```

Note that a WAR file (as we specified in *pom.xml* file <packaging>war</packaging>) is created nd installed in the local repository.

Deploy the Web Application:

We can deploy this application (war file) on any Application Server (Servlet Container) with equired library *jar* files. However, we enabled Jetty Servlet Container (plug-in enabled in *pom.xml* ile) so that we can invoke Jetty to run using the following command, which will automatically deploy our application.

```
C:\Development\eclipse-...-win32\workspace\EmployeeAppWeb> mvn jetty:run
[INFO] Scanning for projects...
[INFO] Building EmployeeAppWeb Maven Webapp
[INFO] task-segment: [jetty:run]
[INFO] Preparing jetty:run
[INFO] [resources:resources]
[INFO] [compiler:compile]
[INFO] [resources:testResources]
[INFO] [compiler:testCompile]
[INFO] [jetty:run]
...
[INFO] Started Jetty Server
```

Testing the Application:

Once, our web application is deployed on application server (in our case, Jetty Servlet Container), we can invoke the application with browser.

Invoke the browser with address *http://localhost:8080/EmployeeAppWeb/empdetails.jsp*

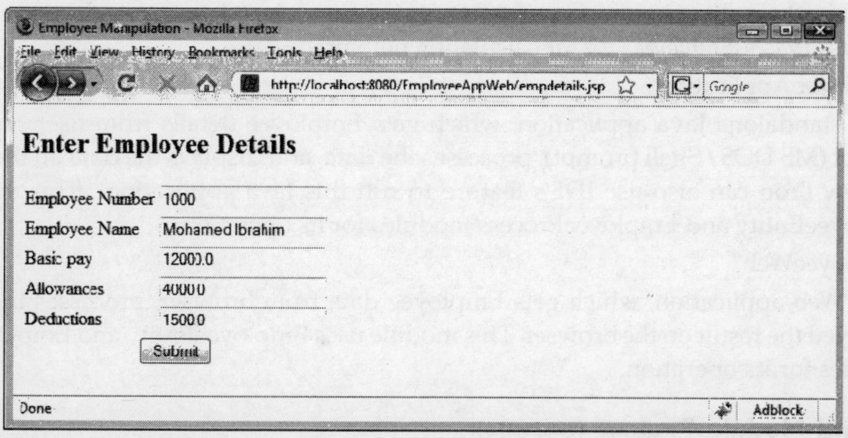

Enter necessary data and click on "`Submit`". Then, the Http request with the data will be sent to he `EmployeeServlet` and the resultant data will be sent back to the browser as Http response fter the manipulation of data.

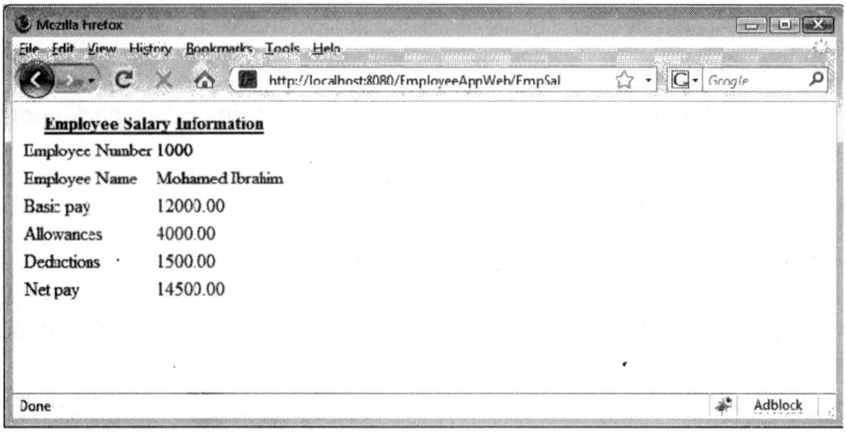

10.8 DEVELOPING A MULTI-MODULE PROJECT: DEMONSTRATION

A multi-module project contains more than just one module (as demonstrated earlier), each for one specific goal. For example, all entity classes form one module, all DAO related activities are grouped as one module, all utilities can be reated as one module, and all controllers are defined in one module. These modules interacts with each other to achieve its goals, thus these modules are separate elements, but parts of a single project.

Generally, Multi-module concept is applied for large projects, not suitable for small applications. However, for demonstration purpose, we will create a multi-module project for Employee Manipulation application.

The parent (main / project) is "EmployeeAppMultiModule". This contains four modules as described below.

(1) "EmployeeEntity"

It contains Java Beans / Value Objects to hold Employee details, in our demo, we have only one value object (*Employee.java*).

(2) "EmployeeProcess"

It contains Java classes / interfaces for processing Employee data, in our demo, we have only one class *ProcessEmployee.java* for calculating netpay.

(3) "EmployeeApplication"

It is a standalone Java application, which gets Employee details from user on command prompt (MS DOS / Shell prompt), processes the data, and displays the data on the command window (You can also use IDE's feature to run this Java application). This module uses EmployeeEntity and EmployeeProcess modules for its operation.

(4) "EmployeeWeb"

It is a Web application, which gets Employee data from browser, processes the data, and displayed the result on the browser. This module uses EmployeeEntity and EmployeeProcess modules for its operation.

Create Multi-Module Project (parent):

Go to the "workspace" directory of Eclipse and create a directory named "Employee AppMulti Module" (Project Directory).

```
C:\Development\eclipse-jee-ganymede-win32\workspace> mkdir EmployeeAppMultiModule
C:\Development\eclipse-jee-ganymede-win32\workspace> cd EmployeeAppMultiModule
C:\Development\eclipse-jee-ganymede-win32\workspace\EmployeeAppMultiModule>
```

Create Modules (projects) in Parent:

All the modules except "EmployeeWeb" are of type Java application project. Create these projects (modules) inside the "EmployeeAppMultiModule" directory.

Create "EmployeeEntity" module:

Go to the workspace\EmployeeAppMultiModule directory and issue the following command (just use mvn archetype:generate for interactive input while creation of project).

```
C:\Development\eclipse-jee-ganymede-win32\workspace\EmployeeAppMultiModule>
        mvn archetype:generate
            -DgroupId=PayrollMultiModule
            -DartifactId=EmployeeEntity
            -Dpackage=com.empbeans
            -DarchetypeArtifactId=maven-archetype-quickstart
            -Dversion=1.0-SNAPSHOT
[INFO] Scanning for projects...
[INFO] Preparing archetype:generate
[INFO] [archetype:generate]
[INFO] Generating project in Interactive mode
Confirm properties configuration:
groupId: PayrollMultiModule
artifactId: EmployeeEntity
version: 1.0-SNAPSHOT
package: com.empbeans
 Y: :
....
[INFO] BUILD SUCCESSFUL
```

Create "EmployeeProcess" module:

Go to the workspace\EmployeeAppMultiModule directory and issue the following command.

```
C:\Development\eclipse-jee-ganymede-win32\workspace\EmployeeAppMultiModule>
        mvn archetype:generate
            -DgroupId=PayrollMultiModule
            -DartifactId=EmployeeProcess
            -Dpackage=com.empprocess
            -DarchetypeArtifactId=maven-archetype-quickstart
            -Dversion=1.0-SNAPSHOT
```

```
[INFO] Scanning for projects...
[INFO] Preparing archetype:generate
[INFO] [archetype:generate]
[INFO] Generating project in Interactive mode
Confirm properties configuration:
groupId: PayrollMultiModule
artifactId: EmployeeProcess
version: 1.0-SNAPSHOT
package: com.empprocess
 Y: :
[INFO] BUILD SUCCESSFUL
```

Create "EmployeeApplication" module:

Go to the workspace\EmployeeAppMultiModule directory and issue the following command.

```
C:\Development\eclipse-jee-ganymede-win32\workspace\EmployeeAppMultiModule>
        mvn archetype:generate
            -DgroupId=PayrollMultiModule
            -DartifactId=EmployeeApplication
            -Dpackage=com.empapp
            -DarchetypeArtifactId=maven-archetype-quickstart
            -Dversion=1.0-SNAPSHOT
[INFO] Scanning for projects...
[INFO] Preparing archetype:generate
[INFO] [archetype:generate]
[INFO] Generating project in Interactive mode
Confirm properties configuration:
groupId: PayrollMultiModule
artifactId: EmployeeApplication
version: 1.0-SNAPSHOT
package: com.empapp
 Y: :
[INFO] Parameter: groupId, Value: PayrollMultiModule
[INFO] Parameter: packageName, Value: com.empapp
[INFO] Parameter: package, Value: com.empapp
[INFO] Parameter: artifactId, Value: EmployeeApplication
[INFO] Parameter: basedir, Value:C:\Development\eclipse-jee-ganymede-
win32\workspace\EmployeeAppMultiModule
[INFO] BUILD SUCCESSFUL
```

Create "EmployeeWeb" module:

Go to the workspace\EmployeeAppMultiModule directory and issue the following command.

```
C:\Development\eclipse-jee-ganymede-win32\workspace\EmployeeAppMultiModule>
        mvn archetype:generate
            -DgroupId=PayrollMultiModule
            -DartifactId=EmployeeWeb
            -Dpackage=com.empwebapp
            -DarchetypeArtifactId=maven-archetype-webapp
            -Dversion=1.0-SNAPSHOT
[INFO] Scanning for projects...
[INFO] Preparing archetype:generate
[INFO] [archetype:generate]
[INFO] Generating project in Interactive mode
Confirm properties configuration:
groupId: PayrollMultiModule
artifactId: EmployeeWeb
version: 1.0-SNAPSHOT
package: com.empwebapp
 Y: :
[INFO] BUILD SUCCESSFUL
```

Create parent *pom.xml* file:

Store the following *pom.xml* file in "EmployeeAppMultiModule" directory.

```
<project xmlns="http://maven.apache.org/POM/4.0.0"
      xmlns:xsi="http://www.w3.org/2001/XMLSchema-instance"
      xsi:schemaLocation="http://maven.apache.org/POM/4.0.0
      http://maven.apache.org/maven-v4_0_0.xsd">
    <modelVersion>4.0.0</modelVersion>
    <groupId>PayrollMultiModule</groupId>
    <artifactId>EmployeeAppMultiModule</artifactId>
    <packaging>pom</packaging>
    <version>1.0</version>
    <name>EmployeeApp MultiModule</name>
    <modules>
        <module>EmployeeEntity</module>
        <module>EmployeeProcess</module>
        <module>EmployeeApplication</module>
        <module>EmployeeWeb</module>
    </modules>
```

```
        <build>
            <pluginManagement>
                <plugins>
                  <plugin>
                    <groupId>org.apache.maven.plugins</groupId>
                    <artifactId>maven-compiler-plugin</artifactId>
                        <configuration>
                          <source>1.5</source>
                          <target>1.5</target>
                        </configuration>
                     </plugin>
                  </plugins>
            </pluginManagement>
        </build>
        <dependencies>
            <dependency>
                  <groupId>junit</groupId>
                  <artifactId>junit</artifactId>
                  <version>4.5</version>
                  <scope>test</scope>
            </dependency>
        </dependencies>
</project>
```

The <modules> element in *pom.xml* adds the specified modules to this parent project.

```
        <modules>
              <module>EmployeeEntity</module>
              <module>EmployeeProcess</module>
              <module>EmployeeApplication</module>
              <module>EmployeeWeb</module>
        </modules>
```

Configure *pom.xml* for modules:

Modify *pom.xml* file of "EmployeeEntity" (*/EmployeeAppMultiModule/EmployeeEntity*) as below.

```
<project  xmlns="http://maven.apache.org/POM/4.0.0"
          xmlns:xsi="http://www.w3.org/2001/XMLSchema-instance"
          xsi:schemaLocation="http://maven.apache.org/POM/4.0.0
          http://maven.apache.org/maven-v4_0_0.xsd">
<modelVersion>4.0.0</modelVersion>
<groupId>PayrollMultiModule</groupId>
```

```
<artifactId>EmployeeEntity</artifactId>
<packaging>jar</packaging>
<version>1.0-SNAPSHOT</version>
<name>Employee Entity Module</name>
    <parent>
        <groupId>PayrollMultiModule</groupId>
        <artifactId>EmployeeAppMultiModule</artifactId>
        <version>1.0</version>
        </parent>
</project>
```

Modify *pom.xml* file of "EmployeeProcess" (*/EmployeeAppMultiModule/EmployeeProcess*) as below.

```
<project xmlns="http://maven.apache.org/POM/4.0.0"
      xmlns:xsi="http://www.w3.org/2001/XMLSchema-instance"
      xsi:schemaLocation="http://maven.apache.org/POM/4.0.0
      http://maven.apache.org/maven-v4_0_0.xsd">
    <modelVersion>4.0.0</modelVersion>
    <groupId>PayrollMultiModule</groupId>
    <artifactId>EmployeeProcess</artifactId>
    <packaging>jar</packaging>
    <version>1.0-SNAPSHOT</version>
    <name>Employee Process Module</name>
    <parent>
        <groupId>PayrollMultiModule</groupId>
        <artifactId>EmployeeAppMultiModule</artifactId>
        <version>1.0</version>
    </parent>
    <dependencies>
        <dependency>
            <groupId>PayrollMultiModule</groupId>
            <artifactId>EmployeeEntity</artifactId>
            <version>1.0-SNAPSHOT</version>
        </dependency>
    </dependencies>
</project>
```

Modify *pom.xml* file of "EmployeeApplication" (*/EmployeeAppMultiModule/ EmployeeApplication*) as below.

```
<project xmlns="http://maven.apache.org/POM/4.0.0"
      xmlns:xsi="http://www.w3.org/2001/XMLSchema-instance"
      xsi:schemaLocation="http://maven.apache.org/POM/4.0.0
      http://maven.apache.org/maven-v4_0_0.xsd">
```

```
<modelVersion>4.0.0</modelVersion>
<groupId>PayrollMultiModule</groupId>
<artifactId>EmployeeApplication</artifactId>
<packaging>jar</packaging>
<version>1.0-SNAPSHOT</version>
<name>Employee  Application  Module</name>
<parent>
     <groupId>PayrollMultiModule</groupId>
     <artifactId>EmployeeAppMultiModule</artifactId>
     <version>1.0</version>
</parent>
<dependencies>
    <dependency>
      <groupId>PayrollMultiModule</groupId>
      <artifactId>EmployeeEntity</artifactId>
      <version>1.0-SNAPSHOT</version>
    </dependency>
    <dependency>
      <groupId>PayrollMultiModule</groupId>
      <artifactId>EmployeeProcess</artifactId>
      <version>1.0-SNAPSHOT</version>
    </dependency>
 </dependencies>
 <build>
      <plugins>
           <plugin>
                <artifactId>maven-assembly-plugin</artifactId>
                <configuration>
                  <descriptorRefs>
                    <descriptorRef>
                       jar-with-dependencies
                    </descriptorRef>
                  </descriptorRefs>
                </configuration>
                </plugin>
           </plugins>
      </build>
 </project>
```

Modify *pom.xml* file of "EmployeeWeb" (*/EmployeeAppMultiModule/EmployeeWeb*) as below.

```
<project xmlns="http://maven.apache.org/POM/4.0.0"
        xmlns:xsi="http://www.w3.org/2001/XMLSchema-instance"
        xsi:schemaLocation="http://maven.apache.org/POM/4.0.0
        http://maven.apache.org/maven-v4_0_0.xsd">
<modelVersion>4.0.0</modelVersion>
<groupId>PayrollMultiModule</groupId>
<artifactId>EmployeeWeb</artifactId>
<packaging>war</packaging>
<version>1.0-SNAPSHOT</version>
<name>EmployeeWeb Maven Webapp</name>
<parent>
    <groupId>PayrollMultiModule</groupId>
    <artifactId>EmployeeAppMultiModule</artifactId>
    <version>1.0</version>
</parent>
<dependencies>
    <dependency>
        <groupId>PayrollMultiModule</groupId>
        <artifactId>EmployeeEntity</artifactId>
        <version>1.0-SNAPSHOT</version>
    </dependency>
    <dependency>
        <groupId>PayrollMultiModule</groupId>
        <artifactId>EmployeeProcess</artifactId>
        <version>1.0-SNAPSHOT</version>
    </dependency>
    <dependency>
        <groupId>javax.servlet</groupId>
        <artifactId>servlet-api</artifactId>
        <version>2.4</version>
        <scope>provided</scope>
    </dependency>
  </dependencies>
  <build>
   <finalName>EmployeeWeb</finalName>
    <plugins>
     <plugin>
        <groupId>org.apache.maven.plugins</groupId>
        <artifactId>maven-compiler-plugin</artifactId>
```

```
            <configuration>
                 <source>1.5</source>
                 <target>1.5</target>
            </configuration>
            </plugin>
            <plugin>
              <groupId>org.mortbay.jetty</groupId>
              <artifactId>maven-jetty-plugin</artifactId>
              <version>6.1.10</version>
              <configuration>
                 <contextPath>EmployeeWeb</contextPath>
                 <webApp>target/EmployeeWeb</webApp>
                 <scanIntervalSeconds>30</scanIntervalSeconds>
                 <connectors>
                  <connector implementation =" org. mortbay. jetty. nio. Select
                  ChannelConnector">
                    <port>8080</port>
                    <maxIdleTime>60000</maxIdleTime>
                  </connector>
               </connectors>
               <requestLog  implementation="org.mortbay.jetty.NCSARequestLog">
                  <filename>target/yyyy_mm_dd.request.log</filename>
                  <retainDays>90</retainDays>
                  <append>true</append>
                  <extended>false</extended>
                  <logTimeZone>GMT</logTimeZone>
               </requestLog>
             </configuration>
           </plugin>
         </plugins>
         <resources>
           <resource>
               <directory>src/main/resources</directory>
               <filtering>true</filtering>
           </resource>
        </resources>
     </build>
  </project>
```

Delete Auto-generated test Case Files:

Delete all auto-generated JUnit test case files such as AppTest.java

Make the project editable with Eclipse:

Use the following commands in the parent module directory.

```
mvn clean install
mvn eclipse:eclipse
```

Open the project in Eclipse:

Choose File → New → Java Project → Specify "EmployeeAppMultiModule" as Project Name, Check "Create project from existing source" radio button and specify directory name (in our case, C:\Development\eclipse-jee-ganymede-win32\workspace\EmployeeAppMultiModule).

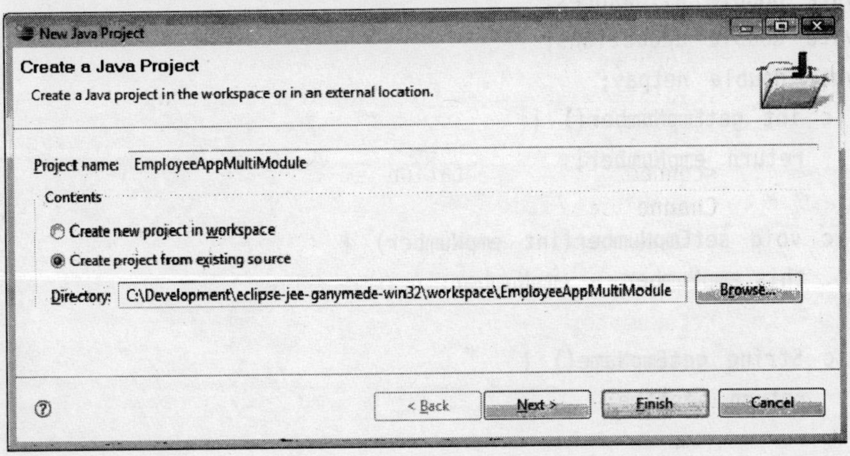

Click on "Finish" button.

Create necessary directories:

Create `/src/main/java` and `/src/test/java` directories under (EmployeeWeb) and make sure that the directory `src/main/resources` exists (already created by Maven). Use "`mvn eclipse:eclipse`" command in command prompt and refresh the project in Eclipse IDE.

The project structure in Eclipse IDE looks below.

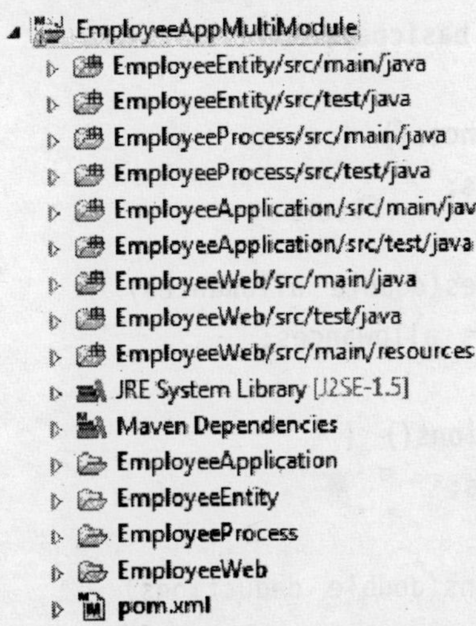

Add Source Files:

Create a package named "com.empbeans" under "EmployeeEntity/src/main/java" and add the following Employee.java file.

```
package com.empbeans;
public class Employee {
private int empNumber;
private String empName;
private double basicpay;
private double allowances;
private double deductions;
private double netpay;
public int getEmpNumber() {
        return empNumber;
}
public void setEmpNumber(int empNumber) {
        this.empNumber = empNumber;
}
public String getEmpName() {
        return empName;
}
public void setEmpName(String empName) {
        this.empName = empName;
}
public double getBasicpay() {
        return basicpay;
}
public void setBasicpay(double basicpay) {
        this.basicpay = basicpay;
}
public double getAllowances() {
        return allowances;
}
public void setAllowances(double allowances) {
        this.allowances = allowances;
}
public double getDeductions() {
        return deductions;
}
public void setDeductions(double deductions) {
```

```
        this.deductions = deductions;
    }
    public double getNetpay() {
        return netpay;
    }
    public void setNetpay(double netpay) {
        this.netpay = netpay;
    }
}
```

Create a package named "com.empprocess" under "EmployeeProcess/src/main/java" and add the following ProcessEmployee.java file.

```
package com.empprocess;
import com.empbeans.Employee;
public class ProcessEmployee {
  public void calculateNetpay(Employee e) {
    e.setNetpay(e.getBasicpay() + e.getAllowances() - e.getDeductions());
  }
}
```

Create a package named "com.empapp" under "EmployeeApplication/src/main/java" and add the following EmployeeManipulation.java file.

```
package com.empapp;
import java.util.Scanner;
import com.empbeans.Employee;
import com.empprocess.ProcessEmployee;
public class EmployeeManipulation {
  public static void main(String args[]) throws Exception {
      Employee emp = new Employee();
      // Get Employee data from user
      readEmployee(emp);
      // Find Net pay
      ProcessEmployee processEmployee = new ProcessEmployee();
      processEmployee.calculateNetpay(emp);
      // Display the Employee data
      printEmployee(emp);
}
static void readEmployee(Employee e) {
      Scanner s = new Scanner(System.in);
      System.out.println("Enter Employee Number ==> ");
      e.setEmpNumber(s.nextInt());
```

```
        System.out.println("Enter Employee Name ==> ");
        s.nextLine(); // Clearing new-line character
        e.setEmpName(s.nextLine());
        System.out.println("Enter Basic pay ==> ");
        e.setBasicpay(s.nextDouble());
        System.out.println("Enter Allowances ==> ");
        e.setAllowances(s.nextDouble());
        System.out.println("Enter Deductions ==> ");
        e.setDeductions(s.nextDouble());
    }
    static void printEmployee(Employee e) {
        System.out.println("\n ================================");
        System.out.printf("\n Employee Number  : %d", e.getEmpNumber());
        System.out.printf("\n Employee Name    : %s", e.getEmpName());
        System.out.printf("\n Basic pay        : %.2f", e.getBasicpay());
        System.out.printf("\n Allowances       : %.2f", e.getAllowances());
        System.out.printf("\n Deductions       : %.2f", e.getDeductions());
        System.out.printf("\n Net pay          : %.2f", e.getNetpay());
        System.out.println("\n ================================");
    }
}
```

Create a package named "com.empwebapp" under "EmployeeWeb/src/main/java" and add the following EmployeeServlet.java file.

```
package com.empwebapp;
import java.io.IOException;
import java.io.PrintWriter;
import javax.servlet.ServletException;
import javax.servlet.http.HttpServlet;
import javax.servlet.http.HttpServletRequest;
import javax.servlet.http.HttpServletResponse;
import com.empbeans.Employee;
import com.empprocess.ProcessEmployee;
@SuppressWarnings("serial")
public class EmployeeServlet extends HttpServlet {
 public void doGet(HttpServletRequest request,
                HttpServletResponse response)
                throws ServletException, IOException {
     doPost(request, response);
 }
```

```
public void doPost(HttpServletRequest request,
            HttpServletResponse response)
            throws ServletException, IOException {
  try {
    Employee emp = new Employee();
    // Get Employee data from user (from browser)
    readEmployee(request, emp);
    // Find Net pay
    ProcessEmployee processEmployee = new ProcessEmployee();
    processEmployee.calculateNetpay(emp);
    // Display the Employee data on the browser (Send as response)
    printEmployee(emp, response);
  }
  catch (Exception e) {
    e.printStackTrace();
  }
}
static void readEmployee(HttpServletRequest request, Employee e)
                                        throws Exception {
  // Assumed that Javascript validation is performed
  // to ensure valid data are entered in the form
  e.setEmpNumber(Integer.parseInt(request.getParameter("empNumber")));
  e.setEmpName(request.getParameter("empName"));
  e.setBasicpay(Double.parseDouble(request.getParameter("basicpay")));
  e.setAllowances(Double.parseDouble(request.getParameter("allowances")));
  e.setDeductions(Double.parseDouble(request.getParameter("deductions")));
}
static void printEmployee(Employee e, HttpServletResponse response)
                                              throws Exception {
  PrintWriter out = response.getWriter();
  out.println("<html> <body>");
  out.println("<table> <caption><b><u> Employee Salary Information
                                              </u></b></caption>");

  out.println("<tr> <td> Employee Number </td> <td> " +
                              e.getEmpNumber() + " </td> </tr>");

  out.println("<tr> <td> Employee Name </td> <td> " +
                              e.getEmpName() + " </td> </tr>");

  out.println("<tr> <td> Basic pay </td> <td> " +
    String.format("%.2f", new Double(e.getBasicpay())) + " </td> </tr>");
```

```
    out.println("<tr> <td> Allowances </td> <td> " +
        String.format("%.2f", e.getAllowances()) + " </td> </tr>");
    out.println("<tr> <td> Deductions </td> <td> " +
        String.format("%.2f", e.getDeductions()) + " </td> </tr>");
    out.println("<tr> <td> Net pay </td> <td> " +
        String.format("%.2f", e.getNetpay()) + " </td> </tr>");
    out.println("</table> </body> </html>");
    out.flush();
    out.close();
    }
}
```

Include `<servlet>` and `<servlet-mapping>` description for EmployeeServlet servlet in *web.xml* deployment descriptor file.

Then, the content of `/src/main/webapp/WEB-INF/web.xml` file is as below.

```
<!DOCTYPE web-app PUBLIC
    "-//Sun Microsystems, Inc.//DTD Web Application 2.3//EN"
    "http://java.sun.com/dtd/web-app_2_3.dtd" >
<web-app>
        <display-name>Employee Manipulation</display-name>
        <servlet>
                <servlet-name>employee</servlet-name>
                <servlet-class>com.empwebapp.EmployeeServlet</servlet-class>
        </servlet>
        <servlet-mapping>
                <servlet-name>employee</servlet-name>
                <url-pattern>/EmpSal</url-pattern>
        </servlet-mapping>
</web-app>
```

To get the Employee data from user, use a JSP file which will submit data to the EmployeeServlet. Store the JSP file named *"empdetails.jsp"* with the following content in the */src/main/webapp* directory.

```
<html>
<head>
 <title>Employee Manipulation</title>
 <!– Write Javascript for validating data on input fields,
      before form submission. –>
</head>
<body>
 <form name="form" method="post" action="/EmployeeWeb/EmpSal">
 <h2>Enter Employee Details<h2>
```

```
<table>
    <tr>
      <td>Employee Number</td>
      <td><input type="text" name="empNumber"></td>
    </tr>
    <tr>
      <td>Employee Name</td>
      <td><input type="text" name="empName"></td>
    </tr>
    <tr>
      <td>Basic pay</td>
      <td><input type="text" name="basicpay"></td>
    </tr>
    <tr>
      <td>Allowances</td>
      <td><input type="text" name="allowances"></td>
    </tr>
    <tr>
      <td>Deductions</td>
      <td><input type="text" name="deductions"></td>
    </tr>
      <tr align="center">
      <td colspan=2><input type="submit" value="Submit"></td>
    </tr>
   </table>
  </form>
 </body>
</html>
```

Add JUnit test File(s):

Add the following JUnit test class in the package "com.empapp" (create this package) under "EmployeeApplication/src/test/java" and in the package "com.empwebapp" (create this package) under "EmployeeWeb/src/test/java".

```
// File Name: EmployeeTest.java
package com.empwebapp;
import static org.junit.Assert.assertEquals;
import org.junit.Test;
import com.empbeans.Employee;
import com.empprocess.ProcessEmployee;
public class EmployeeTest {
  @Test
```

```
    public void testNetpay() {
        System.out.println("Test for Netpay");
        ProcessEmployee processEmployee = new ProcessEmployee();
        Employee emp = new Employee();
        emp.setBasicpay(10000.0);
        emp.setAllowances(3000.0);
        emp.setDeductions(1400.0);
        processEmployee.calculateNetpay(emp);
        assertEquals(11600, emp.getNetpay(), 0); // (Expected, Actual, Delta)
    }
}
```

Install the Application:

Install the Multi-Module application as shown below.

```
C:\Development\eclipse-...win32\workspace\EmployeeAppMultiModule> mvn clean in-
stall
[INFO] Scanning for projects...
[INFO] Reactor build order:
[INFO] EmployeeApp MultiModule
[INFO] Employee Entity Module
[INFO] Employee Process Module
[INFO] Employee Application Module
[INFO] EmployeeWeb Maven Webapp
...
...
...
[INFO] - - - - - - - - - - - - - - - - - - - - - - - - - - - - - - - - - - - - - -
[INFO] Reactor Summary:
[INFO] - - - - - - - - - - - - - - - - - - - - - - - - - - - - - - - - - - - - - -
[INFO] EmployeeApp MultiModule .............................. SUCCESS [2.551s]
[INFO] Employee Entity Module ............................... SUCCESS [1.887s]
[INFO] Employee Process Module .............................. SUCCESS [0.495s]
[INFO] Employee Application Module .......................... SUCCESS [1.569s]
[INFO] EmployeeWeb Maven Webapp ............................. SUCCESS [1.727s]
[INFO] - - - - - - - - - - - - - - - - - - - - - - - - - - - - - - - - - - - - - -
[INFO] - - - - - - - - - - - - - - - - - - - - - - - - - - - - - - - - - - - - - -
[INFO] BUILD SUCCESSFUL
[INFO] - - - - - - - - - - - - - - - - - - - - - - - - - - - - - - - - - - - - - -
[INFO] total time: 8 seconds
[INFO] Finished at: Mon Apr 27 12:07:38 SGT 2009
[INFO] Final Memory: 31M/56M
```

```
[INFO] ------------------------------------------------------------
```

Run the Stand-Alone Application:

To execute this Java application with Eclipse IDE: Select the EmployeeManipulation.java file, Right click on this content → Run As → Java Application.

To execute this Java application with Command Window:

Since, this Stand-Alone Application depends on other JARs (other modules), we need hose JARs to execute the application. We can also create the application JAR with the required dependencies by specifying "maven-assembly-plugin" configuration in pom.xml file and by invoking "mvn install assembly:assembly" command.

```
C:\Development\eclipse-jee-ganymede-win32\
            workspace\EmployeeAppMultiModule\EmployeeApplication>
                                             mvn install assembly:assembly
...
...
[INFO] [jar:jar]
[INFO] [assembly:assembly]
[INFO] Processing DependencySet (output=)
[INFO] Building jar:
C:\Development\eclipse-jee-ganymede-win32\
workspace\EmployeeAppMultiModule\EmployeeApplication\target\
EmployeeApplication-1.0-SNAPSHOT-jar-with-dependencies.jar
[INFO] ------------------------------------------------------------
[INFO] BUILD SUCCESSFUL
[INFO] ------------------------------------------------------------
[INFO] total time: 5 seconds
[INFO] Finished at: Mon Apr 27 16:12:52 SGT 2009
[INFO] Final Memory: 14M/26M
[INFO] ------------------------------------------------------------
```

Change to the "target", where the generated JAR file (with dependencies) presents. And issue the following command.

```
C:\Development\eclipse-jee-ganymede-
   win32\workspace\EmployeeAppMultiModule\EmployeeApplication\target>
      java -cp EmployeeApplication-1.0-SNAPSHOT-jar-with-dependencies.jar
                                             com.empapp.EmployeeManipulation

Enter Employee Number ==>
1000
Enter Employee Name ==>
Mohamed Ibrahim
Enter Basic pay ==>
8000.0
```

```
Enter Allowances ==>
2000.0
Enter Deductions ==>
1000.0
================================
 Employee Number : 1000
 Employee Name   : Mohamed Ibrahim
Basic pay        : 8000.00
 Allowances      : 2000.00
 Deductions      : 1000.00
Net pay          : 9000.00
 ================================
```

Deploy and test the Web Application:

The web application (war file) will be stored in /target directory of /EmployeeAppMultiModule/EmployeeWeb. We can deploy this application (war file) on any Application Server (Servlet Container) with required library *jar* files. However, we enabled Jetty Servlet Container (plug-in enabled in *pom.xml* file) so that we can invoke Jetty to run using the following command, which will automatically deploy our application.

```
C:\Development\eclipse-jee-ganymede-win32\workspace\EmployeeAppMultiModule\
EmployeeWeb> mvn jetty:run
...
...
2009-04-27 16:28:35.518::INFO: Started SelectChannelConnector@0.0.0.0:8080
[INFO] Started Jetty Server
[INFO] Starting scanner at interval of 30 seconds.
```

Once our web application is deployed on application server (in our case, Jetty Servlet Container), we can invoke the application with browser.

Invoke the browser with address *http://localhost:8080/EmployeeWeb/empdetails.jsp*

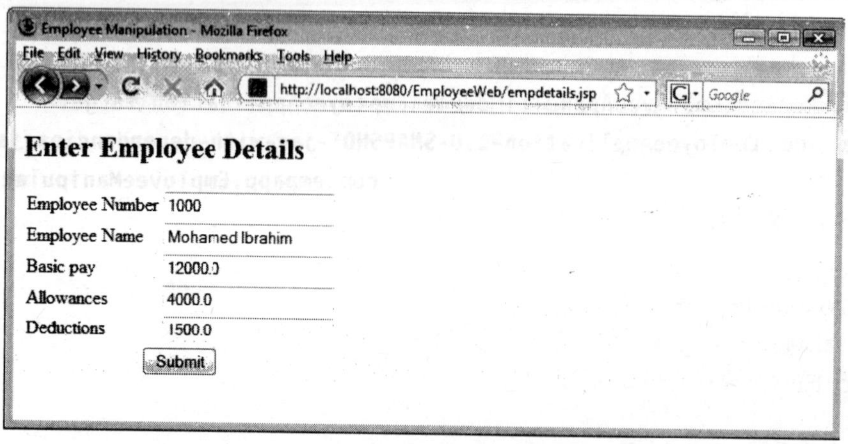

Enter the required data and click on "`Submit`". Then, the HTTP request with the entered data will be sent to the `EmployeeServlet` and the resultant data will be sent back to the browser as HTTP response after the manipulation of data.

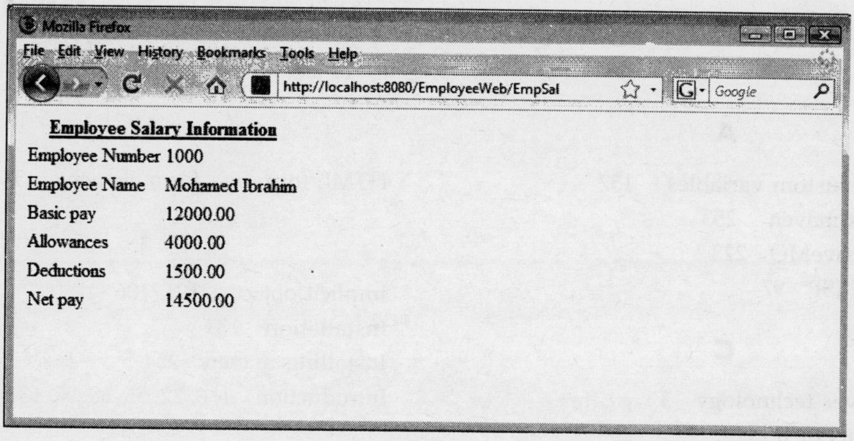

SUMMARY

Maven is a Software Project Management tool, from Apache Software Foundation. It simplifies the all the operations in project development, including downloading libraries, assembling, compiling, building the software. Presently, Apache Maven becomes the developer's choice than Apache Ant, which is another build tool. This chapter started with explain the uses of Build tool and Project, further explained the procedures to create, compile, and execute Java standalone application, Web-based application, and Java Multi-module project.

INDEX

S

T

W